Orientalism and the
Hebrew Imagination

Let me tell you, brothers, that we are not the only ones who look to the East, the entire West has been going eastward for some time now.

M. Z. Feierberg, *Whither? (Le'an?)*

Orientalism and the Hebrew Imagination

YARON PELEG

Cornell University Press ITHACA AND LONDON

First published 2005 by Cornell University Press

Printed in the United States of America

Library of Congress Cataloging-in-Publication Data

Peleg, Yaron.
    Orientalism and the Hebrew imagination / Yaron Peleg.
        p.   cm.
    Includes bibliographical references and index.
    ISBN 0-8014-4376-8 (cloth : alk. paper)
    1. Hebrew literature, Modern—20th century—History and criticism.   2. Orientalism in
literature.   3. Jewish-Arab relations in literature.   4. Zionism.   5. Frischmann, David,
1859–1922. Ba-midbar.   6. Smilansky, Moshe, 1874–1953. Bene 'Arav.   7. Arieli, L. A.,
1886–1943. Allah Karim!   I. Title.

PJ5012.O75P45 2005
892.4'09325—dc22

                                                                        2005002696

Cornell University Press strives to use environmentally responsible
suppliers and materials to the fullest extent possible in the publishing
of its books. Such materials include vegetable-based, low-VOC inks
and acid-free papers that are recycled, totally chlorine-free, or partly
composed of nonwood fibers. For further information, visit our website
at www.cornellpress.cornell.edu.

Cloth printing   10 9 8 7 6 5 4 3 2 1

Contents

Acknowledgments

I am delighted to thank the people who supported and encouraged me in writing this book. Alan Mintz has been a mentor and a friend and a constant source of motivation during the course of writing. The comments of Anthony Polonsky and Ed Kaplan of Brandeis University have also been helpful. Professor Emeritus Gershon Shaked of the Hebrew University in Jerusalem was kind to read the manuscript as well and give me his sage advice. I also want to thank my great friend and colleague Eran Kaplan, now of the University of Cincinnati, whose penetrating insights, rigorous critique, and keen interest and involvement in this project have been truly inspiring and contributed to this study immeasurably. Lastly, my partner Mike has endured the periodic absences I took to research this book with equanimity, grace, and a great confidence in me and in this project. I am grateful to him for his forbearance and love.

I want to dedicate this book to the memory of my late grandfather, Menachem Peleg, whose own life as one of the founding members of kibbutz Usha in the western Galilee in 1937 has always inspired me. As a feeble-bodied intellectual who willed himself into a hard-working pioneer, my grandfather always seemed mythological to me, especially when I was growing up on the kibbutz in the 1970s, when the movement's declining eminence was sharply felt. First as a shepherd and then as a high-school teacher, my grandfather belonged to that first generation of pioneers who came to Palestine from ideological motives and worked consciously toward the establishment of a new Jewish society there. Perhaps because he was so committed to the Zionist ideal, my grandfather was well aware of its paradoxes too; paradoxes that have become so controversial today. And so I want to dedicate this book not only to the memory of my grandfather, and to the memory of his life's work, but even more so to the great modernist ideals that inspired his generation. Israel today may not be the just and righteous haven that these Zionist pioneers imagined back then, but I believe we should aspire to make it so guided by the legacy of their ideals.

YARON PELEG

Boston, 2004

Orientalism and the
Hebrew Imagination

Introduction

In the fall of 1899, Theodore Herzl, the founder of political Zionism, visited Palestine for the first and only time in his life. Traveling around the country with a delegation of Zionist activists, Herzl visited the new Jewish agricultural settlements (*moshavot*) that were established in the Land of Israel about a decade or so before and met with the Jewish farmers who lived and worked there. A moving account of one of these meetings was left by Moshe Smilansky, a pioneer from Rehovot, who met Herzl during his visit to the *moshava*. Eagerly anticipating Herzl's arrival, Smilansky and a small group of young men rode out to meet his carriage and escort it back to the settlement, where a solemn reception was prepared for the important guests.

Stirring and dramatic, the report nevertheless begins with a cautious and skeptical note that illuminates Smilansky's awakening consciousness of his own actions as a Zionist:

> People abroad knew about Herzl. The new Zionism had already begun to make inroads into people's hearts. We, however, did not know Herzl yet. For us, Zionism was still suspect. . . . [Herzl's programmatic book] *The Jewish State* did not appeal to us, it lacked vitality. . . . and from afar we did not see the magic that we longed for without even knowing it. . . . and then, suddenly, the revolution came.[1]

When the young riders spot the carriage in the distance they shout with joy and dash toward it with great excitement:

> We spurred our horses and flew toward the carriage. Our horses ate up the miles in their gallop. . . .

1. Moshe Smilansky, "Yom Herzl birhovot" in *Kitve moshe smilansky*.

From afar I saw that the carriage slowed down, its door opened and a man's head looked out. Then the door closed again. . . .
There was only a small distance between us and the carriage. We stopped our horses and the carriage stopped too. . . .
—"Long live Dr. Herzl!" we all shouted together. . . .
In an instant we were off our horses. The carriage door opened again and with an agile step out sprang a tall man with a black, square and long beard, with big and deep black eyes that expressed great sorrow and sadness that hung over his countenance. Even the light smile on his lips was sorrowful. . . . his face enchanted me. . . . Never before did I experience the trembling that comes from solemn reverence. . . . my knees shook.

Smilansky was initially skeptical of Herzl because he saw his diplomatic attempts to promote Zionism on the international stage as trivial in comparison to the pioneers' efforts to redeem Palestine and establish a Jewish national home there through hard, physical labor and by personal example. Very soon, however, the meeting between Dr. Herzl and the group of riders became an experience of conversion. For Smilansky, the encounter with the messianic figure of the political Zionist leader revealed the full significance of his own actions as a young, Jewish pioneer. And for Herzl, the sight of the fierce-looking Jewish horsemen was an incarnation of his own romantic imagination, in which he envisioned the ridiculed Jewish peddlers of Eastern Europe as proud farmers and fighters in their old–new homeland in Palestine. Smilansky readily describes the profound impact of the meeting with Herzl. But noting the tears in Herzl's eyes, he seems to be aware of the impact the encounter made on the visionary leader, who was deeply moved by the sight of the new Jewish life he had only dreamt about before.[2]

Whether consciously or not, Smilansky brings together in this picture many of the elements that played an important role in the early twentieth-century Jewish cultural revival that changed Jewish society and history so profoundly, especially with respect to the Orient or East: the young Jewish riders, the rustic countryside, the exotic delegation of Sephardi Jews, who later in the report bend down to kiss the footprints of Herzl in the sand and declare, "Thus should be done to the Messiah, son of Joseph!," and the local Arabs, who whisper in awe to one another, "*Malk al Yahood!*" (king of the Jews) at the sight of the tall and

---

2. On October 29, 1899 Herzl wrote in his diary about the very same experience: "A band of riders, about twenty young men, charged toward us from the village of Rehovot and broke into a *fantazieh* before us [simulated war games on horses], they sang Hebrew songs and circled out carriage with laughter. Wolfsohn, Schnierer, Bodenheimer [Herzl's travel companions] and I had tears in our eyes at the sight of these quick and brave horsemen, whom the Jewish peddler boys of Europe may one day resemble." Theodore Herzl, '*Inyan hayhudim, sifre yoman, 1898–1902*, 1:51.

bearded Herzl. All of these elements, described by Smilansky with dramatic flare, highlight the Zionist attempt to construct a new Jewish identity by combining the traditional ties Jews had to the Land of Israel with the modern European attraction to the East as represented by Palestine.

By the end of the nineteenth century, the Orient or East as a place of difference, mystique, imaginative escape, and passion was very much part of Western culture.[3] Beginning with the grand tours, which the nobles of England and France made to Italy, Greece, Turkey, and beyond during the seventeenth and eighteenth centuries, through the widespread trends that these tours inspired in the European bourgeoisie throughout the nineteenth century for "things Oriental," and finally to the actual dominion of European powers over much of the Far and Near East, the Orient had an important role in the development of national consciousness in Europe. At a time when Europe was being divided along ethnic lines, rearranging itself evermore into political entities according to hitherto unacknowledged criteria such as history, language, culture, and ethnicity, the Orient or East became an important point of reference as an ultimate Elsewhere. Culturally different and technologically inferior, Eastern nations became a convenient point of comparison against which Europeans could define themselves as distinct and often superior during their national formation process. The new institutions of the modern state, with its recently established social order and its newly invented collective culture, could be much more sharply distinguished against the ancient cultures of a so-called decaying East. And while the beginning of this process was stimulated by a genuine curiosity about the Orient, at the height of the imperial era prior to World War I much of what Europe called Orient, East, or Levant, came under its direct or indirect political and economic control, transforming Europe's relationship with these far-flung regions from detached interest to an ever-growing tendency to coerce and exploit.

Although West–East relations went through various stages in the modern era, it is the latter dynamic, that of coercion and exploitation, that is most often understood today by the term Orientalism, as defined by Edward Said in his founding study *Orientalism*. Looking at the intricate relationship that England and France developed with the Near East in the nineteenth century, Said's study focuses on the gradual process in which these countries came to dominate the

---

3. I am using the terms Orient and East here interchangeably in reference to both the Near and the Far East. There were nuanced differences in Europe's attitude toward the Muslim cultures of the Ottoman Empire and toward those of East Asia, which stemmed from geographic distances and from the religious and historical affinity that Western Europe had with the Near East. I discuss these differences later on.

eastern shores of the Mediterranean and beyond. The gravamen of Said's argument is that the West never saw the East for what it really was but as a reflection and an invention. This view or approach, Said maintains, was upheld by the very school of Orientalism, which developed as an academic discipline during the nineteenth century to allegedly produce for Western, European consumption an imagined region called "East" or "Orient" about which Europeans could fantasize and which they eventually came to control.

MESSIANIC

Whereas Said's volume focuses on England and France as the major producers of the East's image in the West, the purpose of my book is to examine how Jewish nationalism or Zionism fit into this matrix of Orientalism. The basis of my book is predicated on the fact that the distinction that always existed between Western cultures, such as those of England and France, and Eastern cultures, such as those of Egypt and Persia, for instance, was less clear in the case of European Jews, who were never fully regarded as an integral part of Western culture by other Europeans nor indeed by themselves for much of their history in Europe.[4]

Although they lived on the continent since Roman times, Jews always occupied an unusual position in Europe as both a part of its culture and a foreign element in it. While Christianity retained many of the local customs of the indigenous European tribes that adopted it, Judaism remained much closer to its religious, cultural, and historical origins in the East. For centuries European Jews resisted repeated attempts to absorb them into the local, Christian culture through conversion and chose instead to maintain a distinct minority status. Retaining only tenuous connections to their places of residence, Jews existed for hundreds of years in a unique and peculiar condition that privileged an adherence to abstract law—the Torah—and an essentially Eastern heritage over more tangible Western geographic, cultural, or political allegiances. So long as Jews remained organized as a religious community this existential paradox was not only bearable, it also helped them endure their alienation by giving them a sense of distinction. But as they began to move into the greater, non-Jewish society during the Enlightenment these differences became increasingly problematic.

The secularization of European society after the French Revolution and the extension of civil rights to different social, economic, and religious classes held a great promise for Jews. Here was the first real hope of being integrated into the greater European society without having to give up Jewish religious affiliation. But as more and more Jews left their religious communities and sought

4. Even one of the earliest and most progressive proponents of Jewish civil rights, Christian Wilhelm Dohm, defined Jews as "unfortunate Asiatic refugees" in his famous 1781 treatise, *Concerning the Amelioration of the Civil Status of the Jews*, Ellis Rivkin ed. (Cincinnati: Hebrew Union College, 1957), 1.

entry into the more secular, non-Jewish society, true integration remained elusive for most. Although the Enlightenment diminished the role of religion as a basis for individual and group identity, the Age of Reason ironically brought with it a new set of "scientific" criteria that was used in more pernicious ways to discriminate against Jews and other minorities. The rise of nationalism only complicated this process: as Europeans were forging their distinct and separate national identities, Jews found themselves excluded once more from the majority culture by a new set of standards. This new animosity, which was couched in pseudoscientific terms and renamed "anti-Semitism," proved much harder to overcome than the old, religious bias. Unlike conversion, which was previously a viable option for integration, the designation of Jews as biologically different proved to be an insurmountable hurdle. In the past, even when Judaism was severely discriminated against, it was still viewed with a degree of reverence that stemmed from Christianity's recognized affinity with it. None of this reverence survived the secularism of the nineteenth century. Within the national cultures that were developing in Europe, Jews became marked as anomalous by their very nature—racially inferior, sexually deviant—and no amount of "cleansing" could free them from these damning associations.[5]

The nature of Judaism itself and the unique minority status that Jews had held in Europe for centuries did not make integration easier either. Paradoxically, the attempt by some Jews to become French, German, Polish, or Russian was often viewed with suspicion by their Christian compatriots because Jews were perceived as a cohesive "national" group long before the rise of nationalism. Yet Jews did not conform to the modern definition of a nation because their diasporic existence both predated and transcended it. By virtue of its common ethnic and historic ties as enshrined in its religion, the Jewish community may be regarded as the prototype of the modern nation. While relatively new nations, such as Germany and Italy, attempted to forge national cultures based on common categories such as history, ethnicity, language, and literature, scattered communities of Jews around the world have been sharing many of these attributes for centuries. This peculiarity was always a great source of strength and sustenance for a persecuted minority that was resented precisely for these differences. In the modern era, however, when many of these

---

5. A tragic example of the danger of such anti-Semitic associations was the Austrian philosopher Otto Weininger (1880–1903), a Jew and a homosexual, whose deep sense of inferiority was the impetus for his notoriously misogynistic and Jew-hating tract, *Sex and National Character*, in which he denigrated women as inferior and Judaism as feminine. Shortly after the publication of his book—one of the first scientific best sellers in German—Weininger converted to Christianity and then committed suicide at the age of 23. But his thesis reverberated in German culture for many years to come. Some of it found its way into Nazi propaganda and even influenced early Zionist thought.

categories became the model for the new nation-state, the nature of the Jewish nation as a virtual community that spanned time and space became extremely problematic.

Zionism emerged as a promising solution to these challenges. The inspiring innovation of Zionism was that it recognized, rather than ignored or fought against, the inherent Jewish difference. Deeply rooted in the national revolutions that swept across Europe throughout the nineteenth century, Zionism suggested utilizing the age-old Jewish difference as a catalyst for reform. Adding territory to the other criteria Jews had shared for centuries, Zionists propagated the establishment of an actual Jewish polity in Palestine with all the trappings of a modern state. That the Land of Israel should become the focus of these efforts was both natural and expedient. It was natural because Eretz Israel had always had a central place in traditional Judaism. It was expedient because Palestine's location in the East appealed to contemporary national, romantic sentiments.

This kind of solution was not unique to Zionism of course. As early as the eighteenth century, German Romantics, such as Johann Gottfried Herder, tied together concepts such as folk, history, nation, and literature, and laid the foundations for both Romanticism and nationalism. Herder was one of the first German intellectuals who called for the cultural unification of the Germans, who were scattered at that time among hundreds of small states. Contrary to the spirit of the Enlightenment, Herder and other German Romantics appealed to sentiment, not rationality, in their attempt to promote ethnic group culture, and made language and literature the chief instruments of the attempts to raise German national consciousness.

The usefulness of this combination was so obvious that it became an important element of all the national revolutions in the modern era. Again, European Jews were not different in this regard, as the earlier anecdote by Smilansky illustrates. Many of the elements that influenced the development of Jewish nationalism connected modern Hebrew culture and the Orient through the new ways that they were interpreted during the Hebrew Revival: the conversion of religious difference into ethnic distinction, the use of historical and invented past, and especially the romantic expressions of these attributes.

The very image of Herzl is perhaps the best example of the significant role the East played in the Jewish national revival during the late nineteenth and early twentieth century. To many of his contemporaries Herzl seemed taken out of an Oriental romance. Both Jews and non-Jews alike saw the tall, dark, and handsome Viennese Jew as a living proof of the connection between the ancient Jewish past and the exoticism of the Orient. It was as if time and space were folded into the image of this modern-day prophet, who bridged ancient Jewish history and the modern Levant. "What a striking appearance!" wrote Erwin

Rosenberger, one of Herzl's colleagues, about his first meeting with the Zionist leader at a gathering of the Viennese Jewish Students Society in 1896:

> The prototype of a handsome Oriental. The cut of his features, the dark hair, the dark beard and moustache, the dark eyes all proclaimed eloquently that here sat a son of the East—and one of the noblest blood. I found myself almost wondering, how does *he* come to be sitting on that plain chair? He would look perfectly at ease on the throne of a Babylonian king. How does that slim figure come to be wearing a modern business suit; that figure which was so obviously created for the robes of an Oriental prince? I was convinced that, if we had called a passerby into the room and said to him, "Here among the hundred of us there is a king in disguise; find him," the stranger would have unhesitatingly pointed to Herzl.[6]   *TALL LIKE SAUL.*

What is striking about this quotation is the way Jews themselves seem to have internalized the common European view that classified them as Orientals. In this respect, then, Herzl represented the final stage in a long cultural process. That is, a process of internalizing the very difference that always prevented the complete absorption of Jews into Europe, their perception as "Oriental," and utilizing it constructively by highlighting it rather than by trying to ignore it or eradicate it.

Although Herzl may have been the most pronounced example of this exotic combination, certainly within Jewish circles, he was by no means the first. The British statesman Benjamin Disraeli (1804–1881) comes most readily to mind as someone who was regarded by his contemporaries as princely and Eastern precisely because of his Jewish origins. Disraeli deliberately cultivated an Oriental aura in his politics as well as in his writings. The main character of one of his best-known semi-autobiographical novels, *Tancred, or the New Crusade* (1847), is a young English nobleman who wishes to reinvent himself and revive his English society through a spiritually rejuvenating journey to the Holy Land. The book suggests that the Semitic peoples of the East hold the key to the renewal of Western society.

A literary example of this highly romantic combination is the wistful character of Daniel Deronda in George Eliot's 1876 novel by that name. Either by accident or by intention, Deronda's life reflects Disraeli's and uncannily adumbrates Herzl's image and career (the book was written twenty years before Herzl

6. Erwin Rosenberger, *Herzl as I Remember Him* (New York: Herzl Press, 1959), 13. Herzl's image inspired countless pictures and illustrations in which he was literally portrayed as a king, usually King David or King Solomon, adorned with Oriental robes. See, for example, Moses Lillian's illustration in Julius H. Scheops, *Teodor Herzl, 1860–1904*, trans. Gershon Ritmann (Makhbarot lesifrut Pub., 2001), 105.

published his manifesto *The Jewish State*). The adopted son of an English peer, Deronda captivated readers as a dark and handsome young man of great promise, whose veiled origins only add to his appeal. The notion that a person cannot escape his or her ethnic origin is evident in Deronda's vague existential discontent as a member of the British aristocracy. It is also apparent in his unconscious attraction to things Jewish, so that the revelation at the end of the novel that he was indeed born a Jew is not surprising and confirms his long journey of self-discovery. Along that journey the reader is gradually introduced to many of the elements that combine at the end to create a composite Oriental image. Both in body and mind Deronda represents an Oriental man of noble birth, a visionary leader who epitomizes in his appearance a mixture of the ancient and the modern: the bearing, ideals, and fervor of a biblical prophet; the looks of an Arab prince; and the psychology of a modern European man, cultured and refined.

All three figures, Disraeli, Herzl, and the literary Deronda, exhibit a constructive blend of opposites that stemmed from their unique position as outsiders within. In many ways, Zionism was made up of a similar mixture of opposites: the position of Jews in Europe as outsiders within and later their position in Palestine as the reverse, as insiders without.

The historical period during which Jews began yet another return to Zion affected their revival profoundly. The prevailing attitude toward the Orient in Europe was different at the turn of the eighteenth century than it was a hundred years later. Many images and symbols, especially from the Muslim Near East, influenced European art and letters during the earlier period, before the West exerted its economic, military, and political control over the East. The rose and the nightingale, for instance, two symbols without which European Romantic poetry cannot be imagined, came from Persian and Turkish poetry, and folktales such as the immensely popular *Thousand and One Nights* shaped such Western classics as Swift's *Gulliver's Travels*.[7] A hundred years later, however, when the relationship of Europe and the Near East became more colonial in nature, the need to maintain Western political and economic control considerably diminished the European willingness for cultural exchange. West–East relations became much more adversarial because of the inherent inequality between the European powers and the native cultures they dominated.

Zionism, which emerged during the height of the colonial era, was fraught with many of these tensions. Like the early Romantics, Zionists looked to the

---

7. See Naji Oueijan, *The Progress of an Image* and Mohammed Sharafuddin, *Islam and Romantic Orientalism*.

East for a cultural alternative. But like European colonists, they felt the need to distance themselves from the Arabs in order to maintain the integrity of their emerging national culture. The Arab way of life and the actual Palestinian landscapes were new, different, and mysterious to Zionists, as they were to Europeans a hundred years earlier. But the biblical associations of these landscapes made them part of traditional Jewish culture as well. Similarly, the Jews who came to Palestine feared of "going native," especially since they felt a need to preserve their culture-in-the-making. At the same time, even this typically colonial concern was complicated by the affinity many early Zionist pioneers felt toward the local Arabs, for ethnic and historical reasons. Rather than fantasize a nonexistent East, many Zionist pioneers looked up to the local Palestinian-Arabs and mimicked the Arab way of life in the hope of reinventing themselves and creating a new Jewish culture inspired by their image.

Most if not all of these conflicts were expressed exclusively in writing, because the revolution that created a viable Hebrew culture and eventually a Jewish state in Palestine began essentially as a textual enterprise. In the absence of a living Hebrew culture in a modern, national sense, Hebrew literature at the end of the nineteenth century and the beginning of the twentieth century set out to create that culture from scratch. Given the importance that texts always had in the Jewish tradition, the significance that the literature of the Hebrew Revival assumed during those years is not hard to imagine. When the traditional textual and interpretive library, on which Jews had based their daily existence for centuries, was replaced by a new body of literature and a new set of acquired values, much of the ideological justification and zealous loyalty, which the traditional system commanded in the past, were transferred to the new system almost by default. The literature that was written during the Hebrew Revival can therefore be read not only as a reflection of Hebrew culture or an element of its renewal but as one of the very forces that created it.

The ways in which writers of the Hebrew Revival transformed Jewish ethnicity into elements of modern nationalism; the methods by which they internalized the attraction to the East and "judaicized" it; the devices they used to turn an escapist fascination into a constructive element of a new culture, and their metamorphosis of negative Jewish images were all part of the Orientalist school in Hebrew letters, which flourished briefly during the formative period of Zionism, 1900–1930.

The Oriental cachet that Eretz Israel enjoyed during the Hebrew Revival did not make the Jewish immigration to Palestine less frustrating. Even the most ardent Zionists felt ambivalent about their "return home," an anxiety that was aggravated by the reaction of the Arabs, who saw the Jewish immigration as a Western intrusion. This is one of the main reasons for the relatively short period in the history of modern Hebrew literature—1900 to 1930—in which Orientalism played a discernible role. When the Zionists stepped out of the misty realm of Jewish myth into the real world of Ottoman Palestine, they inevitably discovered that much of the magic had evaporated. The hard facts of life, such as geography, politics, and demographics, dispelled many of the fantastic notions that were cultivated in distant places, far away from the actual land and its people. And because Zionist pioneers, as opposed to European travelers, attempted to revive Jewish culture within the confines of the East itself, Oriental fantasy quickly gave way to the more mundane and sobering facts of life in a materially backward environment.

Hebrew-Orientalist works, therefore, are not only few and far between, many of them tend to be mediocre, motivated by a sentimental Jewish nationalism. For it is one thing to call for the creation of a new literature, even to enumerate the qualities it should have, and quite another actually to create it. At its inception, modern, Hebrew literature was inherently an artificial project because it lacked the most critical element of any living literature—native readers. Well into the 1930s, anyone writing in Hebrew was not only creating a modern, literary idiom but imagining readers as well. Hebrew writers who used Orientalist elements in their works were no different. They too tried to distinguish their modern works from older, Hebrew writings by combining modern contextual and formal elements with older, Hebrew ones.

The following four chapters try to identify, characterize, and evaluate the place and scope of Orientalist elements in Zionist and later Hebrew, Israeli culture. The first chapter traces some of the early associations between Orientalism and Jewish culture. The chapter examines how Hebrew writers interpreted the assumed and actual Jewish connection to the East, as represented by Palestine, by surveying a few of the first literary manifestations of it. The next three chapters examine the works of three important writers who explored the modern Jewish relationship with Eretz Israel/Palestine in greater depths. Chapter 2 looks at David Frishman's anthology *Bamidbar* (In the Wilderness), which combines the language and sensibilities of the Hebrew Bible with modern notions of culture, ethnicity, psychology, and aesthetics; a combination that was designed to breathe a new life into Diaspora Judaism. Chapter 3 looks at Moshe Smilansky's collection of short stories, *The Sons of Arabia* (*Bnei 'arav*), particularly the way the stories present the Arab natives as noble and romantic savages made up of a wishful blend—a negation of the Diaspora Jew and the promise of a New Hebrew that would be created in Eretz Israel. Chapter 4 focuses on A. L. Arielli (Orloff)'s play *Allah Karim!* (Allah the Noble) as a realistic attempt to explore the paradoxes of the pioneering project in Eretz Israel with respect to the East.

Although Frishman was considerably older than Smilansky and Arielli, and belonged to a different literary generation, the works included in this book were written almost at the same time, during the second decade of the twentieth century. This is a relatively short interval, but it was nevertheless marked by an extremely rich and fervent literary activity that was critical for the development of Zionism. I begin with Frishman because he was an important cultural agent during a transitional period, who sought to inspire a profound aesthetic revolution in Jewish culture. Through a reformulation of biblical language and literary motifs, Frishman offered in *Bamidbar* a uniquely Jewish vision designed to address the existential crisis of European Jewry at the turn of the century. Frishman's New Jew was not an actual man at all but an aesthetic notion, like the radically modern world he inhabited. *Bamidbar* thus sets a broad cultural framework for a totally different Judaism. Frishman separates Jews from traditional Judaism and suggests, paradoxically, that a spiritual return to the Eastern cradle of the nation will inspire a cultural revival that would ensure Jewish continuity *in the Diaspora.*

Each person has a role.

and physical

Smilansky's references to the Orient in his immensely popular series *The Sons of Arabia* are much more concrete and incorporate the Hebrew Bible and the native Arabs of Palestine in a romantic blend that has colonial overtones. Although Smilansky's stories are ostensibly about Arabs, they provide a revealing look at the psychological makeup of the New Jew that was unique to early Zionism. If Frishman created an aesthetic Oriental universe, Smilansky may be said to have inhabited it with images of reconstructed Jews disguised as Arabs.

In *Allah Karim!* Arielli questions the validity of some of the assumptions that Frishman and Smilansky make in their works. The possibility that a Hebrew Orient is an ephemeral creation of the Jewish imagination, that it is a delusional invention of questionable value, is explored in the play with surprising integrity by one of the most promising writers of the early Jewish community in Palestine. The book concludes with an examination of the legacy of these trends in contemporary Israeli literature and culture.

Finally, in a more general way, this book addresses some of the postcolonial critique of Zionism, generally subsumed under the post-Zionist critique which has arisen in the past decade or so in Israel in the wake of Said and others' work. Some post-Zionist scholars argue that Zionists' understanding of Jewish history is flawed. They oppose the Zionist view that stipulates that a Jewish state in Some palestine is the only solution to the Jewish problem, arguing that it masks the imperial-colonial character of Zionism. Such critique frequently focuses on the Western character of the State of Israel, and especially Israel's problematic treatment of Palestinian Arabs. At the heart of this critique is the belief that the State of Israel was born in sin, the sin of forceful seizure of the land and the cultural, political, and in some cases physical eradication of its native people, the Palestinian Arabs.[8]

The dispute with those post-Zionists is generally not about facts but about meaning. As Palestinian Arabs are rather obviously the greater losers in the conflict with Israeli Jews so far, the dispute is about intent and malicious forethought and the strident process of deduction that leads to one of the strangest arguments of post-Zionist thought. Unable or unwilling to deal with the responsibility that comes with sovereignty and power, some of the more extreme post-Zionist critics advocate the cancellation of Zionism altogether, the dismantling of the State of Israel and the restoration of Jews to the Diaspora, where they belong. Rather than have power and control over others, powers that have been repeatedly abused by the Israeli establishment in the past and are bound to be abused in the future, these critics argue that it would be better if once again Jews assumed the morally comfortable position of an eternal wanderer. For only by becoming an ultimate Other can Jews preserve their moral superiority and heritage.[9]

The cultural analysis in this book is offered as a reply to some of these extreme claims, whose folly and danger have been demonstrated conclusively by centuries of Jewish suffering in the Diaspora. My book highlights the problems inherent in appropriating the theories of influential postcolonial critics such as Frantz Fanon and Homi Bhabha and applying them to the much more nuanced case of Zionism. By focusing on the instability between "East" and "West" as part of Hebrew culture, I try to show how Zionism, especially in its earlier stages,

8. See for example an article by two leading post-colonial critics of Zionism, Ariella Azoulay and Adi Ophir: "We are the last frontier of the military colonialism that Europe abandoned in shame decades ago. We are a thorn Europe has left in the Orient—now converted into the litmus test Arab countries must take before entering into the New World Order. We are an emblem of Europe's Orientalism, that shamelessly shines in the Orient, Orientalism which has always been devoid of self-consciousness, but is now already empty of desire too, left only with mastery, paternalism, and violence. We are the encounter with the Orient that Europe always fantasized and feared, an encounter that inadvertently became central to the dynamics of Israeli society and its State's apparatuses. Now we have an "inner Orient" and an "outer Orient," and the clear hierarchy of a master relationship between the "White Jew" and his true "Oriental Others." "100 Years of Zionism, 50 Years of a Jewish State," 68.

For a representative collection of articles by leading post-Zionist critics, see *Te'oria uvikoret* 20 (Spring 2002), which is dedicated entirely to a postcolonial critique of Israeli culture.

9. The romance of the Jew as a supreme Other, a disenfranchised vagabond who serves as an eternal moral rebuke in his powerlessness and suffering, has become fashionable in French thought after the Holocaust, by Jews and non-Jews alike. For a poignant example, see Alain Finkelkraut, *The Imaginary Jew.*

For an Israeli example of this phenomenon, see Ilan Gur-Ze'ev, *Likrat hinuch legalutiyut rav tarbutiyut ve hinuch she keneged ba idan ha post moderni.* Although the book is more philosophical than political in nature it essentially advocates the deconstruction of Israel as a Jewish state and the return of Jews to the Diaspora. The title translates as: "Toward an education for diasporism, multiculturalism and counter-education in the postmodernist era."

defies such simplistic and strident categorizations. Moreover, as the literary works I analyze in this book eloquently express, the animosity between Arabs and Jews, which seems so hopelessly entrenched today, was not always so. At its best, the Hebrew Revival offered an inspiring model of cooperation and even integration between Jews and Arabs in Palestine. While these attempts did not survive for long after Israeli independence, their example can serve as hopeful encouragement for the future. *YES.*

CHAPTER I

Orientalism and the Jews

Paradoxes of Time, Place, and Culture

Orientalism was already a significant cultural force in Europe in the middle of the eighteenth century. But its imprint on Jewish culture was not felt until a hundred years later, principally because Jews did not take a significant part in the general European culture until about the middle of the nineteenth century. When they did, much of the European relationship with the East was transformed from an intense but detached enchantment with the region to a more rigid economic and political exchange system with it. This chapter identifies the Jewish encounter with a few of the most resonant elements of Orientalism in European culture at that time; it looks at the Jewish interpretation of these elements and finally traces and evaluates some of the earliest incorporation of Orientalist themes into Hebrew culture and literature.

The publication of *Thousand and One Nights* or *Tales of the Arabian Nights* in France in the mid-eighteenth century (translated by Abbé Antoine Galland) was one of the most significant events in the popularization of the Orient in Europe.[1] The collection of fantastic stories from the Muslim East delighted Europeans tremendously. The vivid emotional and material world of the tales, with their fierce rulers, vicious highwaymen, cunning beggars, and voluptuous maidens, captivated the imagination of a society whose ideas about propriety and etiquette were very different. The fascination with the fictional world of the *Arabian Nights* eventually led to more tangible cultural exchanges when Europeans began to travel to the Eastern Mediterranean. Reports from the Near East soon inundated Europe and supplemented the fantasy of the fabulous Arabian tales with

---

1. See Mia Irene Gerhardt, *The Art of Story-telling*.

varied accounts about actual life in the Orient.[2] Yet despite their attempts to describe the Muslim world faithfully, most European travelers to the lands of the Ottoman Empire were deeply affected by their prior perception of those regions as exotic locations of mystery and passion.

As outsiders who knew little about the places they visited, travelers from Europe naturally invested these "new" lands with associations from their own world. In her study of British colonialism, Elleke Boehmer describes the way in which travelers and later colonizers tried to make sense of the unfamiliar lands they encountered by relying on familiar images and producing stock descriptions of these newly discovered lands for their compatriots at home.[3] But while so-called empty territories like northeastern America or eastern Australia could be named New England and New South Wales, the Near East was different. The peoples and landscapes of the Levant were unfamiliar to Westerners, yet they were not completely strange because of their relative proximity to Europe and especially because of the biblical associations they evoked in the minds of Christian tourists.

James Thompson suggestively terms the peculiar sense of alienation and familiarity Westerners often felt in the Near East as "retrospective anticipation," by which he means the romantic tendency of travelers to see the contemporary Near East as "biblical" and to compare the landscapes they see with biblical scenes they picture in their imagination.[4] Poets like Alphonse de Lamartine (1790–1869), for instance, linked the popularity of the imagined and experienced Levant with the ingrained knowledge of the Bible in a combination that was among the first expressions of Romanticism in French letters. Lamartine and other French poets used biblical plot lines, heroes, names, and landscapes to create an exotic Oriental world that combined past and present in a unique way. Lamartine himself described this process in a book he wrote after he journeyed to the Eastern Mediterranean in 1832–13. When the Oriental landscape unfolded before his eyes, he compared it with a biblical scene that he remembered and pictured in his imagination. The two central images that shaped Lamartine's Oriental epic-poem "La Chute d'un Ange" ("The Fall of an Angel," 1838), for instance, were the expansive natural landscape of Lebanon and the erotic character of Eastern women, which he saw in Beirut and Damascus.[5] These powerful images eventually found their way into Jewish

2. For one of many examples, see a catalog compiled by John Marciari, *Grand Tour Diaries and other Travel Manuscripts in the James Marshall and Marie-Louise Osborn Collection* (New Haven, Conn.: Beinecke Rare Book and Manuscript Library, 1999).

3. Elleke Boehmer, *Colonial and Postcolonial Literature*, 13–14, 16–17.

4. James Thompson, *The East Imagined, Experienced, Remembered, Orientalist 19th Century Paintings*, 7.

5. For more on the influence of the Hebrew Bible on early Romanticism, see Abraham Avni, *The Bible and Romanticism*.

culture as well. Three of these central associations of the East in the West—the *desert* environment as a romanticized wilderness, the *Bedouin* as a noble savage, and the East as a locus of exotic *eroticism*—played an important role in the Hebrew Revival later on as well.

For the English Romantic poets, the *desert* represented an empty space that was both a point of origin and a place that could be filled with any dream or wish. In his study about the influence of Islam on early romantic poetry in England, Mohammed Sharafuddin shows how poet Robert Southey, for instance, believed that the Orient provided a vivid spiritual environment that, unlike modern Europe, was closely connected to the moral world of the Bible. For Southey, the Arabian Desert was not exotic as much as it was an inspiration for a well-balanced relationship between man and nature.[6] As a living metaphor of a biblical-like wilderness, the desert offered an attractive alternative to the material excesses of European civilization, a place that represented a perpetual state of promise. The desert was a paradoxical locus of suspension and movement, as exemplified by the wandering of the Israelites in it. This essentially Greco-Christian pastoral idea of nature as a symbol of simplicity and purity, which was usually contrasted with the artifice of urban life influenced many works of the Hebrew Enlightenment or Haskala during the nineteenth century. Some of the first modern works of fiction in Hebrew, like the late eighteenth- and early nineteenth-century dramas of Moshe Haim Luzzatto, for instance, are transparent adaptations of Christian pastoral love stories.[7] The same is true for the first Hebrew novel, Avraham Mapu's *The Love of Zion* (*Ahavat Tsiyon*, 1853), a pastoral love story set in the days of King Hezekia in the sixth century B.C.E.[8]

However, during the Hebrew Revival or Tehiya at the beginning of the twentieth century, Hebrew writers found such ideas increasingly unsuitable for their new cultural and political agenda. The romantic critique of urban culture, as

6. Mohammed Sharafuddin, *Islam*, 107, 125, 194.

7. Luzzatto's dramas include *Glory to the Righteous* (*Laysharim tehila*, 1743) and *Tower of Valor* (*Migdal oz*, 1837). See Fishel Lachower, who writes that *Tower of Valor* was largely based on a pastoral story by Batista Guarini (1538–1612), one of Italy's foremost Renaissance poets, who had a large following in Italy and beyond throughout the seventeen and eighteen centuries, *Toldot hasifrut ha'ivrit hahadasha*, 1:14–44.

8. Mapu's pastoral romance illustrates some of the fundamentally different ways in which Jews internalized contemporary cultural trends. Mapu placed his novel in the ancient biblical past not only because it afforded him an aesthetic distance that masked his critique of contemporary Jewish culture but also because he perceived that period as purer and closer to a natural Jewish state. The novel combines a classical longing for a simpler life in nature (Greek pastoralism) with a cultural materialism that later characterized Zionism. Mapu carefully creates a biblical composite of an idealized natural existence on one hand—his characters spend a lot of time in the fields and vineyards of Judea—while on the other hand he describes an earthly Jerusalem that is a great material center, urban, political, and religious.

embodied in the ideas of Rousseau, had a diminished appeal for Jews, because a majority of them lived then in small towns in the Eastern European countryside. Moreover, enlightened Jews saw the city as a positive source of educational, professional, and economic opportunity that stood in direct contrast to the backwardness of the small Jewish town or shtetl. Many Jews also identified village life with the largely ignorant and often anti-Semitic peasants of Eastern Europe. Some of these attitudes changed in the course of time, especially after the rise of Zionism, whose call for a return to the land was certainly influenced by Greco-Christian ideas about nature. But they still accounted for the Jewish ambivalence toward notions of culture and nature as part of Orientalism.

Similarly, while the destruction of Jerusalem was always regarded in Jewish tradition as punishment for corruption and hubris, the Hebrew Revival transformed the lamentation over Jerusalem's ruin into a dynamic vision not just of a spiritual renewal but of a material rebirth as well. In the absence of an organized Jewish state, the criticism that the English Romantic poets, for instance, attached to the ruins of ancient empires like Egypt and Babylon was irrelevant.[9] Both Walter Savage Landor in his poem "Gebir" and Southey in "Thalaba the Destroyer" look at the collapse of the great empires of the Near East, such as Egypt and Babylon, as a punishment for their vainglory. Strewn throughout the Near East, these ruins signified for the Romantic poets visible lessons for the folly of man. "The marble statues long have lost all trace," writes Southey in "Thalaba," "Of heroes and of chiefs; / Huge shapeless stones they lie, / O'ergrown with many a flower."[10]

For Jewish nationalists, however, the devastated Jerusalem was not just the remains of a glorious past but a promise of an equally glorious future. By virtue of the historical continuity that was part of their religion, Jews could thus turn an essentially romantic sentiment into a constructive plan for renewal. As I discuss in the next chapter, the Hebrew Revival was fraught with many of these conflicting tensions between West and East, between a wish to create a new material culture in the European mold, and an equally strong, essentially pastoral desire for an idealized return to the land.

The *Bedouin* as a powerful symbol of personal and cultural freedom was first used by the English Romantic poets, who invested him with a deep religious consciousness of both nature and God. Rousseau's critique of tyranny, his skepticism of contemporary cultural constructs, and his belief in the basic purity and innocence of nature made the pastoralism of Islamic nomadic life especially attractive to English poets in the early nineteenth century.[11] The Arab

9. Sharafuddin, *Islam* 10.
10. Robert Southey, *Poetical Works* (Paris: A. and W. Galignani, 1829).
11. Sharafuddin, *Islam*. The poets he analyzes are Landor, Southey, Thomas Moore, and Byron.

nomad suggested the idea of nobility in the midst of unspoiled nature. As a symbol of ascetic simplicity, the Bedouin represented a free and wild being, a noble savage whose direct connection to nature questioned the value of civilization.[12] English and French Romantic poets used this image as a contrast to the contrived and artificial landscapes and characters of classical literature because it fit their ideas of simplicity, innocence, and nature that were nurtured by the geographic discoveries of "new" worlds during the seventeenth, eighteenth, and nineteenth centuries.

But the Arab nomad was different in one important respect from the so-called noble savages of the Americas, the African continent, or the South Pacific in that he was not entirely "savage." As a Muslim who roamed the geographic expanses of ancient Israel, the Bedouin also brought the Bible to life for European travelers. Here was a figure whose solitary, harsh, and fierce life in the desert separated him completely from the European, urban experience. Yet as someone whose religion, manners, and habitat evoked the Hebrew patriarchs in the Western imagination, it was a familiar and welcome image as well. Orientalist writers were deeply inspired by this combination of the exotic and the familiar. While they identified with the Bedouin morally, they also felt far enough removed from him to use his image critically. These associations were not lost on Zionist pioneers. Yet unlike European visitors to the Levant, the Jews who came to make their home there were inspired by Palestinian Arab culture in fundamentally different ways. As I show in chapters 3 and 4, the Arabs and especially the Bedouins were perceived by these New Jews not only as a critique of their old diasporic culture but as an inspiration for the creation of a new Jewish culture in their image in the Land of Israel itself.

Another aspect that was often associated with the Orient in the West was *eroticism*, which was believed to be more pronounced in the East than in the fogs of the north.[13] In its paintings of steamy bathhouse scenes filled with curvaceous nudes, in titillating stories of kidnapping, and in dark conspiracies concocted in shady bazaars, the East was staged in Europe as a sexual fantasy of the proper bourgeoisie.[14] Yet, because anti-Semites sexualized Jews and considered Jewish

12. Neal Hoxie Fairchild, *The Noble Savage*, 2.

13. See Sharafuddin's analysis of Thomas Moore's epic poem "Lalla Rookh," in which the Islamic heroine is portrayed as more voluptuous and passionate than European women. See 183–185.

14. See Hirschfeld, *Kadima*, 14, as well as Abraham Avni, *The Bible and Romanticism*, who writes that the poem, "La Bain" (the Bath), by Alfred de Vigny (1797–1863), which describes the bathing ritual of the heroine of the apocryphal book *Susanna*, had a considerable influence on nineteenth-century Oriental visual imagery. According to Avni, the limited merit of the mediocre poem resides mainly in its rich details of local color, the descriptions of Susanna's beauty, her dress, and the elaborate ceremony of her bath (154). See also Raymond Schwab, who writes that "the French Romantics

men effeminate, not least because they were thought of as Oriental, Zionists had to resolve this tension by internalizing and deflecting it or by adopting masculine imagery that would compensate for it. Indeed, some of the central ideas of the Zionist revolution were predicated on this anxiety.[15]

Many of the works that were written during the Hebrew Revival tried to grapple with this sexual tension. While most of the writers who lived and worked in Europe at the time—major writers like U. N. Gnessin, M. Y. Berdichevsky, and G. Shoffman—described sexually tortuous Jewish characters, writers who lived and worked in Palestine, most notably Moshe Smilansky, created characters whose approach to sex was less complex. Although both trends were expressions of an emerging sexual consciousness in the West, they were also reactions to the special place Jews occupied in it. Writers such as Gnessin reacted to anti-Semitic stereotypes of Jews as oversexed or effeminate by composing literary psychoanalytical narratives that probed Jewish sexuality and used sexual motifs to discuss the problematics of *fin de siècle* Jewish existence. Palestinian Hebrew writers like Smilansky were more interested in creating a new Jewish stereotype that was not so sexually preoccupied.

Although the division between writers in Europe and in Palestine is significant, it is by no means complete, as the case of the well-known writer and literary critic Y. H. Brenner proves. Although Brenner wrote most of his important works in Palestine, his Palestinian-Jewish characters are haunted by many of the sexual anxieties of their European counterparts. But as I show in chapters 3 and 4, with the growth and establishment of the Yishuv—the new Jewish community in Palestine—sexual anxiety gradually changed in the works that were written in the Land of Israel. The image of the New Jew or New Hebrew in many of these works was not only inspired by the fierceness of the Arab in battle but by some of his alleged vitality in bed as well.

Although Orientalism as a cultural trend began in England and France, it was the eventual popularity it gained in Germany and especially in Russia that had the most significant influence on Hebrew culture, not only because of the

---

have been greatly criticized, and not without reason, for having reduced the weighty Orient of the Germans to picturesque exoticism." *The Oriental Renaissance: Europe Rediscovery of India and the East, 1680–1880*, 204.

15. Sander Gilman examines this anxiety in several comprehensive studies. See for example, *Difference and Pathology: Stereotypes of Sexuality, Race, and Madness* (Ithaca, N.Y.: Cornell University Press, 1985) and *Jewish Self-hatred: Anti-Semitism and the Hidden Language of the Jews* (Baltimore: Johns Hopkins University Press, 1986).

See also Daniel Boyarin, who dedicates an entire chapter to questions of Zionism and gender in his book *Unheroic Conduct, the Rise of Heterosexuality and the Making of the Jewish Man*. For a detailed discussion, see chapter 3 of this work.

proximity of most Jewish centers to central and Eastern Europe but especially because of the interesting parallels that existed between Russian and Jewish cultures with respect to the East. The fascination of the Russian Romantic poets with the Eastern parts of the expanding czarist empire in the nineteenth century shaped much of the later attraction Hebrew writers developed to "their" East, to the Land of Israel. Poised between Europe and Asia, Russians were always ambivalent about their Eastern origins and their affinity to the West. Russia's attitude toward the East became even more complex as it joined the colonial race and extended its control over much of central Asia. The territories Russia acquired in the Caucasus in the 1800s aligned it with other Western colonial powers, politically and culturally, and gave Russians the opportunity to assume a superior, Western stance toward the natives of their Eastern provinces. But as Russia also claimed the Caucasus and beyond in the name of its cultural ties with these regions, it used its dominion over the Ural to change its semi-Asian identity from a liability to an asset, just as Zionists would do about a hundred years later.[16]

In fact, Russians used the contemporary popularity of the Orient to support their claims for both Western and non-Western identity and constructed a romantic, Oriental universe *avant la lettres*, as Susan Layton puts it.[17] At a time when their literary development lagged far behind European literary achievements, Russians could immediately claim more imagination, creativity, and originality by virtue of their culturally mixed heritage. Many Orientalist literary conventions were adapted by Russian writers and poets in the nineteenth century to fit their specific national needs, and the wilderness of the sparsely populated Caucasus was dramatized by poets such as Alexander Pushkin, Alexander Bestuzhev-Marlinsky, and Mikhail (Yuryevich) Lermontov, who painted the Muslim natives of the mountains, the Circassians, as savage, noble, and erotic.[18]

The concerns that absorbed Russians during their time of national awakening, such as language, literature, and the creation of a national folk culture, later engaged Jews during the Hebrew Revival. Traces of these sentiments can be found decades later, for instance, in reports from Palestine that Haim Hissin contributed to the Russian-Jewish periodical *Voskhod*. Sent to write about the new Jewish settlements in Palestine in the early 1890s, Hissin traveled extensively all

---

16. Susan Layton, *Russian Literature and Empire.*

17. Layton, 80, 83.

18. Layton writes that in his immensely popular poem "The Prisoner of the Caucasus" (1821)—one of the first poems that touted the Eastern part of the czarist empire as a place of romantic adventure—Pushkin "constructed the Russian encounter with nature as restorative tourism focused on the self," 37.

over Palestine, and the reports from his tour reverberate with many of the sentiments that Pushkin and Lermontov expressed about the Caucasus.

Climbing from the coastal settlement of Hadera to the hilly village of Zikhron Yaacov, Hissin writes ecstatically: "There is grandness in the air, which is both somber and bright, like the suffering and loftiness of a great soul."[19] Later in the report, the affinity between Hissin's descriptions of nature and those of the Russian Romantics of the 1820s and 1830s becomes closer, when the traveler is thrust into the middle of a spontaneous dance put on by local Arab laborers. "Waiting to receive their wages," Hissin writes, "the Arabs broke into a *fantazieh*. Several scores of them lined up, rested their arms on the shoulders of one another and created a strong wall . . . making complicated gestures with their legs."[20] Although Hissin's descriptions of nature and the Arabs are conventionally romantic, he maintains a certain distance from the native dancers, against whose primitive customs he paints the civilized, Jewish *moshava*. Conversely, the dramatic language in which he describes nature early on becomes more personal and poetic when he contemplates the ancient ruins of the biblical city of Dor, which lies at the foot of the new Jewish settlement: "Lonely and sad it stood on a low hill that jutted into the sea, as in protest against its wretched present"[21]

Hissin's reports, which are essentially an Eastern travelogue, also demonstrate the unique ways in which Jews adapted this once-ubiquitous genre to their own needs. Although Jews may have been interested to know about the East, for obvious religious, cultural, and even linguistic reasons, they had little access to the plethora of travel and scholarly literature about the Orient, which inundated Europe throughout the eighteenth and nineteenth centuries.

That Jews were eager to know about the East, especially Palestine, is clear from the following preface to the second edition of an 1858 collection of travel essays, called *An Eastern Travelogue (Sefer halihot kedem)*. "When I first arranged this book to be published in a great number of copies," writes the editor, "I never hoped, nor did I imagine that, after two years the book will be sought after in vain, and that not one copy could be had, not even for five times the price that was initially set for it."[22] Compiled of translated excerpts from travel to the Holy Land, *Sefer halihot kedem* does not distinguish between the modern, Western idea

19. Haim Hissin, *Masa ba'aretz hamuvtahat*, 297.
20. Hissin, 300.
21. "Further north, right on the sea-shore, the unclear lines of some ancient tower . . . As I sat there on a rock I felt a connection to our past. The tower had seen a lot throughout the years. . . . Will it also see the dawn of our renewal?" (Hissin, 337).
22. Kalman Schulman, ed., *Sefer halihot kedem*.

of "East" and the traditional, Jewish idea of Eretz Israel. No doubt that,
initially, the holiness of the Land and not its Orientalist exoticism attracted
Jewish readers to the book. At the same time, the fact that the book was
written in modern Hebrew made it a quintessential project of the Haskala. This
kind of tension between old and new with respect to the East was used to
great advantage during the Hebrew Revival.[23] But when reports of travel to the
Orient by and for Jews finally did arrive in Hebrew, they took on a different
shape. While letters from the Land of Israel throughout most of the nineteenth
century represented it as holy and mythological, later reports, especially
from the growing Yishuv in Palestine, found it increasingly difficult to portray
exotically.[24]

But as Hissin's travelogue illustrates, even when Jewish visitors to the Land of
Israel in the nineteenth century portrayed it as foreign and exotic, much of it
reminded them of their own ancient culture as they romantically perceived it.
In the same way that Orientalist works of travel, scholarship, and fiction suggested alternative cultural realities that helped relativize the European point
of view, the Hebrew Bible prepared Jews to recognize elements of their own,
age-old culture as viable alternatives for renewal. While many different factors
shaped this process during the Revival, the Hebrew Bible became a central

23. Judith Montefiore's 1828 *Private Journal of a Visit to Egypt and Palestine* illustrates this point differently. The journal was written between 1827–28 and published in 1836. (The copy I obtained
was reproduced by the Hebrew University, Yad Ben-Zvi Publishing, 1975, and edited by Yisrael
Bartal. See Bartal's preface for a concise evaluation of the book.) Despite the fact that it was penned
by a prominent Jewess, the journal was written from a Christian-European perspective. Mrs. Montefiore dedicated little space to Jewish matters, and her descriptions from the Holy Land exhibit the
prevailing Christian values of her English society. After arriving in Jerusalem, for instance, Mrs.
Montefiore writes: "while Montefiore proceeded with Mr. Amzlac to visit some of the sacred spots
most esteemed in this revered city [Jerusalem], I accompanied [the others] to Bethlehem." See
Bartal, 82.
    Montefiore's talents as a writer notwithstanding, the book underscores the lack of social, eco-
nomic, and even the cultural sensitivities of Jews for the curious, investigative, and escapist elements
of the genre, both as producers and as consumers of it.
    24. A distinct genre that became popular during the *Haskala* was travelogues to Jewish commu-
nities in the East, which were modeled after the famous twelfth-century traveler Benjain of Tudela,
a Spanish Jew who compiled an extensive report about his travels to Jewish communities in the
Mediterranean basin, Iraq, and perhaps Persia between 1159 and 1167. In the late nineteenth and
early twentieth century, accounts of travel to Jewish communities from Ethiopia and Yemen to India
and the Caucasus grew in the Hebrew press considerably. The pages of the popular Hebrew periodical *Hashiloah* (1896–1926) are full of accounts about the lives of Yemenite Jews, the Jews of the
Caucasus, and the various cultures of Eastern Jews in general. For examples, see 2nd issue, 1905,
18th issue, 1908, and 23rd issue, 1909, respectively.
    In the absence of a Jewish upper or leisured class, these reports were written for the growing
numbers of Jews who, like the *maskilim* before them, used secular Hebrew literature as a language
of transition into the general culture. See Dan Miron's analysis of this interesting phenomenon in
Bodedim bemo'adam, 100.

source of regenerative inspiration and was increasingly given a modern, Orientalist context.

The place and use of the Hebrew Bible as part of the Hebrew cultural revolution cannot be understated. The Bible was already an important element of renewal during the Haskala, although for different reasons. Enlightened German Jews, *maskilim*, used the Bible to reconstruct the Jewish past in order to ease their assimilation into their "host" nations. By showing that they had a national past of their own, prominent and innovative *maskilim* such as Moses Mendelsohn and others tried to prove that they deserved to be included in the German national project as a distinct but worthy ethnic minority. For Jewish nationalists a hundred years later, however, the Bible became more than a testament to a bona fide national history in the ancient East. It was also an essential instrument for renewing Jewish independence in Palestine according to the ideals of modern nationalism. The Bible was perceived as containing both a record of a national past and a powerful promise of a national future. Moreover, both were written in the Hebrew language, which became a major instrument in the Jewish national reform.

One of the biblical words for East, *Kedem*, can illustrate the significance of the Hebrew language as a vital element of the Hebrew Revival. Although the cultivation of "East" as a modern cultural concept by Jewish nationalists was inspired by Western, contemporary trends, the tension associated with the Hebrew word *Kedem* was perceived already in biblical times as a longing for a pure and initial natural condition.[25] In his evocative essay about Orientalism in Israeli art, Ariel Hirschfeld notes the three different meanings that *Kedem* contains—a point of the compass, a movement forward, and the beginning of time. Thus, the use of the word *kadima* in the first stanza of Naftali Hertz Imber's 1886 poem *Hatikva*, which later became the Israeli national anthem, can be read in several ways—

Deep in the Jewish heart	כל עוד בלבב פנימה
The Jewish spirit still sings,	נפש יהודי הומיה,
And *eastward, forward*	ולפאתי מזרח, *קדימה*
The eye looks to Zion	עין לציון צופיה

The geographic movement eastward is a move forward that denotes development. At the same time, it is also a movement backward to primordial time that preserves a notion of a first beginning.[26] *Kedem* has therefore a sense of *tikkun* as

25. Ariel Hirschfeld, *Kadima*, 11.
26. Hirschfeld writes that the longing for an initial state of purity is expressed in biblical verses such as "renew our days as of old" (Lamentation 5:21), and "awake as in the ancient days, in the

well, a notion of emendation or reform that was an important part of Jewish culture since the Middle Ages.[27] Hirschfeld points out that what set the Hebrew Revival apart as yet another formulation of *tikkun* was that it tried to incorporate all three meanings of *Kedem*, not just a move to a geographic location in the East but a progressive move forward that was also perceived as a return to a state of initial purity. These biblical ideas, which were absorbed into Christianity and formed the basis of the Romantic movement itself, came full circle in the Hebrew Revival and nurtured Zionism as well.

This was the essence that imbued biblical themes, which were reformulated in the works of the period, representing the Zionist attempt to "infiltrate" back into history; to step out of what was perceived as a Jewish time-warp and occupy an actual national space. Indeed, the great power that Hebrew literature offered during this initial period of nation-building was a longing not only to the East but also for *an* East.

Orientalist trends in Hebrew literature were most pronounced at the crossroad of three periods—Haskala (1780–1880), Hibbat Zion (1880–1900), and Tehiya (1890s-1920s).[28] The interim period between Haskala and Tehiya, most commonly known as Hibbat Zion (Love of Zion), saw a change in the perception of Eretz Israel among secularized Jews. Hebrew literature, and especially Hebrew poetry at the dawn of political Zionism, between the pogroms in Russia in 1881 and the first Jewish congress in Vienna in 1897, began to soften the rational didacticism of the Haskala with an increasing emphasis on sentiment. Poets Y. L. Gordon, Naftali Herz Imber, Shlomo Mendelkern, David Frishman, and many others began writing works that were much more personal and sentimental in nature than the programmatic literature of their predecessors, who stressed rationalism and scientific enlightenment.[29] The more sentimental poetry of Hibbat Zion was not confined to personal matters only, like romantic love,

---

generations of old" (Isaiah 51:9). Other verses use *kedem* in the sense of distance and mystery, as in "an east wind shall come, the wind of the Lord shall come up from the wilderness" (Hoshea 13:15), and especially in Genesis, where "the Lord God planted a garden eastward in Eden," (Genesis 2:9). Hirschfeld, 11.

27. *Tikkun*, the augmentation of ritual prayers with additional readings from sacred texts as a way to amend cosmic, historical, or personal faults originated as a Jewish mystic or cabalist custom in the Middle Ages. The meaning of the religious costume gradually expanded to include many other actions intended to mend various religious, social, and other ills.

28. For a more considered periodization see the opening chapters of Gershon Shaked's *Hasiporet ha'ivrit, 1880–1980*. Shaked discusses the problems inherent in such arbitrary divisions and gives a concise survey of various critical schools regarding this question. Common to all of these schools, however, is the emergence of a viable Hebrew culture in Palestine sometime during the 1920s and 1930s, a process that profoundly changed the nature and history of Hebrew literature. It is during this time that Orientalism played its most significant role in Hebrew literature.

29. See Hillel Barzel, *Shirat hibat tsiyon*, 35. See also Dan Miron, *Bo'a layla*, 88–99.

but often turned to the old fatherland as well, to Zion, as the name of the movement suggests. In the spirit of Romantic nationalism, an emphasis on eternal Jewish values and a yearning for the Hebrew nation's ancient glory were common to many poets at the time, for instance, Shimon Shmuel Frug (1860–1916), whose work is representative of the period.

Frug's poems were originally written in Russian, but their spirit and their style greatly influenced his contemporaries.[30] One of Frug's Hebrew translators, the poet Mordechai Zvi Mahne, accompanied his translation of Frug's poem "Massiach Ben David" (Messiah Son of David) with an emotional preface about "the new spirit, the spirit of freedom, of the love of ancient history, [and] of tilling the land," which imbues the work, and which "enters as a reviving dew into the heart of our ailing nation."[31] Many of the inspirational sources in Frug's poetry—biblical legends, talmudic legends (Aggadah), Jewish history—were directly related to Herder's national romantic ideas. "The poems connected old man and young boy, grandmother and grandchild. . . . Both the ears and heart [of readers] were riveted by the wonders of the past with the hope of learning from them a messianic lesson for the future."[32]

Hebrew prose at that time was characterized by similar changes. Young writers such as David Frishman, Y. L. Peretz, and M. Y. Berdichevsky still waged the old enlightened or maskilic war against traditional Judaism, but they internalized that war and transferred it from the public to the private sphere, a change that entailed radical artistic changes as well.[33] Unlike the poets of Hibbat Zion, contemporary prose writers called for greater realism in Hebrew literature. Most of them, however, focused their works on Jewish life in the Diaspora and were not too concerned with the desolate and uncultured Palestine. The few writers who did write about Eretz Israel channeled the restlessness of their age into a vision of a new Jewish life in Palestine. This vision was still motivated

30. This was true especially after they were masterfully translated into a beautiful biblical Hebrew by Y. Kaplan in 1899. Barzel, 411. Miron also writes that "the influence of this visionary poem . . . on many poetic works in Hebrew at that time . . . still requires an investigation." He adds that when Bialik first began to write, Frug's presence was central and crucial for his development. *Bo'a layla*, 95.

31. Barzel, 33.

32. Barzel, 411. Miron describes Frug's poetry as eclectic, containing elements of both early nineteenth-century Russian Romanticism and mid-nineteenth-century Russian Realism. "At the end of the 1880s Frug's influence on the Jewish literary intelligentsia reached its highest point. . . . [Frug] regarded the Bible as a semi-mythological wonder-world, he utilized midrashic material . . . as well as later aggadic material. He wrote legendary historical poems about Ashkenazi martyrdom, as well as ballads that incorporated Eastern-European folklore, he conjured up the image of the old grandfather who tells ancient stories to his children [סיפור קדומים], as well as the image of the mother who tells her child the midrash about the wondrous Cup of Tears, in which the tears that God sheds for the destruction of Jerusalem are collected until, when the cup fills up, redemption will come." *Bo'a layla*, 95.

33. Shaked, *Hasiporet ha'ivrit*, 1:219–20.

by religion and by ideas about a Jewish "mythology," but it was a vision that also demonstrated an increasing sensitivity to contemporary political and national-cultural issues.

Two such "proto-Orientalists" were Yehuda Steinberg and Ze'ev Yavetz, whose nontraditional use of traditional Jewish texts positions them between Haskala and Tehiya, between Enlightenment and Revival. Steinberg used the Bible to interpret modern concepts of primitivism, nativeness, and a return to nature in the context of an imagined, futuristic Eretz-Israeli commonwealth. Yavetz used the Hebrew Bible in new thematic and stylistic ways that were aimed at resuscitating a romantically perceived ancient way of life. Both men were among the first Hebrew writers who expressed the changing sensibilities of their age, for whom the ancient Land of Israel became increasingly part of the modern Orient as well.

Born in 1863 in Bessarabia (Moldavia), Yehuda Steinberg first published collections of folk stories and children's books, but his most important contributions to Hebrew literature are three realistic novels and a romantic, pseudo-biblical novella called *In the Days of the Judges* (*Biymey shfot hashoftim*). The novella, published in the early 1900s, recasts the biblical story of Ruth as an ethnographic tale and uses the Bible in a unique way to look at the origins of primitive society from a modern perspective.

In the Days of the Judges can almost be read as a prequel to the biblical book of Ruth. Because of the famine in Judah, Elimelech, his wife, Naomi, and their two sons, Mahlon and Kilion, leave Bethlehem and go across the Jordan to the land of Moab. Elimelech's family sojourns in Moab for ten years among the nomadic tribes of herdsmen, who roam the region east of the Dead Sea. Most of the novella takes place during that time. It follows the settlement of Elimelech's family among the herdsmen, the marriage of Mahlon and Kilion to Ruth and Orpa, the death of the father and the two sons in a battle with robbers, and the return of Naomi and Ruth to Bethlehem.

Shaked writes that the novella suffers from too many discursive elements about the relations of the settled farmers and the nomadic herdsmen, and from too much anthropological data.[34] Yet, the Orientalism of the work resides

---

34. Shaked, 258–59. In a footnote to this remark Shaked wonders whether Steinberg had recourse to an anthropological treatise on the life of primitive peoples and adds that the matter ought to be investigated further, 517. A partial answer to Shaked's query may be found in Fichman's preface to the 1959 collected edition of Steinberg's works. On page viii Fichman writes that among the few books he saw in Steinberg's room when he visited him were a couple of history books: "Steinberg was learning then the history of the Eastern peoples in preparation for writing some historical stories." As this is the only historical work Steinberg wrote about the East, it could very well be that the books Fichman saw on his desk were in fact the sort of literary references of which Shaked writes.

precisely in these alleged faults, which recast biblical material in the spirit of both modernity and nationalism. Throughout the story, Steinberg glorifies the nomadic way of life and the proximity to the wilderness in opposition to the biblical trajectory, which emphasizes the development of the Israelites from nomads to settled farmers. Whereas the Bible tells of the conquest and settlement of Canaan, Steinberg reverses this direction in his story. Ancient Jewish history and ethnic origin are connected in the narrative through the general biblical framework. The sedentary farmer, Elimelech, abandons his land to become a shepherd because it reminds him "that Jacob our patriarch was a herdsman too, and Rachel the matriarch tended the flocks of her father Lavan" (258).

The female characters of Ruth and Orpa link together romantic ethnography and Jewish nationalism. Their beauty is Semitic and breathtaking, and they are delicate and shy, but they are also ready to defend their womanly honor to death. "Do you see this double-edged dagger?" Ruth asks Makhlon, who flirts with her. "With one movement I shall kill anyone who comes near me. [And if I don't succeed] . . . , I shall drive it through my heart rather than become a prisoner" (261). When she finishes speaking, her eyes glimmer with a horrible fire that makes Makhlon shudder.

This is not a description of a submissive and confined Oriental woman, as in Southey's poem "Thalaba," or Lermontov's novel *A Hero for Our Times*, where the female protagonists are completely subjugated by the men. The two girls are portrayed as exotic and wild, as female noble savages. At the same time, like the Bedouins, their savagery is mitigated by the laws of their ancient civilization. Although the Moabites in the story worship the pagan goddess Ashtoret, their ancestral connection to the Hebrews sets them apart from other pagans. "Tell me a little about Rachel the matriarch, about our first ancestors," Ruth pleads with Makhlon, who then tells her the biblical story of the patriarchs.[35]

Both Makhlon and Ruth repeatedly explore their ancestral connections. Ruth, who is the daughter of nomads, is interested in the history of her forefathers, who were farmers. Makhlon, the son of farmers, is interested in his nomadic heritage. The savage nobility of Ruth is thus projected onto the ancient Hebrew culture. The story makes a tacit comparison between the biblical shepherdess Rebecca, or Leah, and Ruth of this story. As a result, both the biblical women and their

35. Our first patriarch was Abraham, he was a shepherd.
   I know that. Abraham was Uncle Lot's brother, and his son Isaac sowed the land and
      became a farmer.
   Yes. But he took a shepherd's daughter for a wife.
   Rebecca, the daughter of Betu'el?
   Yes. Rebecca gave birth to two sons. Esau was a hunter.
   And Jacob wedded Leah and Rachel, the daughters of Lavan.
   Yes, Lavan was also a shepherd.

recreated literary characters become something quite new, a modern Hebrew woman who is natural and free but who is ennobled by her ancient heritage.

The selection of Ruth over other biblical characters creates a spatial link with the modern East as well as a temporal link with the national Jewish past. As a Moabite, Ruth provides a legitimate connection to nomadic tribes, ancient as well as contemporary. But as the great grandmother of King David, she is also an important part of Jewish history. Ruth's character is the axis of the story, connecting time and space, ancient biblical time with contemporary Oriental space through modern notions of nativeness.[36]

Steinberg repeated this model in another novella called "Ram and Ramot." The work is partly a Robinson Crusoe or a Tarzan-like adventure story and partly a biblical romance. It tells of a girl named Ramot, who is born on a desert island after her mother, a wife of King Solomon, is banished from the court because of the jealousy of another wife. After her mother dies, the girl continues to live in a palace on the island where she is nurtured providentially in an Eden-like environment. Meanwhile, fearing the retribution of the jealous queen, the man who put Ramot's mother on the island escapes Jerusalem with his wife and son. He is wrecked on the same island, where his son grows to be a brave hunter. The story ends after the two young people find each other and fall in love. While the story is clearly concerned with the romantic conventions of primitivism, it is deeply rooted in Aggadah (Jewish legend or fable) and the Hebrew Bible. Both children are refugees from a material civilization, and their simple lives in nature stand as a rebuke of it. But while the boy leads a truly primitive life—he lives in a cave, hunts, and can barely speak—the girl leads a much more refined life in a palace. Their meeting on the island is the meeting of a new Adam and a new Eve, the progenitors of a new Jewish generation, one that is cleansed by nature but whose connections to the old civilization hold a promise of a great future.

Unlike Steinberg, who never visited the Land of Israel, Ze'ev Yavetz, who was born in czarist Russia in 1857, came to Palestine in 1887, where he remained for ten years, publishing idyllic short stories, anthologies of rabbinic legends or Aggadah, educational textbooks, and political articles.[37] Before moving to Palestine, Yavetz published a series of important articles in the Jewish

---

36. Ruth's unusual role as an ethnic/genealogical "linchpin" is also noted by David Biale, who comments on the confluence of Israelite (=Jewish) and non-Israelite elements in her marriage to Boaz. See "Sexual Subversions in the Bible," *Eros and the Jews: From Biblical Israel to Contemporary America* (New York: Basic Books, 1992).

37. Lachower, 3:41. Yavetz left Palestine in 1894. He lived in Vilna for a while, where he was active in the religious Zionist organization Hamizrahi; he then moved to Germany and finally to London, where he died in 1924.

press that called for a halt to Jewish cultural assimilation and argued for a return
to Judaism. Yavetz did not mean a religious return but a cultural one, based on
the ideas of Herder and other Romantic nationalists. He suggested utilizing the
problematic Jewish existence constructively by highlighting, not hiding, Jewish
cultural difference, a task for which Hebrew language and literature were per-
fectly suited in his opinion.[38]

Yavetz looked for manifestations of the nation's genuine, creative spirit as a
proof of its uniqueness. According to Lachower, he was among the first to cat-
egorize Aggadah as an expression of Jewish folklore.[39] Like Herder, who urged
German authors to collect and publish folk stories as a way of fostering ethnic
cohesion and pride, Yavetz considered Aggadah one of the chief, if not the only
outlet of the Hebrew creative genius since the days of the prophets and elevated
it to a respectable literary genre. A self-admitted Romantic, Yavetz emphasized
the innocence of Aggadah, its liveliness, its health, and its keen sense of instinct
and piety.[40]

The merging of Bible and Aggadah was an important juncture in the development of a modern, Hebrew literature, especially with respect to the Orient.
Although Yavetz was not the first or the last writer to do so, his works demonstrate a successful literary marriage between two of the most current schools of
his day, Romanticism and nationalism. Both were turned by him into inspiring
forces of renewal within a traditional Jewish context. Yavetz emphasized that
the new life in Eretz Israel must be based on ancient Jewish traditions as
recorded in the Bible, an idea he expressed by merging Jewish folklore and
history or by presenting Aggadah in biblical Hebrew form. This idea was not
unique to him, and he did not change single-handedly the way Jews looked to
the Bible in the modern era. But Yavetz was one of the most effective writers
who drew the biblical world closer to contemporary Jewish life by infusing it
with the simpler spirit of Jewish folklore. His work is distinguished by its com-

38. Zeev Yavetz, *Pri ha'aretz*, 12–13.

39. Lachower, 3:41.

40. Yavetz also insisted on translating the mixed Aramaic and midrashic versions of Aggadah
into biblical Hebrew, arguing that Aggadah, like the German, medieval *Nibelungenlied* before it,
should be made more accessible. "And let us hope," he continued, "that the fair and delicate
Aggadah shall find favor with her lovers when she appears before them clad in the pure robe which
she wore in the days of her charming youth"; that is, in biblical times, 130. Yavetz published three
collections of Aggadot, which he culled from Hebrew literature: *Sihot mini kedem* (Ancient Talks),
Shmu'ot mini kedem (Ancient Instructions), and *Neginot mini kedem* (Ancient Melodies).

Yavetz's consideration of Aggadah was typical of many writers of his generation. The anthologies of *Aggadot* that were collected from rabbinic literature by Bialik and Berdichevsky are good
examples of that. On the increasing use of aggadic material in poetry since the mid-1880s, see also
Miron, *Bo'a Layla*, 90–91.

bination of disparate cultural elements of language, history, folklore, and geography that produces a *futuristic* vision of a new society in the old East.[41]

Most of the short stories Yavetz wrote about Jewish life in the Land of Israel are simplistic formulations of an ideal national future cast in pseudo-biblical form. His story "Passover in the Land of Israel" (*Pesach shel Eretz Yisrael*), for instance, takes place during the eve of Passover in an idealized community of Jewish farmers in Eretz Israel. On Passover eve, the son of one of the farmers arrives with his wife from abroad to celebrate the holiday. He is very impressed with the peace, the harmony, the prosperity, and the piety of the farmers and by the end of his visit decides to remain in the Land and become a farmer, too.[42]

Three of the main devices Yavetz used to construct the idyllic reality of his stories are Arab folklore, biblical language and motifs, and the notion of a return to nature, or in this case, the land. As in Mapu's historical romance, *The Love of Zion*, the farmers in this story are dramatized biblical characters. But although they live in a pseudo-biblical world of rustic harmony, they are also rooted in the modern era. They use modern means of cultivation, and they have a keen sense of history, geography, and politics. Thus, by conflating national past, agricultural present, and folklorist motifs, Yavetz created in the minds of his readers a convincing picture, not of their own time but of the future: a national, Jewish future.

Stylistically, the biblical vocabulary and syntax as well as the allusion to familiar biblical episodes elevate the simple tale to the lofty heights of the ancient original, a move that creates a sense of retrospective anticipation. When Amiel, the farmer, realizes that his small house cannot contain his many guests, he tells his wife Leah to let the guests sit under the fig tree. "[Go] under the fig tree!" (אל תחת התאנה), Amiel instructs her, paraphrasing one of the most well-known biblical references to peace and tranquility: every man shall sit under his own vine and his own fig tree (1 Kgs. 5:5, 2 Kgs. 18:31, etc. איש תחת גפנו ותחת תאנתו). Woven here very naturally into conversation, the reference lends an idyllic quality to the domestic life of these modern Jewish farmers.

41. Yavetz's stories from Palestine were very different from the various utopias about a new Jewish society in Eretz Iisrael that were written throughout the nineteenth century. These utopias were completely imaginary. Most of them were written in Europe without any reference to an actual, Palestinian reality. For a representative selection of these utopias, see Rachel Alboim-Dror, *Hamahar shel ha'etmol.*

42. Lachower labeled these stories idylls that shine with a magnificent light: "The observer is full of wonder, hope, and belief that imbue everything . . . [these scenes of Jewish farm life in Erets Yisrael] are infused with the quiet, beautiful and idyllic spirit of Mapu's *Ahavat tsiyon, but they are presented more realistically here. It is as if legend has become reality. . . . these idylls have something of a new realism . . . a tendency to describe real life . . .* only these real-life descriptions are old and new at the same time, real yet idealistically so." Lachower, 3:33. My emphasis.

The sense of retrospective anticipation is created by the imposition of two transparent pictures one on top of the other. On the one hand, there is the world that is evoked by the Bible, with its deep sense of national independence, self-sufficiency, and emotional immediacy. On the other hand, there is the contemporary agricultural world of the *moshavot* and the local Orient. Yavetz creates an image of an independent, national Jewish future by combining these two worlds. The stature of the Bible elevates contemporary reality, which in turn makes the biblical text more relevant and lively. Both take place in the East, the place of the ancient and future Jewish nation, which is crucial for the production of the effect. The result is a half real–half imagined exotic travelogue/Oriental adventure story that has elements of the folk story in it as well.

Yet even this idyllic story hints at the problems that later characterized the Zionist settlement of Palestine. Despite the phrases that the Jewish farmers borrow from the Arabs, the reformulation of biblical power relations between Hebrews and Gentiles augurs things to come. When a messenger arrives to tell the farmers that Bedouin flocks invaded their fields, his announcement of "Behold, the Bedouins have come with their camels upon the barley field" (הנה עלו הבדווים בגמליהם על חלקת השעורים), conjures up the raids of the Midianites and the Amalekites in Judges 6:3–4.[43] This clear biblical analogy, which perpetuates the mythological tension between Jews and Gentiles, is further complicated later on when the Bedouins are parodied by the Jewish colonists as incompetent and foolish natives. At the same time, Yavetz also borrows positive elements from the local Arab culture that help transform the Diaspora Jew into a new Hebrew man. When the visitors from Europe see the Arab-like horsemanship of the Jewish farmers, they are very impressed and can "hardly believe how these young Jews possess such courage and such force of hand."

Yavetz, who lived during the height of Romantic nationalism, tried to make the internal Jewish world fit the spirit of his age. His literary images link Jewish past and a wishful Jewish future. The imaginary quality of harmony and bliss in his stories was not meant to conceal the hardships of the settlement efforts but rather to provide an encouraging picture of a possible national future.[44] The

---

43. "And whenever the Israelites sowed, the Midianites and the Amalekites would come upon [their fields] . . . and destroy the crop of the land" (והיה אם זרע ישראל ועלה מדין ועמלק . . . וישחיתו את יבול הארץ).

44. Most critics agree that Yavetz's fiction is more important for historic than for literary reasons, for being the earliest nature stories from the *moshavot* in Palestine. For a collection of articles about Yavetz and his work, see S. Ernst, ed., *Sefer Yavetz*. The work is often faulted for purposefully misrepresenting the harsh Palestinian reality. Nurit Govrin writes that Yavetz never intended to reflect reality but to look at the history of the Yishuv as an Aggadah, a legend in the making. It therefore seems irrelevant to me to fault him for faking reality, for creating a romantic illusion, or for deviating from the truth. Rather, one should read them according to Yavetz's own intention, not as an

Orientalist quality of his work resides in his ability to assimilate the Western, romantic notion of a return to nature with other nationalistic notions that circulated in nineteenth-century Europe, like the Russian idea of *Narodnost*. The term, which means "folkness," "nativeness," or "nationalness," and which evolved in Russia at the beginning of the nineteenth century influenced by Herder's ideas of nationality and ethnicity, was another romantic concept that Jewish pioneers from Russia imported with them to the East during the Hebrew Revival. Yavetz combined these ideas and transplanted them into the Orient. Infusing these imported ideas with references to the ancient national, Hebrew past and borrowing elements from the contemporary East, Yavetz created a fictional Hebrew Orient by synthesizing East, West, past, and present.[45]

Both Steinberg and Yavetz expressed a mixture of Western European ideas that was characteristic of the Hebrew Revival. Steinberg, who never came to Palestine, reformulated the ideas of Rousseau and Herder through an abstract but insightful use of the Hebrew Bible that enabled him to combine history (past) with geography (present, East). Yavetz, who lived and worked for a time in Palestine, ignored the harsh realities of the small Jewish settlement there and created a utopian Jewish society modeled on the Bible and on the local Arab culture. In both cases, while the European background remained important, the literary sources and their reformulation were fundamentally and uniquely Jewish.

Steinberg and Yavetz were among the first writers who envisioned the actual reintroduction of Jews into the contemporary Orient. But their works remained naive and for the most part simplistic, and they ignored some of the major problems that inhered in Zionism. The next three chapters look at the works of three writers who were more mindful of the paradoxes of time, space, culture, and politics that Zionism entailed. These are *Bamidbar* by David Frishman, *The Sons of Arabia* by Moshe Smilansky, and *Allah Karim!* by L. A. Arielli.

While these three works represent the major attitudes toward the East in the emergent Hebrew culture of the *fin de siècle*, they are but representative examples of broader and more nuanced contemporary negotiations of the Land of

---

accurate record of the Yishuv's history but as the impression that the efforts of revival made on the national soul. See Nurit Govrin, *Dvash misela*, 38–44. ∕ *HONEY FROM THE ROCK.*

Yavetz thought that literature should be a source of inspiration not of reflection. He believed that it should be nourished by the vast sea of Jewish letters (Bible, Midrash, Aggadah), but at the same time abide by contemporary reality. He theorized that Judaism has always been able to use historical events constructively, even catastrophes. See the discussion of his philosophy in Yaffa Berlowitz's article, "Haseder hashlishi—tor yisrael be'artso," 165–182.

45. On *Narodnost*, see Lauren Leighton, *Russian Romanticism: Two Essays*, 28. The literary nature of *Narodnost* is an important point of comparison between Russian and Hebrew cultures. Leighton writes that the *Narodniks* were primarily concerned with problems of form and content, language and style, theme and motif, folklore, historical sources, literary merit, originality, etc. (45).

Israel as Orient. The Oriental sensibilities of David Frishman's *Bamidbar* (chapter 2) found an equally powerful expression in many works by leading writers at the time, for example, Micha Yosef Berdichevsky, Haim Nahman Bialik, and Shaul Tchernichovsky. Berdichevsky, like Frishman, never wrote about the new Jewish life in Palestine, yet his shtetl Jews, deep in the green fields and forests of central and eastern Europe are often haunted by the free and violent spirits of their biblical ancestors. West and East clash tragically within them, as in the story "Red Heifer" (*Para Aduma*), for instance, in which a group of shtetl butchers, possessed by the spirits of their ancient, Near Eastern forebears, violently slaughter a cow as if they were the Canaanite "priests of Ba'al, dividing the spoils of the sacrifice before the altar." Bialik gives his Arcadian dream of a lost paradise a distinctly nationalist turn when he places it in Zion in his 1891 poem "To the Bird" (*El Hatsipor*). Sitting by his window, the poet welcomes a bird just returned from "the warm lands" (*Atrsot hakhom*, i.e., the Land of Israel). The biblical topoi of Zion in the poem are mythological (the Valley of Sharon, the Hill of Levona, Mt. Lebanon, the Jordan River, etc.), but the contrast with the miseries of the Diaspora and the insertion of Zionist pioneers into this picture creates a jarring clash. The Land of Israel is both a magical paradise and an alluring refuge that promises a new beginning.[46]

Tchernichovsky explored the more pagan dimensions Frishman suggested by dedicating a number of poems to the ancient Near Eastern universe, of which Jews are perceived to be an integral part, together with Canaanites, Babylonians, and other nations. In his poems "The Death of Tamuz" (*Mot Hatamuz*, 1909) and "My Astoreth, Won't You Tell Me" (*Ashtorti li, halo tasikhi li*, 1919), for instance, about the death of the Babylonian god Tamuz and about the Canaanite goddess Astoreth, the ancient Near East becomes a rich source of violent moods and passions aimed at injecting new life into traditional Judaism.[47] Similarly, in one of his most well-known and often-quoted poems, "Facing the Statue of Apollo" (*Lenochach pesel apolo*, 1899), Tchernichovsky declares that he comes as a Jew to pay homage to the youthful and beautiful Greek god, a symbol of

---

46. Yosef Berdichevsky, "Red Heifer" (Tel-Aviv: Dvir Publishing, 1977), 174. Bialik's poem continues:

> And my laboring brothers, who sow in tears
> Did they reap the first of the harvest in joy?
> Would that I had wings so that I can fly to the land
> Where the almond and the date-palm bud!
> Bialik, *Shirim* (Tel-Aviv: Dvir Publishing, 1966), 9–11.

See also Miron, *Bo'a Layla*, 98–99, who calls his own review of this poem, "To the Bird—Giving a Concrete Meaning to a Landscape of Dreams" (*El hatzipor—nof halomi bemisgeret hishtam'ut metzi'utit*).

47. Shaul Tchernichovsky, *Kol Kitve Shaul Tchernichovsky* (Am Oved, 1990), 1:174, 200, respectively.

light and all that is good and noble in life.[48] The poet's worship of the idol is an act of protest against his morbid Jewish ancestors, who suppressed the vigor and fierceness of the ancient Hebrew god; "a god of wondrous deserts / the god of the sweeping conquerors of Canaan / and bound him with straps of phylacteries."[49]

The exotic Orientalism of Moshe Smilansky's *Sons of Arabia* (chapter 3) found a wider expression in the literature of the period, perhaps because it offered a simpler and more alluring view of a new and "wild" Jewish East. In a political ode titled "The Vision of Arabia" (*Masa 'arav*, 1907), a contemporary of Smilansky, Yehoshua Radler-Feldman, a.k.a. Rabbi Binyamin, formulated an idea he called pan-Semitism.[50] Written in beautiful biblical Hebrew, the poem literally sets down a political platform for a Hebrew Orientalism. It notes the historical connections between Jews and Arabs and their influence on contemporary social and cultural relations between the two peoples that ought, in R. Binyamin's opinion, to inspire the national Jewish revival in Palestine. *U.S.A.*

The Sons of Arabia was the most extensive literary conceptualization of R. Binyamin's Romantic sentiments about a Jewish Orient, but it was by no means the only one. The image of the native Palestinian Arab as a model for a new Palestinian Jew became common in Yishuv culture during the 1920s and 1930s, beginning with Hemda Ben-Yehuda's romance *The Farmstead of the Sons of Rehab* (*Havat bnei rekhav*). The story, serialized in the journal *Hashkafa* during 1902–3, followed the romantic adventures of a Jewish immigrant who comes to Palestine to look for the ten lost tribes, eventually finds them, and settles among them after he falls in love with a beautiful Hebrew-Bedouin girl.[51]

Apocryphal legends about independent tribes of Jews, who remained in the Near East after the destruction of the Temple, abounded in Jewish literature

48. Tchernichovsky's use of Greek symbolism here is a protest against excessive Jewish spirituality more than a cultural identification with the Greeks, who along with Turks were considered at least partially Eastern or Oriental during the Romantic period in Europe.

49. Tchernichovsky, 1:85–87.

50. R. Binyamin, *Al hagvulin* (Vienna: Appel Bros. Publishers, 1923), 98–101. See also his 1902 ode titled "Pan-Semitism" (*Panshemiyut*), 18–20. R. Binyamin was the pen name of the Zionist writer, publicist, and activist Yehoshua Radler-Feldman (1880–1957). Radler-Feldman took active part in the literary life of the Yishuv and was one of the founders of the Arab-Jewish friendship organization *Brit-Shalom* in 1925. The small organization sought to bring Arabs and Jews closer together and to accommodate the national aspirations of both communities. R. Binyamin also edited *Brit-Shalom*'s publication, *Our Aspiration* (She'ifatenu). The organization dissolved in the mid-1930s.

51. Hemda Ben-Yehuda contributed many articles to the various newspapers her husband, Eliezer Ben-Yehuda, edited in Jerusalem at the turn of the century, among them several serialized romances. Although she was a pioneering journalist, probably the first female journalist of the modern, Hebrew press, her more literary endeavors were not universally appreciated. Brenner, the great realist critic of the Hebrew Revival, had little respect for some of the more trivial flights of nationalist fancy that both Hemda and her husband expressed in their various venues. "The journals

since the Middle Ages.[52] In the late 1800s, these mythological stories inspired actual searches for the alleged lost tribes, whose existence was reinterpreted in the spirit of Romantic nationalism. Because the Jewish national enterprise in Ottoman Palestine was slow and difficult, the searches were aimed at boosting it demographically, politically, and culturally. It was hoped that the indigenous Jewish tribes, together with the Jews from Europe, would hasten the re-establishment of a Jewish state in Palestine, and create a new breed of Jews—proud, fearless, and independent.

In her story, Hemda Ben-Yehuda gives a literary expression to this romantic longing in the form of a love story between a European Jew and a Hebrew-Bedouin woman. Although the story had little literary consequence even at the time, its constructive interpretation of exotic, escapist elements is noteworthy. Ben-Yehuda takes an old tale out of the confines of mythology and contemporizes it as ethnic folklore. Much like Yavetz, she does that by combining reality and lore, by styling the aggadic quest as a modern, ethnographic journey.[53]

A more sophisticated treatment of this theme is found in Yosef Luidor's short story "Yo'ash," about a wild Jewish nature-boy growing up in Palestine. Yo'ash's dismissal of formal education is a critique of Jewish bookishness. His attraction to the great outdoors and his intimate knowledge of the local Arab culture designate him as the missing link between Jewish Europe and the ancient Hebrew East:

> He did not find his place in school either. . . . The good teacher has never come in contact with an Arab, and the Arab world and way of life were impenetrable to him. In his great love for the Land of Israel and the Hebrew language he only saw the Hebrew residents of the country, Hebrews who speak Hebrew and who sing Hebrew songs. Every child was either "European" to him or "Hebrew and ancient," which he prided himself on knowing aright. But in Yo'ash he found

---

of Ben-Yehuda," he wrote, "appear self-serving and seem to instill in others the earlier illusion of Jews abroad, as if there exists in Erets Israel a miniature Jewish kingdom and that the Ben-Yehuda family is the 'first family' of that kingdom. . . . This is the inspiration for its shameful phraseology, . . . this is the reason for all the lies, the fabrications, the exaggeration, the pompous articles. . . . and the artifice, the ubiquitous artifice of both language and content." See Nurit Govrin, *Dvash misela*, 52.

52. For a survey of these legends and their place in Hebrew literature, see Shmuel Verses, *Mimendale ad hazaz* (Hebrew University Press, 1987), 300–328.

53. Another example is Rachel Yana'it Ben-Tsvi, who wrote extensively on the obstinate searches that her friend and later husband, Yitshak Ben-Tsvi, conducted after these ephemeral tribes. Ben-Tsvi, who later became Israel's second president, was entranced by the dream of "going to the desert with Yehezkiel Hankin. In his imagination he can already see how they initiate the long-lost Jews of Heibar as watchmen in the moshavot." "The Beduins are men of nature," says Avner [Ben-Tsvi's Hebrew name], "we shall let new blood into the veins of the Yishuv, Hebrew blood from the desert." See *Anu olim* (Am Oved, 1959), 83.

neither the "European" nor the "Hebrew and ancient" as he thought of it. But he did recognize in Yo'ash a wild and natural force that yields to nothing.[54]

Luidor is clearly conscious both of the Jewish attraction to the East and its Romantic nature and he creates Yo'ash as a bridge between the two types of Jews, the European, and the Hebrew and ancient. The invention of Yo'ash as a Jewish native, an authentic product of Eretz Israel/Palestine, makes it possible for Luidor to distance himself from the Romantic longing that produced Yo'ash's image in the first place, and even criticize it.

Ya'akov Rabinowitz's 1929 *The Wandering of Amasai the Watchman* (*Nedudei 'amasai hashomer*) ends this trend more or less with the introduction of a composite Jewish hero.[55] Amasai is a Jewish native of Palestine, a watchman who has fully assimilated Jewish, ancient Hebrew, and Bedouin characteristics. He spends much of the book looking for the Sons of Heibar (Heibar is another name for Rehab), but at the end admits the folly of his Romantic dream. "Let us rid ourselves of our excessive cleverness and our Arabisms," he says resolutely, "let us be Hebrew and lead fine lives. . . . Enough with dreams and fantasies! The time has come to begin our work" (227). As the Yishuv grew and developed, this genre became increasingly marginalized and eventually was relegated for teenagers.

Lastly, A. L. Arielli's critique of the Zionist romance with the East (chapter 4) was shared by other writers as well, especially Yoshef Haim Brenner, who was one of the harshest critics of such attitudes. In 1921, shortly before he was murdered by Arabs, Brenner wrote about the folly of such notions. Brenner describes a stroll he took one evening in the orchards of Jaffa, where he encountered several Arabs who sat in front of their house and ignored his neighborly greeting. Smarting from the insult, Brenner wrote: "Even if it were true, that the natives of this land are our kinfolk, and that the *fellahim* [Arab farmers] of Eretz-Israel have some Jewish blood in them, I want nothing to do with them!"[56] But after the strolling writer meets another Arab a little later on, a 14-year-old boy who told him of the hardships of his life as a hired agricultural hand, his reaction becomes mellower. "Whether it is true or not that we are related," Brenner wrote, "I am responsible for you. I must enlighten you and teach you the way of the world!" This seemingly paternalistic, maybe even colonial attitude is explained by Brenner as follows:

---

54. Yosef Luidor, *Sipurim*, 66.
55. Ya'akov Rabinowitz, *Nedude 'amasai hashomer*.
56. Brenner, 2:212. The article appeared on the 20 of Nissan, 1921 in the periodical *Kuntres*.

We must not attempt to revolutionize the East quickly, by the directive of a certain committee and in the name of a certain socialistic policy. No. No politics! This is precisely what our role should *not* be, even though we may be forced to do it, desperately, without a choice!—But no. [It would be much better if we could inspire] a soulful connection (*maga nefesh benefesh*). . . . from this day . . . and for generations to come. . . . for many days . . . with no aim . . . with no purpose . . . except to be brothers and friends.[57]

Brenner quickly discards any romantic notion of affinity between Jews and Arabs, demanding a realistic consideration of the East and recognition of its hostility and poverty. He would much rather base the relations between the two ethnic groups on human empathy and responsibility than on fantastic ideas of kinship veiled by the mists of time. The task of Zionism, in his opinion, was not to bring civilization to a backwards East. Although he was convinced he could improve the lives of the Arab natives, he finally understood that this can be accomplished only after the two groups achieve equality.

Related bodies of works about the Arab and Sephardi communities of Palestine were written by Yitzhak Shami (1888–1949), Yehuda Burla (1886–1970), Ya'acov Hurgin (1898–1990), and other Jewish natives of Palestine, Sephardi, and Ashkenazi. Their works are not included in this study, however, because they were written by natives. As men who were intimately familiar with the Old Sephardi Yishuv and the local Arab culture, these writers lacked the distance and alienation that characterize Hebrew Orientalist literature. Shami's case is perhaps the best example of this. His 1928 novella *Revenge of the Fathers* (*Nikmat ha'avot*) is a rare poetic study of early twentieth-century Palestinian Arab society and culture. But precisely because it deals with local Arab culture from the perspective of a native the work cannot be labeled "Orientalist." As Shaked puts it, *Revenge of the Fathers* is an Arab work of literature that happens to be written in Hebrew.[58]

The same holds true for Burla, who wrote about the Old Yishuv with the knowledge and awareness of a native.[59] One of the chief criticisms leveled at Burla was that his stories suffered from an overabundance of plot lines, characters, and emotions, characteristics that were labeled "Orientalist" by his con-

---

57. Brenner, 2:212.

58. "As opposed to Smilansky, Shami is not an 'exotic' writer, but a native writing about his fellow countrymen, familiar with the ways of the Arab and Sephardi East. Shami does not write about the East, but rather uses it as a background to his stories." Shaked, *Hasiporet*, 2:71.

59. Another writer, Nehama Puchachevsky (1869–1934), dedicated a large portion of her work to the Yemenite Jews of Palestine. But, as Shaked writes, Puchachevsky's stories "are village melodramas that are [artificially] transferred from Ashkenazis to Yemenites." Shaked, *Hasiporet ha'ivrit*, 1:53.

temporaries.[60] Two of his best works, the novels *His Hated Wife* (*Ishto hasnu'a,* 1922–23) and *The Adventures of Akavia* (*'Alilot 'akavia*), are passionate melodramas from the life of the old Jewish Yishuv in Palestine. Their literary value aside, both novels provide an unmediated picture of the Sephardic and Arab communities that disqualifies them as "Orientalist" for the purpose of this study. Burla's native Palestinian world is not imagined, projected, or invented. It is a veritable world that is authentically local and therefore not included among the works discussed here at length.[61]

Ya'acov Hurgin's case is perhaps the most peculiar of the native writers. Although he grew up in a committed Zionist home in Jaffa and belonged to the first modern immigration wave, the First Aliyah, he never wrote about the new Jewish Yishuv, dedicating his entire work to the old Sephardic Jewish community of Palestine and especially to the native Palestinian Arabs. Hamutal Bar-Yosef writes that Hurgin's works resisted the tendency by many in the Yishuv to mythologize and romanticize the East and that he was the only Hebrew writer who was not captivated by the stereotypical Romantic formula, which served up Easternness as a pure and hermetic primitivism.[62] Rather, his naturalistic portrayals of Arabs, Sephardis, and the few Ashkenazi characters that appear in his stories are realistic interpretations of the absurdities of human life that are not confined to region or genre. More important perhaps, Zionism in his stories is always described from the perspective of the native Palestinian, Jew, or Arab, and never from that of the European immigrant, so that it sometimes appears menacing and sometimes unnatural but rarely if ever as a positive development. This unusual literary phenomenon can qualify Hurgin's works as postcolonial perhaps, but they cannot be considered Orientalist in any meaningful way.

As a literary trend, Orientalism played a role in the Zionist revolution only for a short time. None of these trends survived long past the 1930s, when the relationships between Arabs and Jews began to be defined more by the harsh

60. In 1929 Bialik wrote the following to Burla: "You know how to tell a story. . . . And since I do not want to seem too flattering, let me tell you that you have exaggerated a little with the emotional overflowing of your heroes. You went overboard. Still, your stories captivate the reader so." Shaked, *Hasiporet ha'ivrit,* 2:89. Shaked himself writes that Burla's stories are "complex tales whose psychological reasoning and styling is less important than the constant need to create effects of suspense and denouement (something must always be happening), fear and pathos." 2:85.

61. Burla, who was greatly influenced by the writers of the Second Aliyah, actually underwent an opposite development. "The natural wonder of the Zionist immigrants (Vilkansly, Luidor) sometimes became an enthusiasm about the West. Many of his protagonists leave the Jewish East and end up in the kibbutz." Shaked, *Hasiporet ha'ivrit* 1:83.

62. See the afterword by Hamutal Bar-Yosef in *Professor Leonardo,* 261.

realities of politics than by anything else. As the Jewish settlement in Palestine grew and developed, the political consciousness of Palestinian Arabs developed apace. The fierce competition that ensued between the two nascent polities barred a meaningful cultural exchange. Some of the old notions about the East found their way into subsequent literary works and cultural phenomena. For the most part, however, Hebrew writers from the 1930s forword dealt with the cultural meaning of Israel's geographic location and the local Palestinian Arab culture in vague and obscure ways.[63]

63. Even those who wrote about it repeatedly often did so in vague ways. See for example Amos Oz in *My Michael* (Tel-Aviv: Am Oved, 1968), in which Arabs appear mostly in the heroine's hallucinations and A. B. Yehoshua's *Mr. Mani* (Tel-Aviv: Hakibbutz Hame'uhad, 1990), in which the relations between Jews and Muslims have been variously interpreted. For more on this, see the conclusion of this volume.

CHAPTER 2

Staging a Hebrew Renaissance

The Hebrew Bible as an Orientalist Text

In the spring of 1911 the famous author, translator, and cultural agent extraordinaire, David Frishman, visited Palestine for the first and only time in his life. Delighted with the flourishing Jewish community he encountered there, Frishman wrote about his impressions from the trip in a series of letters, which were published in the periodical *Hatzfira* throughout that year. The first letter opened with a paraphrase of Yehuda Halevi's famous medieval poem: "Exile, will you not inquire after the well-being of your Zionists?" (*Galut, halo tish'ali lishlom tziyonayich?*).[1] Addressing himself to the Diaspora or Exile instead of to Zion, Frishman continued:

> I just returned from a visit to [the Zionists in Palestine], and could tell you a great deal, but I must confess the truth: writing has never been more difficult for me. I could have easily written a whole book about Mars, its inhabitants and the colonies on it, about the high-school and the national bank and the old and new Yishuv, and about the hopes for the future on that planet. But Eretz Israel is a different matter all together. Mars, after all, has no place in my soul or in my heart. This is something I cannot say about the Land of Israel. Many people speak of it as the Land of the Patriarchs; others call it the Land of the Sons. Call it what you will, this small matter changes one's perspective a little. Does the air of Eretz Israel make one wise? No. It would be a mistake to think so. At any rate, I cannot say so for myself. On the contrary, the little wisdom I brought with me from home evaporated like thin smoke on the day I arrived in the country. The little cleverness that I carried with me from abroad and with which I planned to observe everything, left me as soon as I saw the first high

---

1. Yehuda Halevi (1075–1141) opens the poem with, "Zion, will you not inquire after the well-being of your prisoners" (‏ציון, הלא תשאלי לשלום אסירייך‏), which has become a quintessential expression of the Jewish longing to Zion. Frishman's inversion of this famous line is thus very telling of the profound effect the visit to Palestine made on him.

mountains in all their splendor. Somehow, this place casts a spell on those who come to see it and baffles them. The cold and calculating spirit of criticism that I brought with me in order to examine everything was completely lost the moment I laid my eyes on the first group of beautiful children.[2]

This letter must have surprised many of Frishman's friends and readers, who never knew him to be a Zionist. Yet in the next few months nine more letters by Frishman were published, expressing surprise, admiration, and hope at the chances of the small Jewish community in Palestine, which the exacting critic had often dismissed before.[3]

The inversion of Yehuda Halevi's words was ironic for a writer whom Brenner distinguished as "*The* European Jew"; someone who never believed in a political solution to the problems that plagued Jews at this time and who advocated Jewish cultural integration into Europe throughout his life.[4] Yet Frishman's visit to Palestine seems to have changed his mind and inspired one of his most "nationalistic" works till then, a cycle of short stories published collectively in 1923 under the title *Bamidbar* (In the Wilderness).[5] The stories, which recount the narrative of the Exodus and the wandering of the Israelites in the wilderness, reveal Frishman for the first time as a Jewish nationalist of sorts, certainly in a cultural sense. At the same time, the cycle has a distinct Orientalist quality that makes it quintessentially European. The exploration of this seemingly contradictory combination, which stood at the heart of the Hebrew Revival, stands at the center of this chapter.

Born in Lodz in 1859, Frishman had a cosmopolitan upbringing at the crossroad of Jewish, Polish, and German cultures, which may explain his keen, lifelong interest in European arts and letters. A harsh critic and an immensely influential editor of Hebrew literary magazines and manuscripts from 1880 to 1920, Frishman was one of the first Jewish intellectuals who opened up the Hebrew press to Western influences and shaped the tastes of subsequent generations of Hebrew readers and writers alike. To his contemporaries, Frishman was a trailblazer, a revolutionary who rescued Hebrew literature from the increasingly irrelevant didacticism of the Jewish Enlightenment, the Haskala. For many young, literate Jews of his generation, Frishman's scathing criticism of the parochial and programmatic literature of the Haskala was long overdue,

2. David Frishman, "Hayadata et ha'arets?", 1.

3. See the title page of *Hatzfira* during May–June, 1911.

4. First issue of Brenner's London-based periodical *Ha-me'orer*, 1906. Quoted in Tsipora Kagan's afterword to David Frishman, *Bamidbar*, 194.

5. Berlin, Hasefer Pub. The first tale, "Meholot" (Dances), was published in 1909 in the periodical *Sifrut* (no. 3, Warsaw), 103–110. The last story, "Hamkoshesh" (The Gatherer), was published in 1921 in *Hatkufa* (no. 12, Warsaw), 7–12.

and his beautiful Hebrew translations of some of Europe's most prominent Romantics—Byron, Pushkin, Heine, Grimm, Andersen, Wilde, and Ibsen— were a welcome breath of fresh air.[6]

As an urbane and cosmopolitan critic of culture, Frishman never made secret his distaste for Jewish political nationalism. Already in his debut as a critic in the early 1880s, first in his article "From the Mysteries of Our Literature" (*Mimisterey Sifrutenu*), and then in his second attack on the world of Hebrew letters, "Pandemonium" (*Tohu vavohu*), Frishman ridiculed Jewish nationalism, especially nationalistic writing, as silly and frivolous.[7] He continued to promote these views vigorously in many of his subsequent writings, which spanned forty years of prodigious output: critical essays, feuilletons, poems, short stories, and translations from various languages into Hebrew. Even after the death of Herzl in 1904, Frishman remained one of a handful of Jewish intellectuals skeptical of Zionism.

Frishman's reluctance to espouse Jewish political nationalism stemmed from his belief that it was simply unviable; certainly not in Europe, and preferably not in Palestine, a "desolate," "wild," and "Asiatic" land, as he put it.[8] Instead, he thought that the problems Jews were experiencing in Europe should be addressed within the confines of the continent. In this respect at least, Frishman remained deeply rooted in the Haskala and, despite his scathing critique of its writers, he still believed that a fuller integration of Jews into European culture would eventually bring social acceptance with it as well. But where Frishman differed from the writers of the previous generation was in his belief in an aesthetic Hebrew revival, a literary nationalism, really, that would facilitate the integration of Jews into Europe. Jewish enlightened intellectuals, or maskilim, throughout most of the nineteenth century believed that the Jewish adoption of Western culture would eventually result in acceptance and integration; Frishman approached the problem from the opposite direction. He believed that integration would not be possible until Jews developed their own distinct, modern culture. Only then, he thought, would Jews be accepted into the family of European nations as different but equal members. As vague, ephemeral, and perhaps even untenable as this vision may seem today, Frishman's idea was not much different from that of Herzl, who believed that in order for Jews to be accepted as equals in Europe they would first need to establish a sovereign state of their own.[9]

---

6. See Gershon Shaked, *Hasiporet ha'ivrit*, 1:116.
7. David Frishman, *Kol kitve david frishman*.
8. Frishman, *Hatzfira*, May 29, 1911 (2nd letter).
9. "I am a German speaking Jew from Hungary and can never be anything but a German. At present I am not recognized as a German. But that will come once we are there [Palestine]." Quoted from Herzl's diary in Daniel Boyarin, *Unheroic Conduct*, 278.

But as his letters from Palestine show, Frishman seems to have had a change of heart in the last decade of his life. Always candid, he admitted to his readers that something happened to him during his visit to Eretz Israel. For the first time, a small hope in the future of a Jewish national home in Palestine seemed possible to him, if not for all Jews, at least "for some several hundreds of thousands of needy Jews."[10] Frishman's conversion to a modified form of Jewish nationalism becomes even more apparent when the cycle of biblical and Orientalist stories he published in the years following his return from Palestine is considered.

Written in a vibrant and searing neo-biblical Hebrew, the stories in *Bamidbar* take place during the wandering of the Israelites in the desert and focus on the tensions between individual and community. Although many critics, including the author himself, regard the tales as his best literary work, the subject of the stories is not typical of Frishman's other writings. For in *Bamidbar*, Frishman considered for the first time Jewish history, religion, and culture in a combination that can be termed as truly nationalistic. As such, the stories became a logical culmination of everything he always preached but never managed to practice.[11]

Frishman's initial call for an aesthetic revival was based on the idea that Jews should substitute their old, dry, legalistic literary tradition with new, secular, and more natural poetic conventions. "How long will you continue to study?" he asked passionately in "Pandemonium."

> When will you stop poring over texts that eat at your souls and consume your bodies as well? . . . When? When? For I know only one nation on this earth whose thoughts are crooked and whose life passes in slothful daydreaming. I know a nation which wanders in the wilderness, wanders in a written world that saps its vitality. . . . Rise, I tell you, lift yourselves up from the dust you lie in, stop crawling on your bellies looking for justice and look instead for life and meaning. . . . You are nothing but a nation of old people. . . . Let a new world dawn, a new world that will be free of Jews and their Torah, their commandments and their bitterness, a world free of petty calculations, doubts and inquiries! Let us have the dew of childhood!"[12]

הּ״נּ = 433

10. Frishman, *Hatzfira*, May 29, 1911, 1.

11. Shaked writes that as someone who belonged neither to the Haskala nor to the revival, Frishman typically wrote about protagonists who were a cross between the wanderer of the Haskala (התועה בדרכי החיים) and the uprooted of the revival (התלוש). He adds that, thematically, most of Frishman's literary work is maskilic in nature and is primarily concerned with the corruption of the religious authorities and the parasitic nature of Diaspora society. The most original stories, Shaked writes, are Frishman's later stories, especially *Bamidbar*, in which individuals succumb to their primeval urges and emotions. See Shaked, *Hasiporet Ha'ivrit*, 1:117.

I agree with Shaked, but I think the stories go beyond that, as I explain below.

12. Quoted by Berdichevsky in his article "Dor dor" in *David frishman*, Menucha Gilboa ed., 55–56, 59.

Strangely, this fuzzy and expansive vision actually breathed a new spirit into the world of Hebrew letters at the time and ushered in a literary revival that later came to be known by its Hebrew name Tehiya.[13] Yet, despite his spirited and dogged promotion of a new Hebrew literary aesthetics, whatever he may have meant by it, until the publication of his first biblical tale, "Dances" (*Meholot*, 1909), Frishman never managed to do so himself, that is, to produce poetry or prose that expressed this ideology in aesthetic terms.

One complaint that was frequently made to Frishman was that he always preferred style over content. Deriding him as an aesthete, Yosef Klausner lambasted Frishman for his "hatred and contempt of any work that hints at social, collective or national issues."[14] Frishman's reluctance to enlist his art in the service of a more political nationalism may explain why he was soon surpassed by writers who better integrated his own ideas into their works; writers like Berdichevsky for instance, and even Brenner.[15] As an essayist, translator, and editor, Frishman remained influential throughout his life, but until he published his biblical tales, his fiction never quite caught up with his own aesthetic standards.

Frishman's call for a Jewish cultural revolution is expressed in his biblical tales in a unique way. Inspired by Schopenauer's ideas about art as a unique, visionary medium and Nietzsche's views about the supremacy of aesthetics over morality, Frishman used the Hebrew Bible as a basis and a catalyst for a neoromantic revolution in the cultural lives of Jews. Informed by psychoanalysis, expressionism, impressionism, decadence, and inadvertently Orientalism as well, Frishman mined the Bible as an ancient literary repository of an Eastern nation's mighty life and blood to breathe new life into its listless body, which was languishing in the West for two millennia.

Undoubtedly, Frishman would have been surprised at the label "Orientalist," as may be clearly surmised from his review of a Hebrew translation of Benjamin Disraeli's Oriental romance, *Tancred*.[16] Unlike most Jewish readers of

13. For an assessment of the profound influence "Pandemonium" made on the Jewish intellectual world at the time, see Kramer: "The literary ground shook to the devilish laughter of Frishman, who provoked with great chutzpa both small and great writers," 49.

14. Yosef Klausner, "Yefe haru'ah," first published in 1910 in the periodical *Hashiloah*. Quoted in Gilboa, 73.

15. Berdichevsky based his influential call for a "transvaluation of values" (שינוי ערכין) on Frishman's criticism in "Pandemonium." When I was a boy of 15," writes Berdichevsky, "when I was enamored with Haskala and read voraciously, a friend of mine gave me a small pamphlet that influenced me more than anything I had read till then. . . . The name of that pamphlet was 'Pandemonium,' and its author was the man we all know, David Frishman," Gilboa, 54. Berdichevsky's call is widely considered as one of the major catalysts that galvanized Hebrew writers at the time, and helped them initiate the first literary movement of the Hebrew Revival, the New Move (המהלך החדש).

16. Frishman, "Al hanes hu nes lagoyim o tancred," *Kol Kitve David Frishman* vol. 4.

his time, notably the nationalist and language innovator Eliezer Ben Yehuda, who credited the novel with converting him to Zionism,[17] Frishman was not impressed with the work. He thought it an example of cheap, English Romanticism, the pretentious ravings of a converted Jew that have nothing to do with the real Jewish condition past or present: *ThE SAME umBRELLA ExCisT TO DAy -*

> Why should we be surprised to see that Benjamin Disraeli, that "new Jew," sees a great future for his ethnic origin, for both Hebrews and British; that he wants to rebuild the ruins of the "persecuted" race, sparing no efforts to achieve that, and to establish a strong political bond between England and Asia? And so he presents to us a Judaism which was banished from its father's table and which is now made whole and returned to its rightful estate, and tells us of the connection between the "great Asian secret" and Israel? . . . What possible merit can there be in such a story for us, Hebrews?[18]

Disraeli was writing of course in the Orientalist British tradition and his book was part of a fairly developed philo-Semitic literature in England that dated back to the eighteenth century and even earlier.[19] But no matter how well the book was received in England and elsewhere or how popular it was even in Jewish circles, Frishman was not swept up by its sappy sentimentalism.

Orientalist tendencies by Jewish writers were equally absurd in his opinion. In a vigorous attack on a Jewish book of travel to the East, Frishman ridiculed the exotic sensationalism of the writer, whose provincial excitement over Eastern curiosities was especially pronounced in his report about Palestine.[20] He considered such writing to be drivel, another form of the misguided nationalism of more important figures, like the writer, publicist, and early Zionist Moshe Lilienblum (1843–1910), whose critique of Y. L. Gordon's maskilic poetry Frishman also attacked in the same missive. Frishman was annoyed at Lilienblum's gripe that the poetry of Gordon was not nationalistic enough, a

---

17. Eliezer Ben Yehuda, "Hahalom veshivro" in *Kol Kitve eli'ezer ben-yehuda* (Jerusalem, 1943), 1:10.

18. Frishman, *Kol Kitve David Frishman* 4:85 (פה).

19. See Ruth P. Goldschmidt-Lehmann, *Britain and the Holy Land, 1800–1914: A Select Bibliography* (London: Jewish Historical Society of England, 1995).

20. Frishman writes: "the moment we leave our town and venture out, suddenly everything we see appears wondrous to us. . . . [and when we return, we rush to print everything in a book for the benefit of our townsfolk] that they may see with their own eyes the visions we saw on our journey to foreign lands; where we ate and drank, sat or stood, where we rode a camel or a horse, where we were promised a good horse, or where we were given a blind horse who looked into the heavens and read the stars, where we wore a hat and looked like Ishmaelites so that the pretty women thought we were Ishmaelites. . . . and the readers of this text, who drink in all of this absolutely necessary information, say to themselves: How great are the works of God! And they thank the traveler's goodness for having bestowed on them such mercy and salvation." "Bashuk shel hasforim vehasfarim, mahazot," 4:98–102 (צח–קב).

view he considered parochial.[21] "Whereas Gordon [the lion] speaks loftily to us," he wrote, "Lilienblum, the cat, is looking for cheap Jewish exotica, such as the red Jews, the river Sambation, and the Queen of Sheba that abound in Jewish folklore."[22] Frishman makes a clear analogy between the sentimental fluff of the traveler to the East and Lilienblum's more serious criticism, both of which stem from a similar, unsophisticated impulse in his opinion.

Frishman believed that a true national awakening would not come about through political action—

> Asia always represented for us a symbol of evil and darkness, ignorance and disaster. . . . When we come to Asia, we must do so as enlightened and educated people who bring with them the culture of Europe. . . .
>
> The spirit of enlightenment has always advanced from East to West. . . . those people who believe that they can restore it to its former glory do so in vain.[23]

—but through a cultural refinement of the Jewish soul:

> Poetry, genuine poetry, is what makes a nation! Poetry, eloquent, beautiful and full of imagination will impress the hearts of young readers and instill in them faith in their nation for ever! The people of Israel were made into a nation only by the magnificent spirit that imbues their Torah; a spirit that is planted in the heart of every Jewish boy at a young age! This is the secret of nationalism . . . only by the power of beauty and the skill of the artist will we gather [the young] under the wings of our *Shekhina* [the presence or spirit of God]![24]

This expansive call to infuse traditional Judaism with the "dew of childhood" (by which Frishman meant the early history of the Jewish nation, when it was young and vigorous), the belief that a focus on a new Jewish poetics based on the Hebrew Bible rather than on irrelevant, legalistic texts would create a new national aesthetics, is very palpable in *Bamidbar*, where Frishman's artistic skill and sense of poetic beauty actually creates this new spirit that he calls *Shekhina*. By invoking hazy but suggestive concepts like "national origin," "ethnic culture," and "folkness," Frishman created in *Bamidbar* a text that, according to

21. Lilienblum was one of the earliest advocates of practical Zionism, long before Herzl's political brand of Jewish nationalism became popular. Gordon (1830–1892) was the most prominent poet of the Haskala. Their disagreements represented the clash of two generations—Haskala and Hibbat Zion—and two schools of thought with respect to the Jewish question, cultural versus political.

22. Frishman, *Kol Kitve David Frishman* 4:106–7 (קו–ז).

23. Frishman, *Kol Kitve David Frishman* 4:144 (קמד). Compare this for instance to the motto of this book from Feirberg's *Le'an?* in which he says the opposite.

24. Frishman, *Kol Kitve David Frishman* 4:116–7 (קטז–קיז).

the central tenets of nineteenth century Romantic nationalism, was indeed uniquely Jewish.

Clearly, Frishman was neither a nationalist nor an Orientalist in the usual sense. He did not believe in the establishment of a Jewish state in the Middle East, and he was certainly not in favor of the creation of a biblical-Oriental world in the Land of Israel inspired by Arab ethnography. His nationalism and his Orientalism in *Bamidbar* are more abstract, aesthetic formulations of a distinct Jewish national culture. The stories in the cycle may be considered "national" only in the sense that Herder, Pushkin, and other Romantic nationalists developed the concept a century or more earlier. As distinctive and ethnically identifiable text, they were designed to express a unique Jewish nationality by bringing together language, history, common ethnicity, and cultural affinity in the same way Germany, Russia, Italy and other European nations forged their separate identities during the nineteenth century. The Orientalist quality of the tales in *Bamidbar* is thus inherent in them because one of the most important elements that makes the stories distinctively Jewish is their connection to the ancient as well to the contemporary East. In addition to the more standard, maskilic use of the Hebrew Bible as a medium for reform, Frishman incorporated modern notions of the native and the savage into the tales, which, placed in the wilds of an imagined East, contemporized the text in new and innovative ways that went beyond the ethos of the Haskala.

While the interpretation of *Bamidbar* as an essentially maskilic critique of organized Jewish religion has been the traditional reading of the stories, it is hard to ignore the fact that they were written well into the Hebrew Revival and that they incorporate a lot of the Jewish *fin de siècle* ambivalence toward the Haskala. Although Frishman's search for an aesthetic expression of a distinct Hebrew voice led him almost inevitably to the Hebrew Bible, he did not just use the Bible for ideologically motivated linguistic reasons. After all, biblical Hebrew was one of the chief vehicles of Jewish enlightenment since the end of the eighteenth century. Neither was Frishman unique in using the Bible for its historical value. Mapu did that already in 1853 with his innovative, historical novel, *The Love of Zion*. Frishman *was* unusual however in the biblical period of time he chose as the theme for his stories—the wandering of the Israelites in the wilderness. The focus on the nation's very moment of birth in the vast, barren expanses of the wilderness, where the new, Hebrew community was forged, enabled Frishman to tap once again the power and energy of that moment and ignite a national rebirth in his own day *avant la lettre*, as Susan Layton puts it.[25]

25. See chapter 1, note 17. Yosef Auerbach writes that many of Frishman's characters appear to have "an internal glow of tragic longings for something ideal and eternal. . . . The period of youth in their lives, the 'pre-historic' time, is like a paradise lost." See Gilboa, 107.

This may well be what he meant by the "secret of nationalism," which, if expressed by the "power of beauty and the skill of the artist," will once again gather [the young] under the wings of a new *Shekhina*—a new Jewish and national aesthetic sensibility.[26]

Choosing the most formative period in the nation's history can be better understood as a reminder of the community's first beginning where Frishman's earlier call to "rise," to "lift yourselves from the dust . . . and look for . . . life and meaning" unfolds through an exploration of the Jewish soul as it is released in the expanses of a symbolic wilderness. This wilderness holds a great promise, not just because it is vast and empty but also because it always had such a symbolic place in Jewish history. This is another aspect that gives an Orientalist quality to the work, which contemporized the biblical desert as an "East" in a modern sense. The East in *Bamidbar* is not located in a specific geographical area, but rather, in a mythological space. It is not set in a particular historical period, but in primordial time. Yet this East contains many of the characteristics that were commonly associated with it by Orientalists as a place where fantasy, displacement, and projection played a greater part than any objective reality.[27] In the same way that some of the early Romantics in England moved the critique of their own contemporary culture to an imaginary, ancient Near East, or the way French Romantics animated the eastern Mediterranean with an equally imaginary world of violence and sex, Frishman used a Jewish East of his own creation as a medium for censure and renewal.

A critique of contemporary Jewish religious establishment and a romantic celebration of Jewish individuality through violence and sex make up a major part of the tales in *Bamidbar*. This is one of the most striking aspects of the eight tales in which Frishman gives a contemporary interpretation to the wandering of the Israelites in the desert. "Interpretation" may in fact be a misnomer as the stories in *Bamidbar* are not a re-reading of the books of Numbers, Leviticus, and Deuteronomy as much as they are creatively informed and inspired by them.[28]

26. Elliot Rabin puts it eloquently when he writes that *Bamidbar* "presents an allegory of Frishman's view of art" in its "development from primitive, individualistic, Romantic vitalism to a higher stage of civilization established after the imposition of Mosaic law." See his doctoral dissertation, "Idolatrous Fictions: Art and Religion in Modern Hebrew Literature" (UMI Microform 9825472, 1988), 197.

27. "Already when I was a boy, I disliked geography, and preferred history much more. History seemed to me something that was created by heaven [whereas geography] was man-made." Frishman, "Yahadut" 8:24 (כג).

28. Tsipora Kagan compares Frishman's interpretation of the biblical text to the dialectical reading of the Laws of Moses in the Midrash, where the laws are re-interpreted to fit specific social-historical needs (210). Kagan claims that Frishman does something similar when he gives positive meaning to concepts such as freedom and individuality, which are portrayed negatively in the Bible. But Frishman's reading of the biblical text is too radical to be considered dialectical. It is a complete inversion of both the spirit of the book and its content.

Written from the perspective of religious authority, the three biblical books portray the Israelites as an unruly mass of frightened slaves, who must be broken and forged into a unified, god-fearing, and law-abiding community. Written at the beginning of the twentieth century, *Bamidbar* is fundamentally alien to the ethos of these ancient texts, whose religious values are replaced by the more pressing concerns of Frishman's own time. The resistance to religious authority in *Bamidbar* is enlightened, the care for the poor is socialistic, the defiance of the rule of law is nihilistic, the pursuit of individual fulfillment is romantic, and the sexual promiscuity and morbid critique of culture in the stories is decadent. All of these are expressed through some of the major imaginary categories that animated Orientalism, categories that shall inform my discussion of the stories below, including the image of the desert, the image of the nomad who inhabits it, and the heightened passion and sensuality that Westerners associated with both.

The desert environment received a uniquely Jewish treatment by Frishman, who assigned two conflicting values to it. In ways similar to the English Romantic poets, Frishman constructs the desert in *Bamidbar* as a cleansing space whose austere, natural purity stands in contrast to urban civilization (Egypt in *Bamidbar*, Europe in the present).[29] But the mythological desert in *Bamidbar* is also the location of a highly developed and corrupt religious establishment—a power-hungry body that subjects individuals to its machinations. In the story "Rebellious Son," the desert is highly stylized:

> In those days the desert was mightier and seven-fold more terrible than it is now, the mountains were seventy-seven times harder and sturdier than they are now and man was fierce and tough and rebellious and restless and resentful of all limitations seven hundred and seven times more than he is now.[30]

בימים ההם עוד היה המדבר איתן ונורא שבעתיים מעתה, ההרים היו קשים ומוצקים שבעים ושבע מעתה והאדם היה עז וקשה ואוהב מרי ומתקומם ומתפרץ ושונא כל-עול שבע מאות ושבע מעתה.

29. See also Herbert Schneidau's analysis of the wilderness in biblical prophecy. According to Schneidau, the shepherd in the Bible was seen as an agent of constant discontent, a symbolic agitator. Free yet at the same time endangered by the hostile environment of the wilderness, the wandering shepherd reminded urban society of its potential for physical and spiritual corruption. This notion is very different from the pastoral idea in Christianity, which inherited it from ancient Greece and not from Hebrew culture. The classical Greek idea of pastoral life, unlike that of the Hebrew Bible, is a somewhat contrived longing for an uncomplicated life in the bosom of a secure and welcoming nature. During the Haskala many Hebrew works were influenced by Greco-Christian pastoral notions: works such as the pastoral dramas of Moshe Haim Luzato *Midgal Oz* (The Fortress of Valor, 1837) and *Laysharim Tehila* (Glory to the Righteous, 1743), and most significantly, Avraham Mapu's novel *Ahavat Tzion* (The Love of Zion, 1853). Herbert Schneidau, *Sacred Discontent* (Louisiana State University, 1976).

30. David Frishman, *Bamidbar*, 53–63. All subsequent quotes are from this edition.

The careful construction of this opening, with its incremental superlatives and the long string of adjectives, highlights the desert as a symbolic location. The harsh physical environment is a reflection as well as a potent source of inspiration for the freedom-loving and rebellious protagonist of the story, Kehat; an environment that provides him with an excuse for his asocial tendencies, for his passion, and for his lust: "The youth was like the northern wind that storms across the big plain unstoppable, without laws or limitations. . . . he was like the burning fire that bursts from the mouth of Mount Sinai" (56). Both violence and religious reverence make up Kehat's complex character and both are responsible for his inevitable demise.

Similarly, the vast expanses of the barren desert in the story "On Mount Sinai" (*Behar sinai*) compete with and reflect the ferocious passion of its protagonists, Moshi and Poa, for one another: "sometimes the sky interrupted their holy worship of one another—their love—at other times, the earth stood as an obstacle between them and their great purpose in life" (38). Yet all along, even though the lovers are unaware of it themselves, they dwell in the midst of holiness, that is, on Mount Sinai itself, a construction that presents their love, their sense of freedom, and their Jewishness as inherent to their very being. The final mention of Mount Sinai in the story frames their devotion to one another and foreshadows their destiny by transforming the desert from the cradle of the couple's love to the cradle of the love between God and his community:

> And suddenly there was a great noise and lightning and torches and a heavy cloud came down and settled on the mountain and on the entire land around it and on every valley and every hill. The whole of the great desert stopped dead in its tracks and stood still and listened. Then there was the sound of *shofar* and of horn, and the mountain filled with smoke that rose up to the heavens like the smoke from a furnace.

Just as the passion of Moshi's and Poa's love became almost ethereal before the revelation on Mount Sinai, the physical environment of the desert is spiritualized during the revelation in a similar but opposite way. The sand, the rocks, and the mountain turn from tactile to sensory elements that can only be heard, seen, or sensed but cannot be touched so that the fervent love of the one man—Moshi, and the one woman—Poa, is transferred now to the equally zealous commitment between God and the nation.

While in Exodus, Numbers, and Leviticus the desert functions as an empty space, a "ground zero," a cultural-historical vacuum that gives birth to a nation and to a religion, Frishman's dramatic reconstruction of it, his emphasis on individual self-expression and the perception of nature as a responsive mirror of the human soul, emanates from a romantic longing for nature as an attractive alternative to urban life.[31] The harshness of the desert in *Bamidbar* is a fitting environment for the First Hebrew, so to speak, the savage before he is tamed and bound to the yoke of religion. As the "womb" of the Jewish nation and the place where it came closest to God, Frishman's desert also signifies the purest and holiest time in Jewish history.

In other stories, however, the desert, or rather the mythological East, has a completely different function—not that of an empty, purifying space but as an alien environment whose deadly elements reflect a highly developed and corrupt religious regime that is just as oppressive.

> The desert was terrible all around—yellow, deep sand that swallowed up any foot that was set upon it. The sand was hot, feverish, burning and the light-blue sky pressed upon it like steam. If a small bush grew on one of the few rocks . . . it was never green, but yellowish-white, struggling up, striving to prosper it would then wither and weaken and perish. Sometimes, a great, frightful wind would rise up and drive new columns of sand that darkened the land. A moment later everything would be over and a great, heavy silence would return, suffocating and stunning. At other times there would be the howl of a hungry young lion, the roar of a lonely beast and after it an owl would shriek with fear and then a vulture would scream in the mountains. And just as suddenly the silence would return. The desert languished in the noon heat, everything was tired, listless, devoid of life. ("By an Awl," 19)

Every element of the desolate environment is deadly: the sand, the sky, the rocks, the wind, and the predatory animals and birds. The destructive qualities of each of them is magnified by double and triple repetitions of either the nouns, the verbs, or the adjectives so that, once again, the physical environment becomes a stylized, conscious device. This is a symbolic desert of desolation and despair that holds no promise but death.

31. Interestingly, one of the major flaws that Auerbach finds in *Bamidbar* is the use of the desert as a twisted, sensual, and lustful metaphor. Auerbach complains that Frishman failed to describe Moses as the real revolutionary hero and instead grossly twisted and dwarfed his image, adding him to the gallery of rogues who populate the stories: "[Frishman's] skepticism of his generation's causes, of Zionism, of social redemption, his fixation on an abstract aesthetic ideal and a vague internal and metaphysical redemption, his dismissal of collective power . . . his obscure cosmopolitanism—in general: Frishman's eternal solitude prevented him from accompanying the people on their way to freedom." Gilboa, 115. Written in 1952, Auerbach's critique is characteristic of the positivism of his generation. He admits that Frishman contributed greatly to the revolution in Jewish values at the turn of the century, but he faults him for the "unconstructive" way he went about it. "Frishman's heroes," he writes, "do not know the march of the achiever toward a lofty goal (מעפיל) ignoring the obstacles on the road," Gilboa, 123.

In the story "The Brass Serpent" (*Nehash hanehoshet*) this symbolic desert works its destructive powers on the wandering Israelites: "Ovot laid withering in the burning noon heat. . . . the people hid from the terrifying heat in the tents and under bushes and in the crevices between the rocks" (30). This passage comes at the end of a story about a young man named Dishon, a Midianite from the tribe of Dodanim, whose men are doomed to die after they fall in love. When the dreamy Dishon finally meets a beautiful girl and falls in love with her, he inevitably begins to wither away. Even the brass serpent that Moses holds up to cure the sick cannot help the innocent youth, whose life and love are crushed by a vengeful god. As the desert sun beats down mercilessly on the listless flock of believers, "on top of the mountain of Nevo the brass serpent [could] be seen from the desolate wilderness. . . . looking into the terrible silence with shining eyes" (30). The serpent is no longer a symbol of healing through faith. It is now as terrible and deadly as the desert and the sun.

In contrast to its function in the Bible, the wilderness Frishman creates in this instance is a highly organized and even decadent social establishment, which appears urban and sedentary rather than nomadic. The oppressive natural environment reflects the fanaticism, the cruelty, the avarice, and the corruption of the ruling, religious order.

> It was in the days of the new regime of priests which was just created on Mt. Sinai and which was still weak and unstable so that priests and leaders, clerks and officers of the law were plotting and conniving how to strengthen and fortify it. . . . but the people resisted their efforts. . . . Then it was decided to try a new way, by force and with iron prods and strict punishments. ("The Gatherer," 45–46)

Although the Hebrew nation is new and young, its ruling classes are already described critically as conniving, contriving, and plotting (מבקשים תחבולות) in contrast to the Bible, which describes the Israelites themselves as corrupt and conniving against Moses and his brother Aaron. Later in the story, one of the priests is described as "corpulent and pot-bellied . . . wearing a headdress and tassels and a checkered shirt," while another priest is a "delicate and spoiled Levite," with beautiful, white fingers and luxurious blond hair "like a yellow forest."[32] These images of corruption and indulgence, typical of the way the Christian clergy were criticized since the Middle Ages, seem out of place in the context of the exodus and the wandering in the desert.

In the same way, the detailed descriptions of the elaborate religious ceremonies that are conducted by the newly established religion seem equally unfitting to either time or place.

32. Frishman, "The Gatherer" (*Hamkoshesh*), 46.

At the foot of the mountain seven altars stand upon seven ramps, and the priests and the sons of the priests and the Levites and the sons of the Levites file through the encamped people. . . .

Then Pinchas, the son of Elazar the son of Aaron the priest came out and after him came the rest of the priests in formation, seven in each line, and they were all led by Pinchas, who was wearing a long crimson robe, a cloth vest, a breast-plate and a tall white hat and carrying a bowl of burning incense. The priests followed him in columns of seven, wearing white robes and carrying burning torches that were placed inside pots. At the edges of their robes hung tassels and bells and as they walked the torches flickered, and the bells rang, and rang and rang. ("The Brass Serpent," 29)

The numerous altars, the great number of priests, and their strict hierarchical ordering as well as their elaborately ornamented dress and the complex rituals they perform stand in stark contrast to the desolation of the desert. Instead of a vast and empty space in which the nation is created ex nihilo and communes directly with God, Frishman describes a complex and tiered religious structure that stands between God and the people and justifies rebels like Kehat, Moshi, Poa, and others. As a consequence, and in contrast to the Book of Numbers, in which the Hebrew nation is forged out of a disparate group of people, *Bamid-bar* privileges the efforts of individuals to express their inner selves, even at the community's and their own expense.

Although the descriptions of the new religion in the Book of Numbers are elaborate as well and the spirit of individual and communal rebellion is very much prevalent in the biblical story, both the impetus for rebellion and the lessons of it are very different. Kehat's defiant cry against "this man Moses who raises himself above us" (מי לנו זה משה האיש אשר התנשא עלינו פתאום) in "Rebellious Son" is clearly a paraphrase of Korach's very words to Moses and Aaron, "why do you raise yourselves above the community of God" (מדוע תתנשאו על קהל יהוה) 16:3). Yet even a cursory comparison between Korach and Kehat would reveal the difference between them. Korach interprets his status as a Levite not as a duty that bears awesome responsibility, like Moses understands it, but as a priv-ilege. His attempt to undermine Moses' authority is motivated by a selfish desire to gain power and the entire incident symbolizes the difficult process of forging a unified community of faith out of the mob of slaves. In Kehat's case, the leadership of the community is not working toward a redeeming national goal but instead exploits the people for selfish reasons. In this sense, Kehat replaces Moses in *Bamidbar* and the moral authority lies with him and not with the priests.

But whether empty or populated, the desert is central to Frishman's vision precisely because it has no *political* significance in Jewish history. The desert figures prominently in Jewish tradition, surely, but more as a symbolic space where the nation began. As a temporary, transitional stage on the people's way to the Promised Land, it lacks the political associations that Romantic poets often associated with the East in their works.

"The romantic sense of distance," writes Thomas Ashton about Byron's *Hebrew Melodies*,

> lured antiquarians back to older days and primitive civilizations, where sublime works that would inspire a fallen present may be found. The principle of national self-determination that had emerged from the ideals of human rights at work in the revolutions of the 18th century, found an outlet when sentiment for the past joined hands with a subdued nationalism as men's minds dwelt upon ancestral freedoms.[33]

Yet Frishman's characters do not live in an actual or even an exoticized East of the kind Byron, his contemporaries, and other Romantic poets who were inspired by them liked to construct (Alfred de Vigny in France or Pushkin in Russia, for example)—they inhabit an imaginary Eastern universe. For Frishman, the collapse of Jewish political independence in the first century C.E. is not a punishment for the "vanity of earthly life," as Sharafuddin reads Landor's epic poem "Gebir," but a result of the flawed national religion that was formed in the wilderness.[34] To be sure, pathos and nostalgia in *Bamidbar* function as a critique of the ills of contemporary Jewish society but not as a concealed judgment of contemporary regimes, which do not apply in the Jewish case anyway. Frishman had more interest in the artistic energy that the ancient, Hebrew East could generate as the point of the nation's beginning than in the practical political lessons the Bible offered for a possible national future.

The image of the nomad who inhabits the desert is vividly invoked in Kehat, who was already mentioned above. Although Kehat is a radical social reformer, a Jewish Robin Hood, his escalating attacks against the priestly authorities and his penchant for carnal and other earthly pleasures finally lead to his capture, to his trial, and eventually also to his execution by stoning according to the biblical law of Rebellious Son (Deut. 21:18–23).

At first glance, Kehat's innate distrust of the religious authorities appears like a typically maskilic theme: Kehat "never rose with respect before a priest, he never honored the prophet, he despised the ruler and whenever he saw a holy man he called him deceitful" (54). But the problem with this interpretation is not only Frishman's choice of subject matter, his focus on the moment of the

33. Thomas Ashton, *Byron's Hebrew Melodies* (University of Texas Press, 1972), 3.
34. See chapter 1, note 9.

Hebrew nation's birth rather than on the time of the nation's demise at the end of the book of Kings, for instance, but also on *Bamidbar*'s date of publication. Authors very often choose remote or imaginary worlds in order to camouflage or deflect criticisms of their own societies (both Avraham Mapu and Jonathan Swift come readily to mind, Mapu in choosing to set his first novel during the period of Hezekia's reforms and Swift in creating the symbolically fictional universe of *Gulliver's Travels*). Yet removing the plot of *Bamidbar* so far back in time for political reasons, to veil criticism of the calcified religious establishment, was unnecessary at the beginning of the Twentieth century. By 1900, many Jewish religious institutions had lost much of their authority, among other things because of a century of harsh critique leveled at them by enlightened Jews. A more plausible explanation, I would like to suggest, would be that the wandering of the Israelites in the wilderness served Frishman as an analog to the fundamental shifts that were shaking the Jewish world at the time, namely the exodus of Jews from Europe and the first Zionist attempts to establish a national Jewish home in Palestine.[35]

Although Kehat is not constructed as the Jewish Bedouin one finds in the writings of other revivalist writers, most notably Moshe Smilansky, his blend of compassion and tenderness with lawlessness and cruelty typifies the romantic image of the desert nomad in Orientalist art and literature.[36] "The stories that were told about the boy were wonderful and strange, and even awful at times"; "The boy is a troublemaker, who breaks all laws or prohibitions whenever his mighty heart tells him to"; "Still, no one has as good a heart or has more kindness than him in all of Israel" (54). Kehat's social awareness develops already at the age of seven when he is overwhelmed with empathy at the sight of a poor, small boy. With overflowing emotion, he hurriedly takes off his coat, gives it to the wretched lad, and then runs away "without looking back, feeling embarrassed by his good deed" (54). He cries when he sees how a priest dismembers two young doves for sacrifice, and he steals bread and cereal intended for the altar to give to the poor. But he is also "cruel and harder than a rock whenever he fought against the officers and the leaders who oppressed the people" (54).

Kehat is neither a social nor a religious reformer in the usual sense, and calling him a rebel would be difficult as well.

35. Kagan and others write essentially the same, see Kagan, 199; and Frishman himself wrote as much in "Pandemonium," when he called Jews "a nation that wanders in the wilderness . . . [of] . . . the written world."

36. For romanticized paintings of desert fighters see for example Yehoshua Ben Arye, *Tzayareha vetziyureha shel eretz yisrael bame'a hatsha'esre* (Yad Yizthak Ben Tzvi, 1993) and James Thompson's catalog of paintings.

> When he heard that there were laws and regulations, a religion and command-
> ments that govern what may or may not be done, he ground his teeth with anger
> and swore: surely it is the invention of power-hungry men who wish to limit
> other men and take away the freedom that was given to them at creation. (54–55)

On the one hand, Kehat's free spirit and his innate resistance to authority
of any kind paints him as a noble savage, the wild, impulsive but innocent
Primitive of Western literature. Yet unlike the graciously guileless natives of the
Americas or the West Indies—Friday in Defoe's romantic novel *Robinson Crusoe*,
for instance—Kehat does not dwell in a new world that has no familiar historical or geographic boundaries. As an Israelite, he is firmly set in a time and a
place that has deep symbolic significance. His innate sense of social justice
reflects this, and his resistance to organized religion suggests it by contrast.

The image of the ancient Hebrews as Noble Savages is much more developed in the story "At Mount Sinai," which tells of two young Hebrew slaves,
Moshi and Poa, who fall in love with one another one fateful day and run away
to the desert to lead a passionate life in the bosom of nature. Eventually, they
settle in a cave on a high mountain. But their blissful life of passion is interrupted—the mountain they chose to live on turns out to be Mount Sinai, where
their fellow Israelites crowd around to receive the Torah. The event has a devastating effect on the couple. Poa leaves the cave to join her people, forcing
Moshi to follow her, and the story ends with the categorical statement: "the
Torah has conquered life and vanquished it" (לכדה התורה את עצם החיים ותכניעם, 42).

Parts of the story read like Steinberg's novella *Ram and Ramot*. The two inno-
cents leave Egypt and march off fearlessly into the desert. They defy the elements—storms, burning heat, ice, hunger, and thirst, which are no match for
their burning love. Unlike the wandering Israelites who often complain about
their hardships, the young couple lives in harmony with the desert. "At daytime,
when it was hot, the boy stood over the girl and fanned her with a branch of
palm; at night, when the ice was biting, they laid together in a hole in the ground,
heart against heart and flesh against flesh, keeping warm" (34). Then, when they
reach an oasis one day, they take off their clothes and frolic naked among
the lush greenery, adorning their "burning foreheads with a crown of red
poppies" (37).

Although this is a picture of an idyllic, natural life that is typical of pastoral
Romance, many of the genre's stylized symbols are orientalized here by setting
them in a symbolic desert. The two children of nature wander aimlessly in the
wilderness, "from the plain of Ramses they came to Sukkot, and from Sukkot
to Eitam, and from Eitam to Migdol near Pih-Herut. They did not know where
they were, nor did they know the names of the places either" (34). Oblivious,

Moshi and Poa chart the course that will later be traversed by the Israelites after the Exodus from Egypt. The analogy between the couple's seemingly random trek in the desert and that of the divinely subscribed journey of the incipient Hebrew nation sanctifies Moshi's and Poa's lives. At the same time, it also infuses the group of Israelites who came out of Egypt with some of the young people's free spirit and passion. The two individuals and the national group are thus cross-fertilized. The "dry" Jewish nation—a transparent correlation to contemporary Judaism—is rejuvenated and enlivened by the intense love of the two, while the fierce individuality of the lovers is mitigated by their acceptance of the rule of law.

The ongoing analogy between the journey of Moshi and Poa and the Exodus gives their lives a very particular meaning. Moshi's name, as well as his rescue from the Nile after being thrown in there by a midwife, is clearly written to evoke the story of Moses. So is Moshi's divine realization, not of his election as a leader but of his romantic destiny as Poa's lover ("they knew in their hearts that at that moment the hand of God was upon them and that there was no escaping it forever," 33). And so is the lovers' escape to the desert, which is motivated by a personal impulse and not by a divinely subscribed plan, like the escape of Moses to the desert. This analogy reaches a climax during the handing down of the Torah:

A heavy fog rises and covers the mountain.
The lightning and the voices and the torches grow stronger and stronger, and suddenly there was a sound, not a sound but a thunder, yet every word was clear amidst the storm. . . .
"I am the lord your God—thou shall not have another god—"
At that moment, Poa's lips whisper silently in Moshi's ears:
"Thou art most beautiful! So beautiful!"
"Thou shalt not make for thyself a graven image—thou shalt not worship them—"
And Moshi holds her hand, drunk with love, his tongue is heavy, and he knows not what—:
"I love thee more than all the women on this earth! I love thee, I love thee!"
"Thou shalt not say the Lord's name in vain—the Lord shall not forgive the man who will say his name in vain—"
And so Poa continues, going on and on: "Swear in the name of God, Swear on the sun at daytime and on the moon at night, swear in the name of heaven and earth! Let me suck with my lips the fragrant wine from thy lips, for I thirst for thy lips, let me make my blood drunk with your burning blood, for my soul craves blood, let me bite the wet flesh with my teeth, for I desire the flesh of a living man, let me strangle thee with these my hands till I kill thee slowly with my own hands!" (40–41)

The sacred communion between God and his congregation at the moment of the nation's birth is interjected into the communion between the two lovers. Against the harsh moral strictures of the Ten Commandments, Moshi and Poa whip themselves up into a morbidly passionate ecstasy. The fact that the law destroys their love at the end is both an indictment of religion and an admission of its power. But although Moshi and Poa succumb to the rule of law, their radical individuality and their animal passion has the potential to change the religious community they join from within. This paradox creates a powerful model of renewal because it censures religion and uses it at the same time. Disconnected from the community, Moshi's and Poa's pursuit of individual happiness ends in self-destruction. As part of the national group, it promises to inject a new vitality into the life of the nation.[37]

Frishman was not the only Hebrew writer who used the ancient Near East as a way to inspire cultural revival. When the butchers of a small Jewish town in Berdichevsky's short story "Red Heifer" (*Para aduma*) feverishly slaughter a cow in secret in the middle of the night, their impassioned crime points an accusatory finger at the moral degradation of the traditional Jewish community. The failure of the townsfolk to adapt their religious way of life to modernity results in their corruption. Lured by the freedom and opportunity of modernity on the one hand and pressured by the still powerful religious tradition on the other, Berdichevsky's butchers find an outlet for their incipient and pent-up sense of self in a morbid but vital ceremony that is inspired by the Bible. "At that moment the [butchers] were like the priests of the Ba'al in ancient times, when they divided the sacrificial offering on the altar," writes Berdichevsky. "Yet this did not take place in Beth-El or Dan," he adds ominously, "but in the Jewish town of Dashia . . . in the year 1885."[38] The analogy to the priests of the Ba'al high-

---

37. "In this work, Frishman's individualism found its most radical expression. Beyond the legendary haze and the clerical tone, the twisted image of nihilism is visible. The drive toward the abyss of the human soul, toward the instinctual, the unconscious, and the critique of religion in the name of sensual freedom remind us of Nietzsche's critique of culture and religion, of Schopenhauer's longing for the primitive and pre-cultural, and of [Frishman's] resistance to Judaism, which, in the name of morality, allegedly constricts human action and weakens his vital powers." Auerbach in Gilboa, 109.

38. M. Y. Berdichevsky, *Kitve Mem-yod berdichevsky* (Tel-Aviv: Dvir Publishing), 184 (קפד). Auerbach writes that "Berdichevsky came closest to understanding the secrets of Frishman's soul not because he was a critic himself, but because he was guided by a vague sense, that despite their differences of character and style, they shared something in common, and that 'something' gave a tragic majesty to their lives and works. They both searched for a life of impulse and instinct (חיי-יצר) and longed for the innocence of Aggada. They regarded European man as perfection itself, and worshipped the lofty essence of this ideal. But the ideal always remained abstract. Since they did not find it in Western Europe, and could not create it among the Jews either, they remained isolated in clinging to a figment of their imagination. Unaware of it themselves, they were stripped of their human

lights the atavistic connections of the butchers not to their Jewish ancestors but to their ancient Near Eastern, pagan neighbors, whose sensuality always threatened the Jewish religious establishment in the Bible. The butchers thus become descendants of an ancient tradition that is Eastern not Jewish and which is aimed at awakening a spirit of revival, a cultural Tehiya in their fellow Jews.

Similar forces drive Kehat to rebel against the religious authorities. There are times when Kehat acts like a prophet. "During the day, he would confront the oppressors . . . ," and at night, he comforted "the slave who suffered under his master. . . . There was not a prophet who spoke better than him, nor a heart that felt more compassion than his" (56). The people's cries to Moses and Aaron, which in the book of Numbers are portrayed as petty and ungrateful, are socially justified here by the corruption of the priests so that Kehat becomes the de facto spiritual leader of a proletarian rebellion. Although he is the only one who dares to speak against the priests, he is executed for it in the end.

At other times, Kehat's rebelliousness turns wild and destructive and his love of justice is overpowered by his love of personal freedom to the point of anarchy. He thinks that "there is no purpose, no reason and no point" to life, and that there is nothing better to do than eat, drink, be merry, and forget "the terrible poverty which is called Life" (55). Kehat's ennui turns decidedly decadent when he bitterly confronts his father:

> Who asked you to satiate your carnal lust and give life to a human soul in order that it should live a pointless, aimless, empty life? Must I thank you and respect you for pleasuring yourself so that I shall be brought into this purposeless life? (55)

With this morbidly vicious invective Kehat reveals himself as a neo-romantic hero, whose supreme individuality does not inspire exemplary and redemptive

---

ideals and lost themselves in the chase after a terrifying image that was adorned with the wings of an angel." Gilboa, 126–127. My point is that like many other European nationalists, Frishman's and Berdichevsky's search for a new kind of "Jewishness" instinctively led them in the direction of ancient history, or more precisely, the spirit of that history. The fact that for Jews that history took place in the East coincided with the increasing popularity of the Orient as an attractive idea. Their efforts to explore that history and examine its relevance for their own, contemporary agenda can therefore be included in the general European interest in the Orient. But as Jews, their abstract interest in the East went further than many of the popular manifestations of this idea, as can be seen from the example of Disraeli.

"Revival," wrote Frishman, "must be inspired by sense and taste, and not by science and historical investigations. Those who think that Jewish historiography can make a genuine national revival possible do not understand the root of the Jewish people's sickness."

acts of creativity, excellence, or heroism, but gloomy self-destruction. Ostensibly, the decadent elements in Kehat's character do not belong in the historical framework of the story, which takes place at the beginning, not the apex or decline, of the nation's history. Yet, from the perspective of Frishman's time, these elements fit well into the framework of the Revival, which, for various reasons that are not related to this analysis, abandoned the positivism of the Haskala for a much darker worldview.[39]

Kehat shares other traits with Moses, whose own sense of self sowed the seeds for his demise later on in his life.[40] "Visionaries," wrote Frishman in an 1886 critique of a German play called *Moses*, "were always attracted by the conflict between individuals and the community. Moses is the Superman [in the Nietzschean sense], whose aspirations reach out to the heavens, and for whom the people at his feet are but riffraff, a mob which does not understand him or his ideas, and which always rebels against him."[41] In "Rebellious Son" Frishman reversed this relationship. But by passing the leadership to the mob, he nevertheless exacerbated the problems that plagued the character of Moses and gave them a modern twist. The conflicting image of Kehat critiques and affirms Western as well as Jewish society at one and the same time. Yet by placing it at Sinai, Frishman gives his critique religious and historical significance. Although Kehat himself does not have a national or a political agenda, he joins a long line of alternative Jewish heroes who crowd the pages of revivalist literature; heroes who eventually informed the New Jew as I show in the next chapter.

The third category, passion and sex, make up an important part of the stories as well. The rich and detailed descriptions of the religious rituals in "The Brass

39. For an analysis of decadent elements in revivalist literature, see Hamutal Bar-Yosef, *Maga'im shel deakadens*. Bar-Yosef argues that European decadent literature influenced the writers of the Tehiya more deeply than some of the events that are traditionally believed to have brought change, such as the pogroms of 1880s. She makes an interesting comparison between decadence and Romanticism, and demonstrates how Hebrew writers settled the paradox between the positivism that was inherent in the revival and the negativism that is associated with decadence. Although Bar-Yosef does not write about Frishman, I think that the mixture of Romantic and decadent elements in *Bamidbar* qualifies the work for inclusion in her analysis as well.

Yosef Auerbach suggests such a reading too when he writes that all of the stories in *Bamidbar* describe demise in one way or another, "the method of the hero's death [being the only difference between them]. This is how the psychology becomes pathology," he concludes. Gilboa, 124–125. But Auerbach ignores the violence that accompanies these deaths, the eruption of desire itself as a revolutionary act that signifies a great awakening force.

40. To the criticism that the modern tendencies of his biblical characters were historically inappropriate, Frishman replied that it was his belief "that the spiritual forces and the mental visions that preoccupy" his generation "were the same forces and the same visions that were found already in our forefathers in the wilderness." Kagan, 219.

41. Frishman, *Moses* (*Moshe*), *Kol Kitve David Frishman* 8:129 (קצב).

Serpent," for instance, and the colorful and exotic tapestry of a decadent priestly kingdom they create are saturated with sexual tension; a tension that is apparent already in the first story in the anthology, "Dances" (*Meholot*). Timna, the beautiful young heroine of "Dances," falls in love with the handsome Poot, who, after giving her a ring to signify their love, abandons her and disappears. Despairing of Poot's return, Timna finally donates her cherished ring to make the molten calf and when the statue is cast, she dances around it ecstatically, transferring her passion for Poot to the idol until she falls down, dead with exhaustion.

Timna's burning love for Poot and her fervent hopes for his return are given much more importance in the story than the profound religious events that the nation experiences at the same time. The casual mention of the momentous revelation at Sinai in the story is trivialized still more when both God and idol are equally marginalized: "And in another few days there were yet other news: the people were tired of waiting for God in the fog . . . and wanted a god they could see" (11). As far as Timna is concerned, the true God and the false one are one and the same because love is greater than both.

> The next day was as hot as a furnace. A big new wagon came out from of the high priest's quarters drawn by two red oxen. The gilded edges of the wagon glowed as it turned and so did the gilded horns of the oxen, which were adorned with ribbons of crimson and blue flowers. . . .
> As the wagon was nearing Timna women began throwing down their jewelry from the rooftops and from the windows and from the balconies. A golden nose-ring came falling down from the balcony near her and was buried immediately in the moving mountain of gold before her, then a golden goblet came down followed by a big golden bowl. A spirit of drunkenness came over the people. ("Dances," 14, 15)

Frishman must have realized that the decadent urban scene he describes here was absurd in the context of the wilderness of Sinai, yet he still uses it here, as in other stories in *Bamidbar*, to reflect and amplify an emotional state. The contrast in "Dances" between the arid surroundings and the richness of the idol-worship ceremonies reflect Timna's inner conflict. Against the scorching desert that mirrors Timna's pure and intense passion, gold vessels, jewelry, and other ornaments are thrown in a confused mass into a wagon led by the high priest. The jumble of precious trinkets is not only a reflection of Timna's own mixed emotions but also a reflection of the moral decay of the people, who abandon themselves in a sensual orgy to the worship of the calf.[42] The death of Timna

---

42. Sharafuddin writes that the contrast between the desolate desert as "an empty plain and sterile mountains . . . with sands and dust and magnificent sunsets," and the richness and color of

ends the orgy like a sexual release: "And she continued to dance with no end, no aim, no limit. Her lips were covered with white foam and her limbs were listless, until suddenly she fell to the ground and when they lifted her up they saw that she was dead" (17).

It is not only Timna, Dishon, Moshi, and Poa who pursue their true love until death. Many other characters are just as passionate about forbidden love. In the story "Devious Woman" (*Sota*), for instance, a priest lusts after a beautiful and virtuous young woman, Shifra, who agreed to marry her husband I'ezer only after he divorced his previous six wives. Although the woman rejects the repeated advances of the priest, her husband still suspects her. He accuses her of adultery and demands that she be brought to trial for it. The woman, who cannot bear her shame, expires during the trial before the leering mob and her guilt-ridden husband. Frishman intensifies the sexuality of each of the characters in the story. First he gives I'ezer six wives, who are then removed to make room for a seventh, Shifra, who is worth more than the previous six combined. The priest, too, has an exaggerated sexuality that finds an outlet in his shameless pursuit of another man's wife. Finally, even Shifra's love for her husband, although legitimate, is ferocious. When I'ezer returns home at night, "she threw herself on her husband and hugged him and kissed him with great passion" (68–69).

A combination of promiscuity and chastity, which is often associated with the harem in Orientalist art, pervades the last story in the anthology. "The City of Refuge" (*'Ir hamiklat*) is about a wild, free-spirited, and devastatingly beautiful young woman named Noa who celebrates her sexuality freely with any man who desires her. But when a chaste young priest offers to marry her, Noa refuses because she believes she is unworthy of him. After the young man leaves the priesthood to be with her and is still rejected by the girl, he commits suicide and Noa seeks asylum as a murderess in one of the cities of refuge, where she remains until her death. Like the desert itself, Noa's face looks like "copper that was burned by the sun, her bones were like hot and sharp rocks, and she was as wild as the wind that blows from the north" (89). The fact that she may have been responsible for murder is not perceived as an indictment in the story, but an accomplishment, especially as a crime of passion. Noa's ready admission of guilt flies in the face of her peoples' sanctimonious belief that the cities of refuge will never be populated. "There are no killers among the Jews, and there shall never be any," the people reassure one another (97). The mixture of opposites that characterize Noa—piety and profanity, agitation and serenity—are typical

---

the nomadic material culture, with its embroidered linens and wools, jewelry and abundance of food during feasts, was a common device in oriental literature and art," 7.

of Frishman's other heroes in *Bamidbar* as well, all of whom mount a romantic rebellion against "the wilderness of the written world," as Frishman himself put it.

Sexual abandon, including sadism and death, is intensified still further in stories like "Beheaded Heifer" (*'Egla 'arufa*), which tells of Hogla, a young Midianite concubine who runs away and drowns herself after she is raped by her master, the priest Elitsafan. A year later her body is found and she is buried according to the law of Beheaded Heifer, in which a young female calf is sacrificed as a communal cleansing ceremony to atone for an unknown killer. Elitsafan is present at the ceremony and he too chants the customary prayer, "our hands did not spill this blood and our eyes did not see—but the words whither on his lips and cannot be heard" (87).

The story begins with a gruesome battle between the Israelites and the Midianites and dwells especially on the fanatic fulfillment of the biblical law concerning prisoners of war and spoils of war. The Israelites perform the religious commandments with a bloodthirsty frenzy, killing, burning, and destroying their enemy. The accumulation of loot is staggering, especially the number of women who are captured, "three hundred and twenty six thousand, aside from the sheep and cattle and asses." The victorious Israelites then take "all the women who already knew a man and molested them all night long, then, when morning came, they killed them all" (77). This morbid orgy of sex and death frames and foreshadows the more personal story of Hogla, who is subjected to the same carnivorous sexual appetite by her master the priest.

The captured Midianite virgins are displayed for purchase in the market, their nakedness covered only by a thin blanket that is lifted every time a potential buyer approaches. "The sun burnt high in the heavens and shone on the bare, smooth flesh. . . . One moment the rays of light would sway and wash the uncovered splendor and in the next the blanket would envelop everything again" (78). But the brief moment of revelation is enough to excite the lascivious priest Elitsafan, a connoisseur of feminine beauty, "who has the prettiest women in his tent." At the sight of Hogla's nakedness his eyes shine, the veins on his forehead bulge, and he begins to salivate. After he buys the concubine and turns to leave, his legs shake under him with lust, the veins on his temple throb again, and he suddenly whacks a sycamore tree on the side of the road with his staff, evincing his raging desire through violence.

In the story "By an Awl" (*Bamartse'a*), sexual deviance is directly tied to sadomasochism and humiliation in one of the most subtle but profound expressions of decadence in the entire anthology. Yerak'am, the Hebrew slave of Elitsafan the Levite, refuses to leave his master's service, even though seven years have elapsed since his indenture. "But I do not love you!" his master replies, "you were always despised in my household, spat on, beaten, chased by the dog" (20–21). When the slave still insists on remaining with his master, the priest orders his ear cut with an awl as a sign of permanent indenture: "Let his ear be nailed to the door for three days and three nights and every man and every woman who pass before him shall spit in his face," commands the priest (22). Elitsafan pins the slave to the door and the slave, who seems to be relishing the pain and humiliation and seeks to perpetuate them with sickly pleasure, "opened his lips and appeared to be laughing as the spit touched his face" (22).[43]

Although Frishman frequently uses sexual imagery in *Bamidbar*, the erupting lust of his red-blooded Hebrews does not suggest a revolutionary sexual agenda but rather a repudiation of what he and his contemporaries considered the stagnant and artificial Jewish way of life in Eastern Europe; a longing for a more "natural" existence, inspired by the passions of yore. Many revivalist writers dealt with this theme (Berdichevsky, Bialik, Berkowitch, and even Gnessin), although Frishman is perhaps the only one among them who created a biblical-Oriental universe where these passions can be distinctly designated as "Jewish" or "Hebrew." Instead of using the heightened sexuality of non-Jews as example, as most of his contemporaries did, Frishman went back in time and used the Jewish past itself as a source of inspiration. Unlike Bialik in "Behind the Fence," for instance, Frishman did not invest his Jewish heroes with the pronounced and unruly sexuality Jews usually associated with their non-Jewish neighbors, the *goyim*. And unlike Tchernichovsky, who admires the figure of the Greek god in his poem "Facing the Statue of Apollo" for the non-Jewish characteristics it symbolizes, Frishman used a *Jewish* past for precisely the same effect. The sexual abandon in *Bamidbar* is directly inspired by biblical stories of passion, lust, and wantonness. The heroes in *Bamidbar* are semi-pagan Jews, who exhibit the ferocity and vitality that both the Bible and subsequent generations of Jewish writers denigrated as non-Jewish. In *Bamidbar*, as in much of the literature of the revival, these tendencies are perceived positively, of course, as a reaction against the so-called degeneration of Eastern European Jewry.

The sexual projection that takes place in *Bamidbar*, the investment of a distant region, a distant people, and a distant time with forbidden sexual fantasies is perhaps one of the most significant elements that lends Frishman's Hebrew text its Orientalist quality.[44] The combination of license and censure that intensifies the sense of passion in the stories typifies the Orientalist perception of sex in

---

43. Tsipora Kagan sees the slave's refusal to go free as another formulation of the rebellious individualism that permeates the anthology (212–213). I agree with her, but I think the perversion that is expressed here is important as well, especially as an interpretation of the Jewish condition in Frishman's time. Kagan also acknowledges this.

44. See Hirschfeld's discussion of this in chapter 1, note 25.

the East, which Westerners considered as licentious and restrictive at one and the same time, especially with respect to women. The harem as an Orientalist locus is probably the most obvious example of this contradiction. Although the seraglio promised fantastic sexual pleasures, Muslim customs imposed tight restrictions on these pleasures by limiting men's access to it as well as the movement of women in it. Because very few men could keep harems and fewer still could gain admission to them, the harem was always more of an alluring idea than an actual location one could visit on a trip to the East. This did not diminish its appeal, of course, but rather increased it.[45]

But the stories in *Bamidbar* go even further than this. The abundance of precious trinkets and jewels, the ornate and colorful robes, the elaborate religious rituals, the overwrought passions, the killing frenzy, and the feverish and morbid lust also conjure up the Latin concept of *luxuria*, which early Christian theologians associated with the declining Roman Empire and regarded as the gravest of sins. The evil of *luxuria*, a term that can be best understood as abandon, was not necessarily the sexual acts themselves, but the violent eruption of disordered desire, the complete submission to the senses.[46] Although the Roman custom gradually disappeared after the fall of the empire, it became an integral part of the Christian moral universe during subsequent centuries, most often with respect to pagan cultures that Christianity sought to defeat and subjugate.[47]

The sexual license that permeates *Bamidbar* and other Orientalist texts and paintings may perhaps be understood as another version of *luxuria*; a genre that can be said to have resurfaced in the modern era in secular guise first and foremost in the *Arabian Nights*, in which the strange and removed East functioned as a convenient place for repressed desires; where lust, luxury, and death came together in a macabre dance.[48] In *Bamidbar*, Frishman combined this modern,

45. For some works on the mystique of the harem in Western culture, see:
Barnette Miller, *Beyond the Sublime Porte: The Grand Seraglio of Stanbul* (Conn.: Yale University Press, New Haven, 1931).
Leslie Penn Pierce, *The Imperial Harem: Women and Sovereignty in the Ottoman Empire* (Oxford University Press, 1993).
Reina Lewis, *Gendering Orientalism: Race, Femininity and Representation* (Routledge, 1996).
46. See Mark Jordan, *The Invention of Sodomy in Christian Theology*, 37–40.
47. Jordan writes that "when Jerome chose the Latin *luxuria* to translate several different terms in the Old Testaments, he imported into Christian theology a moral category with an ancient Roman pedigree. . . . *luxuria* recurs in Latin moral texts as the opposite of the stern virtues of the Republic. It is often coupled with *licentia*, with the threat of a general social dissolution. . . . In the Latin Old Testament, *luxuria* is associated with drunkenness or gluttony and with sexual excess," 37.
48. For a quintessential example of this combination in art, see Eugene Delacroix's 1827 painting, "The Death of Sardanapalus," in which fantasies of sex, violence, and death are played out in an overwrought fashion. The painting shows the ancient Assyrian ruler Sardanapalus reclining in his bedchamber surrounded by a number of his naked wives and concubines, who are frantically

Orientalist sense of *luxuria* with examples of extreme sensual abandon that he culled from the Bible. Words and images from the debauchery of the Golden Calf in Exodus and from the rich descriptions of gross carnal transgressions that the prophets Amos and Ezekiel rail against are worked into many of the stories in a rich and intricate manner.[49] But while the ancient Hebrew prophets, like their later Christian disciples, used these passions as examples of terrible sins, Frishman and other contemporary writers, treated the eruption of desire as a positive element designed to shake Jews back into a more "natural" existence by resurrecting their primordial selves.

As someone who was especially suspect of literary artifice, Frishman wrote in his second batch of "Letters Concerning Literature":

> Our writers [the Jewish writers of his generation, Y.P.] lost almost completely any sign of originality, the ability to express truly what is in their own hearts and lives. They live in an alien world and write to us only of those things they absorb from the outside. They write about nature. . . . but I suspect that these good people were born blind and can see nothing. . . . They frequently write about Women and Beauty and about Love and Longing—though I suspect

---

clutching the bed in an attempt to escape their execution, ordered by the king so that they do not fall into the hands of the approaching enemy. For a reproduction, see *Orientalism, Delacroix to Klee*, Roger Benjamin, ed., 8.

49. See Amos 6:4–7: "You that lie upon beds of ivory, and stretch themselves upon their couches, and eat the lambs out of the flock, and the calves out of the midst of the stall; that pluck the strings of the lute, and devise for themselves instruments of music, like David; that drink wine in bowls, and anoint themselves with chief ointments: but they are not grieved for the ruin of Yosef. Therefore now they shall go into exile at the head of the exiles; and the revelry of those who stretched themselves out shall pass away" (*Koren bible*, Harold Fisch ed., 1998).

השוכבים על מיטות שן וסרוחים על ערשותם ואוכלים כרים מצאן ועגלים מתוך מרבק. הפורטים על פי הנבל כדוד
חשבו להם כלי שיר. השותים בנזרי יין וראשית שמנים ימשחו ולא נחלו על שבר יוסף. לכן עתה יגלו בראש גולים
וסר מרזח סרוחים.

For staggering descriptions of outrageous sexual license, see Ezekiel 23:5–8: "And Ahola played the harlot when she was mine; and she doted on her lovers, on those of Ashur her neighbors, who were clothed with blue, captains and rulers, all of them charming young men, horsemen riding upon horses. Thus she committed her lewd practices with them, with all them that were the choice men of Ashur, and on all on whom she doted, with all their idols she defiled herself. Neither did she give up her lewd practices brought from Mizrayim: for in her youth they lay with her, and they handled her virgin breasts, and poured out their lust upon her."

ותזן אהלה תחתיה ותעגב על מאהביה אל אשור קרובים. לובשי תכלת פחות וסגנים בחורי חמד כולם פרשים רוכבי
סוסים. ותתן תזנותיה עליהם מבחר בני אשור כולם ובכל אשר עגבה בכל גלוליהם נטמאה. ואת תזנותיה ממצרים
לא עזבה כי אותה שכבו בנעוריה והמה עשו דדי בתוליה וישפכו תזנותם עליה.

In both cases, the English translation fails to express adequately the fantastic sexual crimes, the outrage, and the near hysteria that permeates the accusatory language in Hebrew.

they long for nothing . . . , and that being the meek, decent fellows that they are they probably blush when they sit next to a girl they do not know. I do not doubt that they lust a little and sin a little in their hearts. After all, they are young, healthy men. But can such a great and expansive eroticism [that one finds in the works of the great European writers, Y.P.], or anything remotely similar, can really be part of such sick and wretched human beings, who sat and rotted for hundreds and thousands of years in their holes and in their study houses, until their skin was like the parchments they scrutinized. Is it possible that by some miracle a new life was breathed into those dry bones overnight? [This is something] I cannot believe, I cannot believe, I cannot believe.[50]

It seems here as if Frishman confuses human nature with the ability or even the facility to express it adequately in Hebrew, that is, according to literary conventions that were developed in Western Europe over hundreds of years. For some reason he also seems to ignore a fact he must have known well, that he and his peers lacked the literary tradition as well as the linguistic means to express it in ways that would come close to the impressive [secular] fiction that accumulated in national libraries across Europe. But the consideration of such monumental obstacles never stopped Frishman and others from making such incredulous pronouncements. It may be argued, in fact, that such grandiloquent statements actually inspired the suggestion of remedies that were equally demanding; remedies that were designed to fundamentally mend the maligned nature of Jews. Perhaps this is why Frishman traveled so far back in time and so far out of Europe. Although obviously imaginary, the passions of his heroes in *Bamidbar* are deeply rooted in a mythological Jewish context. At the same time, they also reflect the conventions of an imagined East, an Orientalist universe in which love and passion are perceived to be stronger than in the temperate climate of Europe.

This kind of love and passion, which were believed by many Jewish nationalists to be dormant but nevertheless extant within the Diasporic Jewish soul or psyche, were meant to be aroused by Frishman not only through the choice of subject matter but also through language; a vibrant, pseudo-biblical language that was designed to echo the epic passions of the ancient heroes of the Hebrew Bible. The palpable sensuality in *Bamidbar* advocates a national awakening through a synergy of biblical vocabulary, grammar, syntax, and nomenclature that create a radically new Hebrew sensibility; a mixture of both ancient and modern idioms that engage in a poetic dialogue with the old biblical text. The Hebrew language of *Bamidbar* is so striking that it still remains one of the most powerful messages of revival in the entire anthology nearly a hundred years after

50. Frishman, *Mikhtavim al hasifrut* (Letter 5), 150–151.

it was first published.[51] Even those critics who doubted the literary quality of the stories agreed that their searing Hebrew is one of the most marvelous literary achievements of the revival.[52]

Because the idea of reintroducing Hebrew as the national language of the Jews was a conscious decision, the ideological and political reasons behind it naturally shaped the kind of Hebrew that was revived. The rise of European nationalism, with its preoccupation with ethnic origin, national history, and folklore made biblical Hebrew, and not rabbinic Hebrew, the preferred choice for Jewish nationalists. But while the revived language remained very close to its biblical origin in its basic vocabulary and structure, the inner form of the language—the tense system, the verbs and adverbial expressions, the shifts in meaning, the syntax, etc.—inevitably became Western, or European.[53]

In his analysis of the peculiar character of contemporary Hebrew, Haim Rozen suggests that the Semitic identity of modern Hebrew is more a genealogical question than a typological one, by which he means that the Hebrew that developed during the Haskala, and especially during the revival, differs from other modern languages in that it lacks chronologically detectable stages of development. Whereas different stages of the development of French or English, for instance, can be detected through centuries of common, widespread use, the history of modern Hebrew is of course materially different.[54]

Most writers at the time Frishman composed his stories preferred the more synthetic Hebrew style (the *nosach*) of the Russian-born writer Y. L. Abramowitz, a.k.a. Mendale Mokher Sforim (1835–1917), who made the literary Hebrew of the Haskala more supple by synthesizing its biblical core with lexical and syntactic rabbinic and Yiddish elements.[55] Frishman, however, chose the opposite

51. See Kagan, Kramer, and Rabin's dissertation for comprehensive analyses of various elements of Frishman's language.

52. Some critics faulted Frishman for his beautiful language and believed it came at the expense of substance. Auerbach sums up this notion when he writes that Frishman's biblical tales are fiction in prose. "Substance," he writes, "the deep examination of the complexity of life and the expression of ideals, do not interest Frishman, who is far more concerned with words, the spirit of lyricism, and the shimmering brightness of Aggadah." Gilboa, 125, 126. While one may debate these assessments, their very premise proves the point I am trying to make about Frishman's style.

53. Haim Rozen, *Contemporary Hebrew*. By "contemporary" Rozen means the Hebrew that developed during the revival.

54. Rozen lists numerous examples, although the most obvious one would be the introduction of a clear distinction between tenses into contemporary Hebrew—past, present, future—a distinction that is far less clear in biblical Hebrew. For a concise discussion of this shift, see Eliezer Rubinstein's *Ha'ivrit shelanu veha'ivrit hakduma*.

Rozen attributes this phenomenon to the cultural and linguistic background of the arduous revivers of the language—linguists, writers, educators, ideologues—none of whom spoke Hebrew as a first language. He does not say this specifically, but he implies it when he lists the various traits of modern Hebrew and the influences it received during its revival.

55. For an evaluation of Abramowitz's linguistic contributions, see Shaked, *Hasiporet ha'ivrit*, vol. 1.

way to achieve the same goal. Rather than modernize his Hebrew by incorporating post-biblical elements into it, he confined it more strictly to its ancient, biblical form in order to express modern ideas more radically. Surprisingly, this counterintuitive strategy worked—not only because of Frishman's linguistic dexterity and his impressive ability to manipulate biblical idioms nimbly but also because of his ingenuity in turning the revolutionary elements in the Bible itself into a critique that went beyond the anti-rabbinic agenda of the Haskala to accommodate the complexity of the human and the Jewish condition at the dawn of the twentieth century.

The most obvious examples of this are those parts in the stories that serve up modern philosophies in ancient biblical form. When Kehat is accused of stealing, he flies into a rage and yells:

> There is no such thing as property; there are no property owners, nor masters who own! All that is upon the earth belongs to the people of the earth, who can reach out and take it for themselves. Man was born naked and naked he shall return to his soil. ("Rebellious Son," 55)

The radical socialism and even the anarchy of this speech are unmistakably modern, as the Bible recognizes the right of ownership and sets clear laws for preserving it. Yet the speech also reflects the Bible's concern for social justice. After he announces the abolition of property, Kehat begins the next sentence with the relative clause, כל אשר יש על פני האדמה, all that is upon the earth, which is a common rhetorical device in the Bible.[56] Frishman uses this device here to emphasize an utmost social justice: כל אשר יש על פני האדמה לכל יושבי הארץ ישנו, all that is upon the earth belongs to the people of the earth. Then, to end his cry, Kehat rephrases Job's words: ערום יצאתי מבטן אמי וערום אשוב שמה, naked I came out of my mother's womb and naked I shall return there (Job 1:21). Job's philosophic reaction to the loss of his property and his family, which in the Bible is part of the book's religious message, is incorporated here as part of Kehat's radical socioeconomic message.

But Frishman's more significant achievement in *Bamidbar* is the tension that he managed to create between the ancient means of expression—biblical Hebrew, and the modern, contemporary issues they express. Consider this brief passage from "Dances," for instance, which tells of Timna's spurned love for Poot, and her great longing for him after he betrothed her with a ring and then disappeared and abandoned her.

---

56. It is designed to emphasize its importance over the subject unit, as in God's instruction to Abraham in Genesis 21:12: כל אשר תאמר אליך שרה שמע בקולה, all that Sara says to you, obey her. See Wilhelm Gesenius, *Hebrew Grammar*, 457–458, which deals with this rhetorical device called *casus pendi*.

And even when they came to Alush the youth did not return. A long wrinkle appeared one night across her forehead and split it in half, and her eyes were covered with mist. A silent, heavy sadness grew around her. The women who saw her stopped mocking her and spoke kindly to her, and there were tears in their eyes when they spoke. And the girl did nothing but look at the ring on her finger time and time again, sometimes she would laugh and sometimes she would cry, and sometimes her eyes would fill with light, and sometimes she would close the door behind her and she would hide so that no one would be able to see her face, and sometimes she would still continue to hope. (10)

ובבואם עד אלוש לא שב העלם גם אז. קמט ארוך פרח בן לילה אחד במצחה ויחץ אותו לאורכו, ואת עיניה הגדולות כיסה אד. צמחה פתאום מארץ תוגה חרישית ועמומה וכבדה ותרבץ סביב סביב לה. הנשים אשר ראו אותה, חדלו פתאום מללעוג אחריה, כי אם דיברו אליה רכות; ובעיניהן נראו דמעות בְּדַבְּרָן. והנערה לא עשתה דבר, בלתי אם הביט מרגע לרגע אל הטבעת אשר על אצבעה, ויש אשר שחקה ויש אשר בכתה, ויש אשר אורו עיניה ויש אשר סגרה את הדלת בעדה ותתחבא, לבעבור לא יראה איש את פניה, ויש אשר שבה וַתְּקַו.

The most remarkable feature of this passage is the sense of arrested action or stative condition it creates. The first sentence contains the only verb in the passage that is used actively to denote a movement and a completed action in the past (and when they came, ובבואם). Having set the scene, then, in one short and succinct sentence, all the following verbal expressions, whether perfect, imperfect, or converted imperfects, express a continued state, a condition or a mood in which Timna is trapped. Even though the next three sentences use simple perfects to denote new developments in Timna's life (a wrinkle "appeared," the sadness "grew," the women "stopped"), the effect is not even that of a past-progressive but of a stative condition that is usually achieved in Hebrew by the use of the passive participle. Thus, as Elliot Rabin writes, "the participial form employed here functions ambiguously between its biblical and modern usages."[57] Each of the words used in this passage is extant in the Bible in some form. Frishman does not use neologisms here at all. But he rearranges the ancient idiom and harnesses what he called its "wild and elemental force," its "ecstatic validity," and its "kind of suddenness" and "wildness" and uses it as a literary device for a highly romantic purpose.[58]

An even more radically modern usage of biblical idiom here is the unique expression ויש אשר in the sense of "would" that dominates the latter part of the passage. This prepositional expression, which appears only twice in the Bible

57. Rabin, 205.

58. See Kramer, 122 as note 61 reads.

(Num. 9:20, 21 and Neh. 5:2, 3, 4), is closer to its use in Numbers, which describes how the presence of God in the form of a cloud would sometimes linger upon the tabernacle. Since "would" is inherently vague, inconclusive, and even mysterious, it is almost never used in the sparing text of the Bible, except with respect to God, who may of course be capricious, inconsistent, and above all mysterious. These divine qualities are reinterpreted here as romantic characteristics. Expressed by an extensive use of "would," which is not a Semitic but a Western linguistic modality (for instance, "would" in English, "würde" in German), these characteristics are associated with love as a vague and mysterious but very powerful force.

Ostensibly, this kind of Western, European Hebrew, either Latinate or Germanic, is what Frishman advocated all his life, if not precisely in these words then certainly in spirit.[59] Except that *Bamidbar* presents a radical interpretation of this call. "Dances" was unusual even for Frishman, who, like most of his contemporaries, began to adopt a more synthetic Hebrew toward the end of his life.[60] But after his 1911 visit to Palestine, it appears that both the content of the stories and their language were made to express a newly found nationalism through a deliberate and energetic return to an improved and "purer" biblical style.

Frishman's encounter with the young Yishuv was a deep spiritual experience that shook him to the core and when he returned from Palestine he could no longer return to his old biblical style, according to Kramer. The visit to Palestine appears to have mollified Frishman's long skepticism of the possibility of a national revival in Eretz Israel and reduced his deep skepticism of the revival of the nation's original culture, especially the revival of the nation's language,

59. Consider by comparison the works of two contemporaries of Frishman, Uri Nissan Gnessin and Gershon Shoffman. Like Frishman, both of them were modernist writers, thoroughly steeped in the culture of Europe. Gnessin's modernity, however, was conveyed through what Shaked calls, a Europeanized Hebrew and an innovative literary style that resembles in many respects what later came to be known as stream of consciousness. Shoffman's impressionistic sketches were also written in a modernized Hebrew that was not influenced by older sources. Both Gnessin and Shoffman were well versed in Jewish literary traditions but preferred to express their existential concerns in modernistic, Western fashion.

Shaked provides a concise and illuminating assessment of both writers, whom he considers much more European than Jewish, both in the subject matter of their works and in their language. He writes that Gnessin borrowed models from European languages (Russian and French) and combined them with Hebrew words creating a new model that neither mimicked other languages nor bastardized Hebrew, but was an original phenomenon that opened up new stylistic directions for Hebrew. See Shaked, *Hasiporet Ha'ivvit*, 1:423.

60. Kramer writes: "I specified at length and in depth the changes that occurred in Frishman's language, because of the tremendous and sudden difference between his excellent biblical Hebrew, which he used for a very long time, and his later language. Even Frishman, who was a biblical purist most of his life, to the point of anachronism, could not ignore the changes that occurred in the language in the last twenty years of his life. Although he was late in absorbing this process, he too was swept in the stream [of new Hebrew], which he used with considerable talent," 121.

which was the only possible link between the different groups within the nation.[61]

The assertion about Frishman's invention of a modified biblical style to suit his new sense of nationalism may be further strengthened by this reference he made in a 1908 letter intended for publication: "The Bible! No matter how much I work my poor brain to understand the nature of its wonderful and secret charm I still do not understand the great mystery. [The text] erupts with wild and elemental force, an ecstatic validity, a direct access to nature, a kind of suddenness and a great wildness, something which is beyond grasp and beyond man, a kind of human and worldly greatness."[62]

To express the deep impression of his experience in Palestine and his cautious conversion to the cultural and political possibilities of Zionism, Frishman chose to contemporize the Book of Numbers through a conscious restyling of its language, perhaps because he saw an analogy between the national promise that inhered in the wandering of the Israelites' in the wilderness and that of the inchoate Jewish Yishuv in Palestine. But the biblical universe that Frishman evokes in *Bamidbar* transcends its narrow ethnic confines to suggest not just a Hebrew but a Canaanite, or pre-Israelite space as well.[63] In addition to Hebrew or Israelite names, like Zavad ben Yarcha, Reggem ben Mrary and Evyasaf ben Machly, which in "Rebellious Son" for instance are crowded into one sentence in a stylized proximity, Frishman also used explicitly non-Hebrew names such as Poot, Dishon, Gog, and Dodanim, from the numerous lists of Gentile names that abound in the Bible. This repeated and at times almost campy biblicism reflects some of the blurry family lines between Hebrews and Gentiles that often occur in the Bible, especially in the books of Genesis and Chronicles.

Beginning with Adam through Noah, Abraham, Isaac, and Jacob, many of the offspring of the Hebrew patriarchs in the Bible blossom into foreign nations, and vice versa. The same is true for intimate relationships between Hebrews and non-Hebrews, of which Abraham and his Egyptian maid Hagar are a notable example. Frishman recreates this expansive and borderless world of Eastern antiquity in the relationships he portrays, as well as in the geographic territory he charts in his stories. As can be seen from many of the quotes provided throughout this chapter, Timna, Poot, Dishon and the Hebrew girl he falls in love with, are modern formulations not only of ancient passions but of an

---

61. Kramer, 122.

62. Frishman, *Kol Kitve David Frishman* 5:173 (קעב).

Elliot Rabin thinks that *Bamidbar* "is a culmination of decades of experimentations in forging neobiblical prose," 204.

63. See Kagan, 209.

ancient culture and an ancient geography that are neither Jewish nor Eretz-Israeli but Canaanite, that is, Eastern and mythological.[64]

In one of his "Letters Concerning Literature," Frishman discusses at length the inimitable power and vision of the Hebrew Bible. "When I think sometimes about the Bible," he writes, "strange and wonderful ideas come to me:

> Say for example that I wished to be someone in the Bible, let's say Isaiah, and the heavens opened before me ninety nine times: I would have probably stood there wide-eyed, unable to utter a word. I would not know what to ask, because I do not know the first thing that is needed for such a task, and I do not know the secret of their wonderful charms or where to find it. It seems to reside between the lines. The word alone does not convey the idea, yet I do not understand what it is. . . . Something like that happened to me only with some of Shakespeare's works. . . . here too, I could not exactly locate his wonderful power. It does not reside in a single word or in a single sentence, nor can it be found in the content—but there is a wonderful power in the greater whole.[65]

Frishman did not really wish he were a prophet. He believed that the modern era required the mediation of art not prophecy. With a romantic flare, he wrote that the artist can still touch humanity by appealing to its senses and by stirring its soul. He did not speak specifically of himself, but his great affinity to the Hebrew Bible, and the romantic analogy he makes between the prophet and the artist, somehow lend *Bamidbar* a prophetic quality. It is a prophecy for the modern era; a prophecy that is written in the language of the Bible but imbued with a very modern sense.

"Eretz Israel," began his fourth letter from Palestine,

> seems like one big resort . . . even the sight of men working . . . seems somehow picturesque to the traveler. . . . as if it were taken from the One Thousand and One Nights or from the fairytales of Hans Christian Andersen. [This is] a land whose grown-ups seem like children, so that sometimes you are surprised to see that they actually have beards and mustaches.

64. In his critique of Karl Hauptman's play *Moses*, Frishman ridiculed the use of biblical names for aesthetic purposes: "this is a well-known recipe, you mention once or twice the name of the divinity YHWH, you mention names of cities and of men who are noted in the Bible—and suddenly the whole thing becomes holy and Hebrew," *Kol Kitve David Frishman* 8:197. I bring this quote as an example of the difference between such a facile use of the Bible and Frishman's much more extensive and complex use of it in *Bamidbar*.

In any event, the reference to an East that is both Hebrew and pagan was made by contemporaries of Frishman as well. Berdichevsky did the same in his short story "Red Heifer" when he compared the Jewish butchers to priests of the Canaanite god Ba'al. Tschernichovsky also wrote several "Canaanite" poems, which I mention in chapter 1.

65. Frishman, *Mikhtavim al hasifrut* (13th letter), 174 (קעד).

Suddenly, the youth and the vigor Frishman wrote about with so much longing already in "Pandemonium," his cry to "Let us have the dew of childhood!" have all materialized before his eyes in Palestine. So that after a visit to Tel-Aviv, which rose before his eyes like a "magical island from the sea," he looked at the wondrous world around him as if it were a fairytale, an Aggadah that "has something of the dew of childhood upon it."

Frishman's use of the East was never more than an aesthetic formulation. The actual lands and cultures that lay east of the Mediterranean never interested him in or of themselves. He made this very clear in his second letter from Palestine, when he noted prophetically that only if England were somehow to take charge of the region, build it up and then hand it over to the Jews, will the land be made decent and livable. But the simple and natural Jewish life he saw in Palestine mollified his cosmopolitan skepticism and did stir in him some sense of nationalism.[66]

Although Frishman did not have a national epiphany in the wake of his visit to Palestine, the developments he saw in the Yishuv softened some of his more categorical objections to Zionism, especially in its political form. The potential importance of space, not just time, for a Jewish revival, was perhaps one of the most important realizations Frishman took with him from his visit. As a result, he recreated in *Bamidbar* a primordial Jewish space that accommodated these conflicting impulses in the only way that was possible for a rigorous critic such as himself. In some ways, Frishman's "return" to the Bible in *Bamidbar* can be understood as a literary analogy of the Zionists' "return" to the land. His modern formulation of a biblical world was an attempt to describe a meaningful "late return," a re-entry into Eden after the banishment, as Ariel Hirschfeld puts it, a progressive move forward as well as a return to a state of initial purity.[67] The next chapter looks at how other writers developed Frishman's aesthetic Eastern space and populated it with one of the most original creations of the Orientalist Jewish imagination, a noble *Jewish* savage.

66. Iris Parush maintains that Frishman's basic objection to Zionism as a political solution for the Jewish problem did not change after his visit. See pages 29–30 in her book.
67. See the discussion in chapter 1.

CHAPTER 3

Out of the Book and into the Desert

The Invention of a Native Hebrew Culture in Palestine

"At the edge of the rocks," writes Moshe Smilansky in one of his earliest short stories, "a man as mighty as an oak sat on a magnificent mare, his thighs tightly wrapped around her, his hair coming down in curls, golden curls, with eyes as blue as the sky, gleaming with strength and courage."[1] This unusual description of a blond and blue-eyed Arab "Jew," a combination of Semitic manhood and Western European features that abounds in early-twentieth-century Hebrew literature, was one of the most innovative ways that Jews, especially Zionists, grappled with anti-Semitic stereotypes that portrayed them as racially inferior, weak, and cowardly.

Moshe Smilansky belonged to the first generation of pioneers who reinvented themselves in Eretz Israel as New Jews. Arriving in Palestine from the Ukraine in 1890 at the age of sixteen, he soon settled in Rehovot—one of the first agricultural settlements, *moshavot*, that were established in Palestine. Like many of his contemporaries, Smilansky was not only a farmer but a writer as well, who was deeply engaged in the cultural life of the small Jewish Yishuv of his days. A prolific writer, he published farming manuals, programmatic essays, and Zionist novels, but he is best known for his documentary and fictional stories about Palestinian Arabs, which appeared regularly in the Hebrew periodic press between 1902 and 1934. The stories, which often describe Arabs as Oriental supermen, "primitive" natives who possess all the traits that Jews wished very

---

1. Moshe Smilansky, "Niqmat humadi," *Kitve moshe smilanski*, 5:151. All subsequent references to these stories are from this edition.

much to adopt, like courage, pride, constancy, passion, a strong sense of self, and love for the land, were extremely popular—so much so that a selection of them was published as an anthology as early as 1910. Entitled *The Sons of Arabia* (*Benei 'arav*) the anthology went into several reprints for the next thirty years and eventually became a founding text of the new, Hebrew culture of Palestine. The popularity of Smilansky's Arab stories was a strange phenomenon not only because of the unusual subject matter but especially because the stories captured the hearts and minds of Hebrew readers in Palestine and abroad during one of the most astonishing periods of renaissance in *Jewish* history.[2]

The very naming of the anthology is also noteworthy. According to Yaffa Berlowitz, Bialik, the editor of the first edition of the anthology, was the one who gave it the highly suggestive title.[3] In his article about the origin of the Palestinian Arabs, A. B. Polack charts the historical changes in the use of the appellation "Arabs" for the natives of Palestine. He writes that after the Turkish conquest of Palestine, the term usually referred to Bedouins, who, by their customs and language, were considered to be descendants of the "original" Arabs. The Arab farmers and townspeople were called *wallad al Arab*, or children of the Arabs, which marked them as less "purely" Arab. During the First Aliyah, the appellation *wallad al Arab* was translated into Hebrew as *benei 'arav*, or the sons of Arabia, to denote both Bedouins and other Arabs.[4]

In her book *The Arab in Hebrew Prose, 1911–1948*, Risa Domb suggests that Smilansky did not fully understand this distinction, and that his use of it as the name for his anthology points to his superior, Western stance in relation to the Arabs. Aside from the fact that Bialik, not Smilansky, gave the anthology its title, this imprecision underscores my contention that the Arab natives of Palestine were viewed by Smilansky and others as an inspiring cultural symbol and not as subjects in an ethnic or anthropological study.

For many of these reasons, and because they are considered adolescent literature today, the stories in *The Sons of Arabia* have always attracted more political than literary attention. This is especially true of the first two out of the three groups that the stories are usually divided into—the patronizing stories and the social-critical stories—and much less so of the third group, the folktales.[5] In fact,

---

2. Unlike many of his fellow pioneers, Smilansky was greatly interested in the Arab natives of Palestine, whose simple lives close to the land shaped his Zionism profoundly. This was such an unusual phenomenon that Smilansky himself was asked about it. Berlowitz quotes a conversation that Smilansky relates in his memoirs between himself and Yosef Aharonowitz, who could not understand Smilansky's choice of subject matter. She does not mention whether Aharonowitz ever received a reply. See Yaffa Berlowitz, *Lehamtsi erets, lehamtsi 'am*, 405.

3. See Berlowitz, "Sifrut utehiya le'umit," *'Iyunim bitkumat yisra'el*, 4:409.

4. See Polack, "Motsa'am shel 'arviye ha'aretz," 297–99.

5. Gershon Shaked, *Hasiporet ha'ivrit*, 2:50; Domb, *The Arab in Hebrew Prose*, 61–63. Both divide the stories more or less along the same lines. Berlowitz concurs and writes that the first group

what is generally referred to as the image of the Arab in Hebrew literature and the numerous studies devoted to it are largely based on Smilansky's stories, which are usually understood to represent the meeting between a developed West and a backward East and to express the colonial essence of the Jewish settlement of Palestine.[6] As sometimes implied by literary critics such as Risa Domb, Gila Ramraz-Rauch, and Yaffa Berlowitz, and clearly articulated by cultural critics such as Daniel Boyarin, Smilansky and his peers represented Zionism as a domineering movement that sought to establish in Palestine a colonial society of "white" settlers.[7] While literary critics focus on Zionist paternalism toward the Arabs, who are ostensibly portrayed as inferior and uncivilized natives, cultural critics explain the origin for this stance in the Jewish desire to gain the respect of white Christian Europe by mimicking its ways.

This is not surprising, as the omniscient narrator in many of Smilansky's stories relates to the Arab protagonists either patronizingly, as children, or critically, as miserable or misguided wretches who wallow blindly in their own backwardness and naïveté. Although Smilansky's didacticism is not much different from the critical spirit that animated Hebrew writers during the Haskala, it is the Arab subject matter and the fact that he is an outside observer that give his stories their "colonial" nature.

While this is true of the first two groups of stories, a close examination of the distinct third group of stories, the folktales, would reveal an alternative image of Arabs, one that differs from what traditional critics of the stories and postcolonial critics of Zionism suggest. These tales—"The cry of Tsalhia" (*Yillelat tsalhiya*) and its sequel "Humadi's revenge" (*Nikmat humadi*), "The hill of love" (*Giv'at ha'ahava*), "The work of the devil" (*Ma'ase satan*), "The scroll" (*Hamgila*), "Shaitana," "Sa'id the Bedouin" (*Sa'id bedui*), "The sheik's daughter" (*Bat hashech*), and "The blood avenger" (*Nikmat dam*)—do not condemn the Arab society as primitive but actually present it as a preferred cultural option to Diaspora Judaism. In a unique move that characterized early Palestinian Zionism, Smilansky's folktales offer an alternative model to Diasporic Jewish life in the way they incorporate and adapt modern notions of nationality, ethnicity, and nativeness and locate them in the East. By looking at Smilansky's treatment

---

includes stories that look at the Palestinian natives from a Western perspective as primitive and backward; the second group of moralistic stories is critical of both the Arab and the Jewish Palestinian society; the group of folktales differs from the previous two, because it examines the non-Jewish history of the land and the nature of Arab nationalism from an aesthetic point of view.

6. The most recent study of the stories offers a limited exception to this rule. See Berlowitz, *Lehamtsi erets, lehamtsi 'am*, in which she charts the gradual change of Smilansky's attitude toward the Arabs, from ambivalent separation to enthusiastic integration. Earlier studies include Domb, *The Arab in Hebrew Prose* and Gila Ramraz-Rauch, *The Arab in Israeli Literature* . For articles, see notes below.

7. Boyarin, *Unheroic Conduct*.

of race, gender, and sexuality in these tales, three of the most debilitating aspects of anti-Semitism, which plagued enlightened Jews at the turn of the century and animated much of early Zionism, I hope to demonstrate some of the innovative ways that Zionists used the East to reconstruct their image as Jews.

Although Smilansky's folktales do not compensate for his other, more oppressive, stories about Arabs, they do serve as an example of the complex nature of Zionism as a political and cultural movement and highlight the conflicted attitude that Zionist pioneers had toward their reclaimed homeland in the East. Moreover, precisely because these tales are not especially sophisticated, they offer a rare glimpse into some of the most telling Jewish fantasies about the East during the Hebrew Revival. The tales capture the virtual character of the First and Second Aliyah and paint a world made up of the wishful thinking of a small group of Jews who willed themselves into a new community and eventually into a new nation.

One of the most striking aspects of Smilansky's tales was the way that they managed to cast Zionism's new ideal of Jewish manhood in native Palestinian form and transferred the inspiration for Nordau's "muscular Judaism" from the Slavic peasants of Eastern Europe to the society of fighting Bedouins in the eastern Mediterranean. In principle, this shift was not new, of course, as many writers of the Hebrew Revival, the Tehiya, moved their Jewish protagonists closer to nature and away from the study house. By giving them traits that were not typically associated with Jews, such as physical or sexual prowess, and a keen sense of self-respect, they reconstructed those Jewish heroes in the image of Gentiles.[8] Smilansky's innovation, however, was to locate this dynamic in a native Palestinian context. This was one of the main reasons for the popularity of his tales, which struck a chord with contemporary readers who longed for the regenerative promise the tales held. Instead of the young shtetl Jew who "goes Gentile," Smilansky created in *The Sons of Arabia* a young Palestinian Jew who "goes native."[9] In both cases, the desired transformation of the Jew, from a bookish weakling to a strong and forthright man, was inextricably tied to the non-Jewish society through the adoption of its values.

Such, for example, is the hero of "The Hill of Love" (1916): Hamdan, a noble savage and a handsome son of Arabia whose association to Jews is vaguely hinted at in the story.[10] The son of a respected sheik, Hamdan becomes a daring

8. Bialik's "Me'ahore hagader" comes readily to mind. The protagonist is a wayward Jewish lad who prefers the carefree life of Gentile youth and their proximity to nature to his restrictive Jewish environment.

9. On the place and evolution of "muscular Judaism" in Zionism, see Shmuel Almog, *Tsiyonut vehistorya*, 78–115.

10. Smilansky, 6:5.

highway robber, falls madly in love with the young Turkish wife of an old, decrepit Bedouin sheik, kidnaps her, and, after two days of ecstatic happiness in a place called the Hill of Love, kills her and then falls on the swords of the soldiers who come to arrest him.

The tale itself starts with a stock description of a harmonious universe, part biblical, part Eastern that is typical of many Orientalist works of art and literature of the fin de siècle. Against the setting sun, the fighting young men of the tribe ride playfully on their beautiful mares, "talking, laughing, exchanging words with ease" (5). The mares are followed by their dancing colts, "who jump and fly in all directions, or come together and neigh at one another" (6), after which the shepherds with their flocks arrive, "filling the air with the fragrance of milk, saturating it with pleasure" (7). At last, the sun sets and heaven and earth prepare for the night.

Into this pastoral panegyric Smilansky inserts the laughing young fighters whose "long spears laugh as well, laugh and turn in the air. Every spear is ten feet long. The sharp spears glimmer in the light, reddened by the sun's rays as if they were covered with blood" (5). This peculiar addition to an otherwise peaceful and harmonious picture directs attention to one of Smilansky's most frequently recurring images: the overtly masculine Bedouin who always carries a long rifle (in this case, a spear) as an extension of his pronounced and menacing manhood and who rides mares, not stallions, as an expression of his mastery over the female.

The placement of the fighters as an integral part of the rustic tableau, directly after the setting sun, as well as the extended description of their spears, underscores the importance that Smilansky gives them, consciously or not. The spears—which are described as measuring ten cubits long (עשר אמות אורך כל רומח) and which conjure up the words with which God instructs Moses to build the wooden beams in the Tabernacle (Exod. 26:16)—are sanctified, in effect. The association between the native Arabs and the Bible repeatedly informs Smilansky's characters, Jews as well as Arabs. Such is also the description of the mares, who, like the daughters of Arabia, "know their masters' hearts" (5), and the rider, "who sits with his neck outstretched, close to the back of his mare, as if he were one with her" (6). In a language usually reserved for lovers, Smilansky describes the close connection between man and beast as well as the Bedouin's mastery over it.

Smilansky is repeatedly preoccupied with making clear distinctions between masculine and feminine in his stories. Hamdan is a wild and passionate man. He is a "tall and thin man with black eyes that burn like the eyes of the *debba* [hyena] and curls that are blacker than black. His brave face is tanned by the sun, and all of his being radiates courage and might. . . . The daughters of the

Bedouins coveted his beauty in their hearts" (14).[11] Smilansky builds up Hamdan's Semitic masculinity with additional traits that make him into a superman, like most other Bedouins in Smilansky's works, whose "eyes are sharp, piercing hearts and minds alike. At night they see as well as the fox, and during the day nothing escapes them on the whole wide plain" (18).

An integral part of Hamdan's masculinity is his irresistibility to women, who all "coveted his beauty in their hearts." Hamdan's manliness is so pronounced that at the tender age of ten, "he began loving the beautiful daughters of the Bedouins, especially the more mature and prettier of them" (13). The girls naturally make fun of the little boy, who nevertheless threatens to kill the lover of an eighteen-year-old maiden, with whom he is infatuated. But after Hamdan runs away to join a band of highway robbers, and then reappears as a strikingly beautiful young man, "the daughters of the Bedouins did not make fun of him any more. . . . In the dark nights, the girls wrapped themselves around his neck, and his searing kisses intoxicated them" (14). Hamdan's appealing darkness, like his exaggerated bravery and sexuality, set him up as an ideal model of Oriental manhood and an inspiring example for his Jewish cousins.

If the association between Hamdan and his Jewish cousins is vaguely suggested in the pseudo-historical beginning of the "The Hill of Love,"[12] the ethnic and cultural proximity of Arabs and Jews is much more explicit in "The Cry of Tsalhia" (1909), and more so in its sequel, "Humadi's Revenge" (1910), where Smilansky eloquently portrays the image of the Bedouin hero by blending Oriental fantasies and Jewish wishful thinking.[13]

"Tsalhia" tells the story of the loveless marriage of the son and daughter of two rival sheiks. The marriage is dissolved after Tsalhia gives birth to a child she conceives from a former lover. The boy, Humadi, is taken away from his mother, who is tied to a tree and left to die of hunger at the foot of Mount Tabor. In the sequel to this story, "Humadi's Revenge," Humadi avenges his mother's death. After years of exile, he crosses the Jordan in search of those who stained his family's honor in order to settle his score with them. He meets a witch who tells him that he should inflict on his enemies the same curse that his mother suffered from, the curse of hopeless love. Humadi agrees and taunts the daughters of the tribe with his dazzling good looks until the tribe-girls' obsession with

11. The dark coloring of the hero recurs frequently in *The Sons of Arabia* and seems like a conscious overcompensation for the Aryan analogy between fairness and nobility that preoccupied assimilating Jews in Europe. See Boyarin's discussion of this neurosis in *Unheroic Conduct*, 246, 275–76.

12. The beginning tells how the Jews lost their right to the land, which was then entrusted to their Muslim brethren.

13. Smilansky, 5.

him ruins their reputation and renders them ineligible for marriage, leading to the demise of the tribe.

With his golden curls and blue eyes, Humadi is not typical of most of Smilansky's Arab characters, most of whom are handsome variations of the tall, dark, and fierce-looking Oriental man encountered in countless literary and artistic depictions of the Orient at the turn of the century.[14] Still, Humadi is a rugged, independent Bedouin, a cross between the ambiguously admired Gentile-like Jewish lad of Hebrew literature, and the native, noble Semite who figures in many stories by Smilansky and other writers of his generation.[15] "Humadi grew up in the plains of the South. . . . a lad among the young shepherds. . . . He grew up wildly; no one commanded or controlled him, for the shepherds were free to do as they pleased. . . . He loved the wide plains and the tops of the mountains that stood above the clouds. . . . and most of all, he liked his constant wandering with the herds of camels" (134–135).

Humadi is described here with the admiration that Hebrew writers had for what they imagined to be the carefree and natural childhood of Gentile children, who were not subjected to the regime of Torah study and corrupt teachers. Many revivalist works, such as Bialik's "Me'ahore hagader" (Behind the fence) and Y. D. Berkowitz's "Yom hadin shel feivka" (Feivka's day of judgment), were predicated on these notions. But the reference to shepherds, deserts, and tents places the story in the East, literally and historically. Smilansky uses an imaginary, idealized Arab to contrast common images of weak Jewish masculinity and construct it anew. The wistful and, at times, even homoerotic way in which he describes his ruggedly beautiful sons of Arabia marks him not only as an Orientalist but also as a representative of a nineteenth-century culture that correlated nationalism and masculinity.

George Mosse points to the surprising extent that depictions of manly beauty symbolized moral and physical value after the French Revolution—a notion that leads directly to the modern perception of masculinity as a totality that includes body and soul, outward and inward virtue as one harmonious whole.[16] In "Humadi's Revenge," the young Bedouin hero is "most beautiful and very strong. His muscles were iron and his hands were stone. . . . He knew no fear

14. See, e.g., Ze'ev Raban's 1923 illustration to the Song of Songs, Tzalmona, "Mizraha!" *Kadima; Hamizrah be'omanut yisrael* (Jerusarem, Israel museum, 1998), 53.

15. I am referring here to the plethora of revivalist literature that celebrated physical strength, which was often associated with the non-Jewish farmers of Eastern Europe. Many Hebrew writers during that time took the Jew out of the study house and placed him closer to nature, giving him "non-Jewish" traits and constructing him in the image of a *goy*. The desired change from a weak and diminutive Torah scholar to a strong and courageous man was achieved in stories like Bialik's "Arye the Hulk" or Gnessin's "In the Gardens" by internalizing traditionally non-Jewish values.

16. George Mosse, *The Image of Man*, 5, 24.

and no awe entered his heart" (135). Similarly, in "The Hill of Love," Smilan-sky compensated for two of the most common faults associated with Diaspora Jewry when he writes that the hero of the story, Hamdan, "did not like all his friends. He only liked the brave of heart. The weak, those who met their shame without retaliation, he hated and despised in his heart. . . . Neither did he like his older brother, a weak and gullible lad, who sat in the tent all day" (13).

An even stronger suggestion of Humadi's pseudo-Jewish heritage is offered by Smilansky's combination of biblical vocabulary, syntax, and imagery with ethnographic details from the lives of the Arab natives. This was one of the most compelling strategies that Hebrew writers of the Tehiya adopted to express their renewed connection to the land, and it provided them a uniquely Jewish way to express their national ideology. When Humadi sees the Sea of Galilee and the Jordan River for the first time, he is filled with awesome reverence and remembers the legends that the elders of his tribe had told him about them:

> In the beginning, when Allah created the heavens and the earth and all their hosts (בראשית הימים, כאשר ברא אללה את השמים ואת הארץ ואת כל צבאם), he also created the Jordan and the Kineret [Sea of Galilee]. Allah created them in one day (130). And there came a day . . . when the Jordan furtively left its place of hiding. . . . and stole and wound itself around . . . and came and reached the big valley and made its way into the Kineret's heart. (131)

The almost word-for-word rendition of the opening of Genesis, as well as the repetitive uses of vav conversive (ויתגנב, ויעבור, ויבוא, ויגיע, ויפתח) and the absolute infinitive (הלוך והתגנב, הלוך התפתל), immediately flags the text as biblical. This is not striking in itself, as it was a common literary convention of the time. What is striking is that Allah takes the place of the Hebrew god, and that the origi-nal Hebrew text is "appropriated" to relate a Muslim historiography of the Land of Israel. "Humadi's Revenge" is full of biblical allusions to the land designed to welcome Humadi as a returning native, reintroduce him to his mother's country, and enable him to renew his claim to it. As such, Humadi is not only written as a model for the New Jew by his looks and temperament. His life in exile and his return to the land—of which he always dreamed and to which he feels deep connections—are a reformulation of the Jewish connection to Eretz Israel in native form.

In the same way that Humadi is more of a Jewish literary creation than a lit-erary verisimilitude of a real Arab, his native land is also a Jewish projection. In a reformulation of Jewish, not Muslim, history, Humadi first longs for the land: "Whenever the shepherds and the camel caravans returned from [the North], Humadi drank with thirst their stories about the Jordan, the Kineret, and Mount Tabor" (135). Humadi then crosses the Jordan to return to the land. Finally, Humadi reclaims the land by riding around it on his mare. He rides to the Gilead, to Mount Tabor, and to the mountains of Naftali. When he comes to the Gilboa Mountains, the Arab youth is reminded of the way in which the elders of the tribe used to refer to them, saying: על במותיהם נפלו חלל המלך ובנו אל ... טל ואל מטר ("The beauty, O Israel, is slain upon thy high places. . . . Mountains of Gilboa, let there be no dew, neither let there be rain, upon you," 142). The reference to David's eulogy for King Saul and his son Jonathan in 2 Samuel 1 is strange only if Humadi is thought of as an Arab. But as a reconstructed Jew, he reflects in his conduct the actions of many idealistic Jewish immigrants during the revival who made trips to biblical sites around Palestine, retracing their forefathers' footsteps.[17]

Humadi's conduct can actually be read as a symbolic restaging of Abraham's arrival in Canaan and the entry of the Israelite tribes and their settlement in it later.[18] The "Grand Tour" that he embarks on after crossing the Jordan effectively amounts to a heritage tour in which he husbands the land and reclaims it by physically walking all over it.[19] In the same way, his meeting with the old–new land is fraught with a conflicting sense of intimacy and alienation that was characteristic of many pioneers upon their arrival in Palestine. As with Humadi, the disappointment of the Jewish immigrants, whose preconceptions of the Land of Israel clashed with the bitter reality of Palestine, was also stirred by a sense of a spiritual intimacy with the land.[20] The displaced pioneers, who came to Palestine with dreams of a new society and a new land, felt alienated from the physical environment, yet they also felt close to the land, as if they had always known it.[21]

When Humadi crosses the Jordan, he is spiritually uplifted: "In another moment, his feet will tread the land where his mother lived. . . . His heart stirred

17. This was a common practice at the time. Rachel Yana'it Ben-Zvi, who relates such a trip to the cave of Adulam, near Bethlehem, in 1908, writes: "This must be the cave of Adulam, then. We forgot how tired and hungry we were. We drink from our water and feel around us. . . . We ask ourselves again: Is this really the cave where David escaped from Saul? We light a candle and read 1 Sam. 24:3. . . . We listen to the words, and before our eyes the ancient figures come alive." *Anu olim*, 163.

18. Shaked, *Hasiporet ha'ivrit*, 52.

19. These heritage trips on foot that began during the first Aliyot have long been enshrined in Israeli culture. High-school children from all over Israel go out every summer on long treks in different parts of the country. The trips are usually taken in historically significant areas, where the teenagers are acquainted firsthand with the topography and its significance in biblical history. A telling development of recent years is the diminishing popularity of these trips among secular high schools in Israel and their growing popularity with national-religious high schools, which wish to reassert the Jewish right to all parts of Israel through these ritualistic treks.

20. Sadan-Loebenstein, Nilie, *Siporet sel shenot ha'esrim be'eretz yisra'el*, 48.

21. Ibid., 47.

. . . [Yet] "his soul did not burn any more, as it had in the morning. . . . A deep and heavy sadness descended upon him" (140). The cold and silent night that greets him after his crossing distorts the contours of the land that was made familiar to him by countless stories. He feels deeply connected to it yet at a complete loss as well. "Mother!" he cries, when "out of the darkness that envelops the mountain [Tabor], he saw the shape of a woman" (143). For a moment, the land literally takes the shape of Humadi's mother. But after the young man rushes toward it frantically, with burning eyes, "his heart beating violently, his trembling arm outstretched forward in the air," it disappears, and "the rider stands on the hill of Ein-Dor facing Mount Tabor" (144).

If there were any doubt as to Smilansky's attempt at constructing a new model of Jewish manhood through his depictions of Bedouins, his cultural agenda becomes quite obvious in stories such as "Avner," in which many characteristics of the Arab natives are transferred to the New Jew.[22] Avner grows up on a *moshava* in the upper Galilee that is menaced by the Druze of Lebanon. From early childhood, he is inexplicably drawn to those fierce mountain fighters, who fatally wound his father one day, capture the boy, and carry him off to their secret hideout in the mountains. After spending time with them, Avner is released and returns to the *moshava*, where he vows to avenge his father's death. He becomes a night watchman, a *shomer*, and uses the skills he learned from the Druze to kill his father's murderer one night during an Arab raid on the *moshava*.

Avner's resemblance to Humadi or Hamdan is striking. Like the two Bedouins of the folktales, Avner is eager to experience "the joy of war," to taste "the sweetness of revenge," and to "laugh at death" (24), all of which he associates with the mountain Druze. The brave lad is tormented by the cowardly behavior of the men in the *moshava*, and wonders why they do not fight back, "like Yoav Ben-Tsruya fought in the nearby Avel Bet Ma'acha" (84).[23] The difference between the brave lad and his cowardly parents is designed to illustrate the profound change that Jewish youth is, or should be, undergoing. A subtle analogy is being made between Avner's father and his mother, which paints the father as a coward and womanlike. When shots of attacking Druze sound in the night and excite Avner, his father calls out to him to "Lie down! . . . and [his] mother hides under the blanket and cries." Their weakness offends and enrages Avner, who cannot understand why the men from the surrounding Jewish villages will not behave as men should and "go out to fight." Later, when the father and son meet three armed Druze on their way home, the father whimpers and cowers before them.

---

22. Smilansky, 3:83–110.

23. The reference here is to the siege that Yoav, King David's chief of staff, lay to the city in 2 Sam. 20:14–15 in pursuit of the rebellious Sheva ben Bichri. Avel Bet Ma'acha was located in the northern Galilee, just north of Metula.

"Avner's heart was bitter. A dull pain filled him, and he felt utterly ashamed. . . . Something in him made his blood boil. He began to shake with anger. A feeling of deep hatred seized him, and his hand rose involuntarily and lashed the face of [one of the riders] once, and then a second time" (86). Against repeated warnings of Druze savagery and the fear they strike in the hearts of the Jewish settlers, Avner's action becomes an impressive act of courage. His anger is so great and his sense of indignation is so natural ("something" he is unaware of awakens his rage) that his hand rises involuntarily to strike his aggressor. Just as the cravenness of the father is innate and represents his generation, Avner's natural sense of honor and his courage represent his.

Although Avner is kidnapped by the Druze as punishment, he experiences his incarceration by the untamed tribesmen as a conversion in which he is "baptized" as a real man, that is, Druze-like. His initiation into the fierce manhood of the Oriental natives is complete when his benefactor, Hamdan,[24] hands him his mare and gun as presents before his return to the *moshava*. With these two gifts, Avner begins his new life as a real man, according to the codes of the native, Eastern culture, codes that he has a chance to implement even before his actual return to the *moshava*. Passing by the place where his father was shot and where he himself was captured, Avner uncannily senses the blood of his dead father crying to him from the ground. Avner "winced, his heart rose in him, and he began to breathe heavily. He felt as if his blood were on fire. . . . He jumped off the mare and fell down with his face to the ground. Here, on this spot, his father's blood was spilled" (100). Although Avner is saddened by his father's demise, the father's death is justified poetically by his weakness. In fact, the cowardly father is much more useful to Avner as a dead man, because he enables him to become a blood avenger.

Back in the *moshava*, Avner feels too restless to return to farming. The need to avenge his father's murder consumes him, and he finds that he "misses the mountains and the Druze" very much. In his frustration, he channels his pent-up indignation and anger to his mare and his gun. Avner quickly gains a reputation among the Bedouins of the valley as a swift rider, and he eroticizes his gun, the extension of his manhood, in what can be read as a displaced act of onanism that validates and intensifies his status as a man and a warrior. Every night, he takes his gun "out of its crate, . . . cleans and polishes it, and looks at it fondly."

Smilansky's preoccupation with masculine ideals becomes still more pronounced through Avner's homoerotic relations with his Druze friend Hamdan and with Zevulun, a young assistant he employs on his farm. Hamdan and Avner

---

24. Smilansky uses the name Hamdan over and over again in his folktales.

learn to love each other like brothers during Avner's captivity. Before Avner returns to the *moshava*, the two friends undress in order to exchange their clothes, face each other in the nude, and take a vow of friendship. But the love between Avner and Zevulun is even stronger and more suggestive than the love between the Jew and the Arab. When Avner first meets Zevulun, as a young pioneer who comes to work on the *moshava*, he notices that his "eyes are blue and dreamy like a girl's. [Avner's] heart went after him, and he gave him his hand and said: 'What is your name?' 'Zevulun.' 'Will you come to work with me?' 'I will'" (102).[25] From then on, the two men are inseparable. They till the land together and roam it side by side, familiarizing themselves with its geography and its biblical history.

Smilansky probably had no intention of suggesting that Avner was a homosexual. More likely, Avner's exclusive associations with men and his obsession with manly codes of honor constitute an overcompensation for the prejudice that linked Jewishness with effeminacy. This neurosis was not peculiar to Jews. It was part of the masculinization process that accompanied the development of nationalism in Europe, which was greatly inspired by ancient Greek culture. The consolidation of national culture in the West contained a homoerotic tension that was evident, among other things, in the stricter division of gender roles, and the creation of exclusive male organizations such as the German youth movement, the *Wandervogel*.[26] The founders of the *Wandervogel*, which greatly influenced Jewish youth movements as well, encouraged their members not only to get acquainted with the German land by taking long trips into the countryside but also to get intimately acquainted with one another. Avner and Zevulun fulfill the first part, when they roam the Galilee with hearts "overflowing with song and endless love for the land of their fathers," invoking legends about biblical heroes, whose example they wish to follow. They fulfill their daydreams when, tired of farming, Avner turns his sense of honor, his courage, and his indignation, as well as the fighting ways he learned from the Druze, into something useful and fulfilling. Prompted by Zevulun, the two abandon farming in order to establish a Jewish militia:

> In the dead of night, when all our brethren will be soundly sleeping, we shall be awake. . . . Don't you love the night? . . . Every tree shadow looks conspiring. . . . [and] every stone and every bush lie in wait for you. . . . The air is full

25. This construction is typical of the meeting of destined lovers in the Bible, such as Jacob and Rachel or Ruth and Boaz.

26. Mosse writes that homoeroticism was an integral part of the ideal of normative masculinity in the West (*The Image of Man*, 32). Writing about German nationalism and masculinity, he also points out that "the *Turnplatz*—the field on which gymnastics took place—was likened to a public sanctuary where . . . legends about Germanic heroes sprang to life and the past informed the future" (44).

of suspicion, hundreds of eyes are watching you and hundreds of ears are listening for you, and a deathly silence lies heavy all around you. . . . Don't you love it? . . . And we shall ride our horses with guns in our hands, laughing at fear itself. How beautiful is the night! (105)

The land becomes mysterious, a symbol of fear, a dark side that must be overcome physically, as well as mentally, in an ultimate act of heroism. And so the two men vow to remain "brothers for life or death!" by becoming *shomrim*, watchmen, who would defend the Jewish settlements from marauders at night. But there is never a suggestion of sexual intimacy between them. Rather, their close bonds serve to intensify their association as men, new Jewish men, by doubling and refraction. Hamdan, the Oriental prototype, imparts the fighting ways of the East to Avner, his Jewish disciple, who transfers them to Zevulun and from him to all the others who would soon follow in their footsteps.[27]

Smilansky's famous pseudo-documentary story "Hawadja nazar" is similarly concerned with the construction of an alternative Jewish masculinity that is deeply homoerotic. Lazar, the hero, is a strapping young man of mixed Russian-Jewish parentage who is drawn to farm life in Eretz Israel through his love of the Bible, but who dies shortly after his arrival in a drowning accident in the Jordan River. Smilansky's attraction to the Russian-Jewish giant is unabashedly physical: "Every morning, I saw him as he passed through the yard near my window, . . . carrying a hoe and basket. I used to look at him and delight myself with the sight of his beautiful, strong body" (6). Yet his attraction is never really sexual. The narrator's admiration of Lazar is designed to direct the reader's attentions to precisely those traits that Smilansky and other Zionists wished to transform in Jewish culture, such as physical strength and valor.

As farmers and militiamen, both Lazar and Avner are portrayed as "Jewish Cossacks," who represent the link between East and West, as well as past and present that the Cossacks symbolized in Russian culture. The Cossacks provided Russia with a forceful and picturesque portrait of their past and themselves and were often portrayed in Russian literature as true, or original, Russians. Living at the fringes of Russia, geographically and culturally, the Cossacks came to symbolize the tension between East and West that characterized the expanding

27. In a short report called "Gever-isha," on which Zevulun's character was probably based, Smilansky writes about a meeting with a sixteen-year-old Russian-Jewish boy whose face was as delicate as a girl's, with light blue eyes, who dreamed of becoming a farmer. "The day was clear and beautiful," he writes. "Mount Hermon behind me, and the Hula Valley and the Jordan River before me were so splendid, so full of majesty and charm. But more beautiful than the day and more charming than the landscape was the dreaming boy" (Smilansky, 8:227). Years later, he meets the boy and waxes about his metamorphosis into a splendid *shomer*, who, "when he rides, becomes one with his horse; [and] when he fights, is coolly magnanimous and heroically enthusiastic," but who, nevertheless, still has "something of the woman in his face" (8:228).

czarist empire in the nineteenth century. More important, the myth of the Cossack enabled nineteenth-century Russians to cast themselves in an exotic, native context. In fictional works such as Tolstoy's *The Cossacks*, Pushkin's *The Captain's Daughter*, and Gogol's *Taras Bulba*, the fascination with Cossacks was not merely a yearning for the exotic or the fantastic; it was also motivated by a passionate interest in Russian national history.[28]

"The three principle producers of romantic Caucasus [Pushkin, Bestuzhev-Marlinsky, Lermontov]," writes Susan Layton in her analysis of Russian imperial literature, "invented Muslim tribesmen as shadow selves endowed with heroic machismo, a love of liberty, instinctual authenticity, simplicity and an aura of Homeric song."[29] The Bedouins and the Druze in Smilansky's tales have a similar role—so much so that Avner's trip to the Druze village reads like a children's version of Lermontov's Orientalist novella about the Caucasus, *A Hero of Our Time* (1839–1840). Avner's horse and gun are symbols of manhood that were frequently associated in the West with native and, in this case, Oriental exoticism.[30] As tools of war, the gun (or any other manual weapon) and the horse were not exclusively Western, of course. But since they were not part of Jewish culture at the time, Smilansky probably adopted them from his native Russian culture. Eventually, these symbols became staples of Jewish-Israeli manhood.[31]

The image of the Cossack that was imported to Palestine at the turn of the nineteenth century from popular Russian culture was connected in the minds of many pioneers with the Bedouin and the Arab farmer.[32] The example of the Cossacks inspired the new national image that Jews wished to cultivate because it fit the security needs of the Yishuv by containing a model for a farmers' army and because it combined the exoticism of the Oriental natives with the ancient Jewish heroes of the Bible.[33] It also enabled Jews to recast themselves as the Gentiles whom they feared and admired in Eastern Europe in a "native" context

28. Judith Kornblatt, *The Cossack Hero in Russian Literature*, 15, 25.

29. Layton, *Russian Literature and Empire*, 192.

30. The Russian Romantic poet Vassily Andreyevitch Zhukovsky portrays the Circassian tribes in his poem "To Voeikov" as "mountaineers [who] value their weapons as their treasures and their gods and prize a fine horse as a 'fleeted-footed comrade in arms'" (Layton, 94).

31. See, for example, a *New York Times* review of the arts in Israel: "At the opening of the Israeli Festival in 1995, the Batsheva Company dancers sat with their backs to a capacity audience. . . . They appeared to be simulating masturbation until they turned to reveal that they were cleaning their army-issued guns." Debora Sontag, "In Israel, Free to Be Personal, Not Political," *New York Times*, 24 October 1999, Arts & Leisure section, 33.

32. Yisrael Bartal, "Kozaq ubedvi: 'Olam hadimuyim hale'umi hehadash," *Ha'aliya hashniya*. Itamar Even-Zohar also writes about this inspiring connection and its importance in shaping the emerging Zionist culture in his seminal article "Tsemihata shel tarbut 'ivrit be'eretz yisra'el 1882–1948," *Studies in Zionism* 4 (1981): 450–482.

33. Bartal, "Kozaq ubedvi," 488.

that only the Land of Israel could provide. Avner's daydreaming at the beginning of the story about Yoav Ben-Tsruya, King David's army chief, and his biblical battle at the nearby site of Avel Bet Ma'acha (2 Sam. 20), and his initiation later as a "Druze" bring together East, West, past, and present.[34]

Avner and Zevulun's transformation into *shomrim* completes their metamorphosis from farmers to fighters and marks "Avner" as one of the first stories to depict this shift in modern, Hebrew culture. The end of the story brings the gradual construction of Avner's image as a fighter to its logical conclusion. He alone defends the *moshava* against a whole band of Druze that raid it one night, and avenges his father's death by killing his murderer in a face-to-face fight. By losing his father, Avner is tied to the soil by blood. By avenging his father's death in the manner of the natives, he is linked to the East by custom.

Although Smilansky did not write "Avner" or any of his other stories for children, by the end of the 1930s his naive tales appealed mostly to the Jewish youth of Palestine.[35] Designating *The Sons of Arabia* as "teenage literature" certainly diminishes its literary value, but it also underscores its important place in early Zionist culture. The Hebrew-Oriental universe of the tales shaped the worldview of younger Zionists, who grew up in Palestine with little knowledge of the Jewish Diaspora. Smilansky's stories, like those of the American frontier, provided the children of Zionist pioneers with an attractive interpretation of their environment, a "Wild East" of their own, onto which they projected themselves as new Jewish men.

The exclusive brotherhood of men in stories like "Avner" and the absence of women as objects of desire may be another reason why Smilansky's stories were eventually relegated to teenage readership, although even in Smilansky's other tales the eroticism of the Arab men is surprisingly subdued as well. The ambivalence toward Oriental erotica may be an expression of the sexual confusion of Jews at the time. The correlation of Jewishness with Orientalism and femininity was a staple of anti-Semitism during the late nineteenth and early twentieth century, which the popularity of the colonial East complicated even further.

34. This perception was very common at the time. In a chapter called "Where Are You, Descendants of Bar-Kochva?" Rachel Yana'it Ben-Zvi compares the skirmishes between Arabs and Jews in the Galilee to the ancient wars of the Israelites: "The spirit of the Galilee rebellion comes alive in us, and the heroes of Judea appear before us as if they were alive. Was not Bar-Kochva like Yechezkele?" *Anu olim*, 147. It is very telling that Yana'it Ben-Zvi uses the Hebrew name Ezekiel with its Slavo-Yiddish suffix of endearment together with the ancient Hebrew figure of Bar-Kochva.

35. The naive literature of the First, Second, and Third Aliyah, by Smilansky, Nehama Pukhachevsky, Vilkansky, Yosef Luidor, Yehuda Burla, and others, writes Shaked, was first written for Jewish readers abroad "who enjoyed the innocence and the heroism of the protagonists and the sacrifices they made in the Holy Land. It finally appealed to Jewish-Palestinian youth, whose imagination and dreams about a legendary world began to fill up with Jewish and Arab heroes who fight, wrestle, draw swords, and ride well, and who will inherit the land." Shaked, *Hasiporet ha'ivrit* 2:54–55.

Boehmer writes that "the characterization of colonized people as secondary, abject, weak, feminine, and other to Europe . . . was standard in British colonial writing. Time and again, the derogation of other cultures was used to validate the violence of invasion. . . . Within the terms of colonialist representation it was possible to style any incident of conquest as demonstrating the power of the invader and the inferiority of the conquered."[36]

One such example is Wali Dad in Kipling's "On the City Wall." Wali Dad, an effete young Muslim who spends most of his days in the perfumed rooms of Lalun, a pretty prostitute, is sensualized to the point of decadence. His image exemplifies the Western perception of the Orient as an orgiastic universe, to which Jews were thought to belong as well. A tragic example of the consequences of such anti-Semitic associations was the Austrian philosopher Otto Weininger (1880–1903), a Jew and a homosexual, whose deep sense of inferiority was the impetus for his notoriously misogynistic and anti-Semitic tract *Sex and National Character*, in which he denigrated women as inferior and Judaism as feminine. Although Weininger's thesis was extreme, the popular notions about race, sex, and Judaism that it propagated made it a long-standing best seller.

When Smilansky constructs his alternative Oriental world, he must contend with such perceptions. Perhaps this is why, in most of his stories, passion is more a woman's prerogative. To create a clear division between the sexes, Smilansky exaggerates the traits of both according to Western conventions of respectability. The adoption of sexual paradigms from the West, especially the stricter definition of gender that attended the rise of nationalism in Europe—confining women to the home and men to the world of action without—plays an important part in his folktales, as Hamdan and his lover Hemda clearly demonstrate in "The Hill of Love":

> [Hamdan's] left arm supports her, and his right hand—the hand that could wield a sword like a toy. . . .—caresses with the tenderness of a child her gleaming black hair, as soft as silk. His face is lit by heavenly bliss. . . .
> "Hamdan!"
> Her small and soft white hand passes over his hard face, his tanned cheeks, his forehead, his eyes, and his mustache, as if to say, "How strong you are, how brave, how courageous!" (23)

The Western, chivalric conventions of masculinity and femininity, both physical and temperamental, are illustrated almost didactically here. The tough

36. Boehmer, *Colonial and Postcolonial Literature*, 80. See also Boyarin, *Unheroic Conduct*; Paul Mendes-Flohr, *Divided Passions*; as well as Jacques Kornberg, *Theodore Herzl*.

warrior is tamed by the tender proximity of the woman, while the softness of the woman's features and her long black hair are contrasted with the man's ruggedness. Both are conveyed through a limited and recurring vocabulary that draws attention to the importance that Smilansky gave these Oriental signs of manhood. Smilansky's reverence toward this new manhood is not only expressed through the fetishist enumeration of its signs—hard face, tanned cheeks, mustache, sword wielding—but is further intensified through the woman's passion for her beautiful Semitic lover.

In "Humadi's Revenge," the hero's masculinity is so conspicuous that Smilansky can display him as a sexual object without jeopardizing his manliness. To take his revenge on the offending tribe, the young man passively sits on his horse and lets his good looks drive the beautiful daughter of the sheik mad with lust as she bathes in the nude before him night after night, transfixed by *his* ravishing good looks. "The sickness of the sheik's daughter inflicted the other girls of the tribe. The eyes of the modest tribeswomen began to gleam with lusty fires. . . . and many of them started talking of the mighty fellow who appears before them at night on the rock, high above the spring. They were all sick with love" (152). Although Humadi is an angry young fighter who is eager to engage his enemies in a manly battle face-to-face, his revenge takes a different form. Instead of confronting his enemies as a true Bedouin, the young man subjects himself to the leering girls in a passive, feminine way that becomes an aggressive act of revenge. Unlike the lascivious Jews of anti-Semitic lore, Humadi lets himself be sexually objectified by the women whom he watches without ever losing his composure. It is the women who are consumed with excessive lust for him to the point of insanity.

This peculiar Zionist formulation is important, especially in light of the common postcolonial criticism that exotic images in nineteenth-century literature are often portrayed as sexually forbidden or deviant. This theme recurs frequently in the Indian stories of Rudyard Kipling. "Beyond the Pale," for instance, is a story about the secret love of an English official to a young and pretty Muslim widow, whose hands are chopped off after she is discovered flirting with the Englishman. The story dwells on the deviance of the two lovers, who defy the norms of their respective cultures, as well as on the cruel and, in Western terms, unusual punishment the woman receives. Both the woman and the culture she represents are portrayed in a mixture of allure and menace that examines cultural limits. The story acknowledges the Western fascination with exotic Indian culture, exemplified by the widow's beauty and attractiveness. But it also punishes for the attempt to mix culturally.[37]

---

37. Rudyard Kipling, *The One-Volume Kipling, Authorized.* See also Boehmer, 27.

In Smilansky's folktales, however, even the prurient draw of the harem, a topos of Oriental erotica, is reevaluated. In "The Hill of Love," the harem does not signify the titillating sexual escapism that it usually had in Orientalist literature. It is portrayed as a prison, a symbol of enslavement that is associated with the corruption of Muslim culture. Hamdan first sees Hemda, a beautiful Turkish woman, during one of his raids on a convoy of rich merchants. The robbers are surprised to find that instead of gold, the merchants are carrying women to the harem of the pasha in Damascus. "From the top of one of the camels, a woman lifted her veil and looked at Hamdan. Hamdan . . . stared back. . . . Never had he seen a face like that . . . as white as the snow on Mount Hermon [with] eyes as black as the deepest night. . . . The moonlight was dancing on the wonderful, sad face" (16–17).

Hamdan is a romantic at heart, like all of Smilansky's Arab men, and once he is struck with the woman's beauty, he decides to give up his life of crime and seek the forgiveness of the authorities so that he can marry her and settle down. He asks the holy bek, leader of all the northern Bedouin tribes, to intervene on his behalf with the pasha. The old man agrees and puts Hamdan in charge of his harem during his embassy to Damascus. But one night, before the bek returns, Hamdan is asked to fix something in the tent of the bek's new Turkish wife.

> A small lamp illuminated the darkness of the big tent. In the middle of the tent, on a large and embroidered Persian rug, sat a young woman on a heap of pillows and blankets. . . . Her face was as white as snow and pale with sorrow. There was deep sadness and pain in her big black eyes, which shone with tears. Her long lashes cast a shadow on her pale face. Her long hair fell down on both her sides and covered her body.
> "It is she!" flashed a thought in the Bedouin. . . .
> "*Haidud!*" cried the woman. Her voice was frightened, but she seemed pleasantly surprised nevertheless.

Smilansky is clearly more interested in the woman, whose features are spiritualized rather than objectified, than in the mystery, color, and ornament of the harem, which he mentions in passing (darkness, rug, pillows). He emphasizes the mutual and genuine attraction of the man and the woman, whose purity is intensified in contrast to the decadent surroundings that bespeak sexual excess and lascivious desire. "No one can imagine the things I saw in these tents! The love, the tears, the cries!" laments the old female attendant of the young wife, who reassures Hamdan that "the prettiest Arab girls were here, whose blood is fire and whose kisses are honey." Finally, the immorality of the old bek's lust for his young wife is personified in his degenerate harem guard, "the old, one-eyed, and wrinkled guard, who has the heart of a chained dog, [and who] looked with hate and contempt at the trespassing young guard [Hamdan]."

Significantly, the harem is not presented as an exotic location of forbidden pleasures but as a place of confinement, from which Hamdan releases the young wife. This critique continues in the nightmare that the young Turk has during her first night as a free woman. The dream recaps Hemda's confinement, her sale to the pasha, and the repulsion that her aging masters awoke in her. Ultimately, the story becomes an indictment of the Oriental commoditization of sex that the harem symbolizes, a sentiment that is underscored by the bliss that Hemda finds at the end of the story in the arms of her true lover, Hamdan:

> The two of them hug and fall on the Persian rug of the holy bek. . . . Their kisses ring in the dead of the night. An enchanting whisper flutters through the air. The canopy of the heavens above them stretches wide . . . [and] covers them and separates them from the world. The moon stands still and smiles at them and blesses them. And far, far away the stars twinkle at them and send their blessings, too.

The stifling confinement of the harem is contrasted by nature itself, which welcomes the true and right love of the young couple by stretching its skies over them like a bridal canopy. In further contrast to the material luxury of the harem, Hemda decorates herself the next day with flowers. "She put a garland of white flowers on her head, tied blue flowers to the tips of her hair, and hung a thick rope of red flowers around her neck. On her chest, on her white robe, she stuck red lilies, and around her white arms she wrapped strings of small flowers of all kinds and all colors." The amassing of colors, shapes, and materials reads like a subversive Oriental description in that—unlike the description of the colorful fruit of precious stones in the cave of Aladdin, for instance—it celebrates natural, not artificial, luxury.[38] The excessive blend of colors and flowers gives the impression that nature itself approves of the young lovers by providing abundant decorations for their makeshift wedding.

Smilansky's reevaluation of the harem, however, does not extend to his portrayal of the young Turkish woman. Her image is strictly constructed according to Western conventions of erotic Orientalism, which usually serve up Islamic women as innocent but voluptuous maidens who are less domesticated, less socialized, and closer to nature than Western women, and as women who regard

38. "The trees of this garden were all full of the most extraordinary fruit. Each tree bore a sort of a different color. Some were white, others sparkling and transparent, like crystal; some were red, and of different shades, others green, blue, violet; some of a yellowish hue. . . . The white were pearls; the sparkling and transparent were diamonds; the deep red were rubies." *The Arabian Nights*, rev. and corrected from Lane's edition (New York: David Francis, 1869), 87.

their lovers as their masters.[39] Like her male lover, the beautiful Hemda is characteristic of most other women in Smilansky's stories. The brief history of her childhood, in which we learn of the attempts to domesticate her and then sell her to the pasha, is designed to convey her innocence and juvenile intelligence. In her childlike ways, the girl does not understand her parents' destitution, their intentions to sell her for profit, or the sexual greed of the old men who buy her. The same innocence that prompts her to bite first the pasha and then the bek, who both approach her for sex, makes her appear initially less socialized, although later it makes her submit completely to Hamdan, for whom she willingly dies at the end.

At the end of "The Hill of Love," Smilansky brings all these conflicting notions to a climax, in his ecstatic blending of nature, love, and death. The love of Humadi, the ultimate Semite, and Hemda, his consummate Oriental lover, ignites into fiery passion in a natural environment aptly called "The Hill of Love." The last portion of the story is dedicated entirely to the description of their burning passion and its reflection and amplification in the fecund nature around them: "The Bedouin [Hamdan!] jumped up, lifted the woman . . . and pressed her against his heart. Suddenly, he roared like a lion and ran with [her] cleaved to his heart around the tower, jumping and galloping like a horse" (24).

The next morning, after the two lovers awake, nature itself bursts into song in honor of their sacred love, exploding in colors and shapes that pour forth uncontrollably. But just as quickly as their passion ignites, it is extinguished by Hamdan's dramatic killing of his mare, his concubine, and himself when the Turkish soldiers approach to arrest him. But because he lived his life to the fullest, Hamdan's death is not perceived as pathetic but as enviable—the only end that befits his noble and heroic free spirit. Hamdan's image thus shines in all its Oriental glory. His love of war, his passion for women, his honorable willingness to die, and his deep connection to the unspoiled land make him a powerful romantic model for a new Jewish generation.

This kind of Oriental "camp" that distinguishes Smilansky's work was a uniquely Jewish formulation. The heroes of Smilansky's folktales embody a new model of Jewish masculinity, fashioned according to the conventions of Romantic Orientalism. Just as the male body itself became a symbol of the healthy nation in nineteenth-century European culture, the exotic, Oriental men in *The Sons of Arabia* informed the new Jewish masculinity that Zionists sought to create. But instead of the clean-cut Englishman or the all-American boy, Smilansky

---

39. See Sharafuddin's discussion of Oriental poetic conventions in Romantic English poetry, 184–185.

created a dashing figure of an all-Semitic boy; a figure that was both Arab and Jewish or better still—Eretz-Israeli.

Although Smilansky made a strong case for considering the Bedouins as inspiring images of reform for the Jewish "colonists" in Palestine, not everyone shared his views. In 1905, J. Klausner published in the periodical *Hashiloah* his well-known article "Fear" (*Hashash*), in which he warned of going native in Palestine: "If a Jew happens to adopt Bedouin customs; if he manages to ride a horse and shoot a gun and wear an Arab robe—right away our Hebrew writers get excited. If a Jew shows a spirit of untamed bravery that makes the Arabs respect him—our writers scramble to praise him. With strange delight, they paint every Palestinian Jew who speaks Arabic and looks like an Arab. . . . If [the establishment of a Jewish Yishuv in] Erets Israel [means] . . . assimilation into Arab backwardness, it is better to stay in the Diaspora and assimilate into the enlightened Western culture."[40]

Theodore Herzl, too, promoted Zionism as a wall that would protect Europe from Asian barbarism, and his right-hand man, Max Nordau, vowed that just as the British did not become Indians in America or Hottentots in Africa, the Jews shall not adopt the inferior culture of Palestine either.[41] The Jewish society that both Herzl and Nordau envisioned in Palestine was essentially colonial. Herzl expected Palestine to be acquired, domesticated, and then civilized by Jews through the wholesale importation of Western culture, just as the British transferred their religion, social structure, and economy, including the names of cities and towns, to places like North America, Australia, and South Africa. Herzl made no secret of his admiration for the British colonial administration, although his views on the relations between the would-be Jewish settlers and the Arab natives of Palestine are less clear. At any rate, the social interactions between Jews and Arabs in his utopian novel *Altneuland* seem more benign than the British reluctance to mix with the natives of some of their colonies or the British tendency to represent natives as racially and culturally inferior and consequently to impose physical and legal restrictions on them.

One of the most provocative interpreters of Herzlian Zionism, Daniel Boyarin, contends that the literary heroes of the Hebrew Revival were indeed created in the image of Gentiles and made to conform to the codes of European chivalry, and that Jewish nationalism did not develop out of a wish to separate from the Gentiles, but rather, Zionists imitated Christian European

40. Quoted in Berlowitz, *Lehamtsi erets, lehamtsi 'am*, 120.
41. Tom Segev, *Hatsiyonim hahadashim* (Jerusalem: Keter, 2001), 30.

culture in order to be accepted by it. But as Smilansky's Oriental universe suggests, many Jews in Palestine dreamed of becoming dark, not white, men.[42] This is true even if the impetus for making up the image of the all-Semitic boy, repeated over and over again in Smilansky's stories, was motivated by the need to create an alternative to the denigrated Jewish man. Ido Bassok writes that in *The Sons of Arabia,* Smilansky tried to understand his own mental world by projecting it onto and displacing the world of the Arabs, thereby making them part of the Jewish-Zionist search for identity. The Arab, writes Bassok, is the Jewish Other, but he is not exactly the mirror image of the Jew, the place onto which evil, or the shadow, is projected, because in many ways he is an Other that one desires to become.[43] Similarly, Boyarin writes that, "in the colonial/postcolonial moment, the stereotyped other becomes the object of desire, of introjection rather than abjection, and it is the stereotyped self that is abjected."[44] Although Boyarin makes this observation with regard to Herzl's and Freud's obsession with Christian, Western-European values, I think it applies better to the metamorphosis of these desires in *The Sons of Arabia.*

Boyarin's postcolonial critique of Zionism has influenced critics in Israel, who, beginning in the late 1980s, began to examine the relations between Jews and Arabs using the colonizers/colonized paradigm. Hanan Hever, a prominent post-Zionist literary critic, acknowledges the violence that usually comes with the attainment of national independence.[45] "The establishment of a sovereign nation on its soil," he quotes the contemporary French philosopher Derrida, "requires the use of violence, of forceful seizure of the desired territory and also of expulsion that enables the institution of sovereignty."[46] This necessary stage of establishing a coherent sovereign identity, writes Hever, is a violent stage that never really ends and must be repeated forever in order to justify itself and its control over the national territory, which continues to be physically and morally threatened.

Although this model of power relations is perpetuated in some way or another in the literature of all nations, Hever warns that the postcolonial reading of Hebrew literature must take into account the special case of Zionism within the common colonial model. Hever describes this Jewish or Hebrew colonialism as doubled. On the one hand, Jews were Europeans who came to the East from

---

42. Boyarin's contention is not entirely groundless, especially with respect to Herzl. See chapter 1, note 15. But I think that Smilansky's work is more representative of the alternative that was adopted by Zionists in Palestine.

43. Ido Bassok, "Psikho'analiza beheksher tarbuti ufoliti," 78.

44. Boyarin, *Unheroic Conduct,* 304.

45. I focus on Hever in particular because he is not only a prominent and prolific post-Zionist critic but a leading literary critic as well.

46. Hanan Hever, "Mesifrut Ivrit lesifrut Yisre'elit," 167.

the West with plans to take over. On the other hand, these same Jews existed as colonial subjects in Europe for centuries. While this complexity makes their relationship with Palestine and its Arab natives ambivalent, Hever still maintains that it cannot and should not obscure the violent enactment of sovereignty that Hebrew texts try to conceal.[47]

But, as I have shown in this chapter, the early works that were written during Zionism's most formative years defy such dogmatic categorizations. Not because they necessarily negate them but because they complicate them even further. Against the stereotyped Jewish weakness, Smilansky creates in *The Sons of Arabia* an alternative Semitic masculinity—one that draws heavily on romanticized elements from the native Arab culture. As a result, the "stereotyped other," that is, the Bedouin, becomes indeed the object of Jewish desire, whereas the "stereotyped self," that is, Diaspora Jewishness, is dismissed. The improvement of the inferior Diaspora Jew is achieved through a cultural assimilation into the superior, native, Arab, so that the society of Jewish settlers in Palestine mimics the native Arab society and not the other way around, as the colonial paradigm usually worked.

This move not only defied usual colonial patterns; it ran contrary to central Jewish historical patterns as well. For within the imperial dynamics that govern the relations between the center of an empire and its colonies, how should we understand the centrality that the Land of Israel always had in Jewish culture, and the fact that communities of Jews outside the Land of Israel, in the Diaspora, were traditionally referred to as settlements, or *moshavot* (the very word that was used for the new, Jewish agricultural settlements in Palestine at the beginning of the twentieth century)?! Whereas England always remained the undisputed heart of the British Empire, politically, economically, administratively, and culturally, the Land of Israel maintained a similar centrality in Jewish culture throughout history, at least symbolically. This was so even though most Jews resided elsewhere throughout history and were subjugated by the people among whom they lived, not the other way around. The same holds true for the traditional Jewish fear of "going native," which historically was directed at the white Christian society in Europe. Despite constant pressures to convert to Christianity, Jews resisted these pressures for centuries and disdained almost any kind of association with Christians. In Smilansky's folktales, however, this Jewish anxiety all but disappears and becomes a strong desire to assimilate into the Arab culture of Palestine and acquire many of its traits.

Smilansky's infatuation with the foreign and exotic culture of the Arabs was undoubtedly Western and Orientalist. It may also be that Smilansky imposed

47. Ibid., 168.

his Western values on the Arab culture by choosing those Arab traits that best
fit his need to create a new, Hebrew culture. In many cases, Smilansky did not
even describe actual Bedouins but fictional images, products of his Orientalist
imagination. Despite his intimate knowledge of Arab culture, he remained an
outsider to it. But the important difference here is the psychology that motivated
Zionists like him. As opposed to similar dynamics in contemporaneous colonial
cultures, it seems doubtful that Smilansky wished to establish his superiority as
a white European over the dark, primitive native. Rather, he seems eager to
become *native-like*. While Boyarin asserts that Herzl wished that Jews in Uganda,
Argentina, or even in Palestine would "turn into people 'English in tastes, in
opinions, in morals and in intellect,'" Smilansky clearly held the Arab culture
in reverence and in many instances placed it above his own Jewish-European
society as an inspiring model.[48]

Smilansky's colorful and dramatic descriptions of a mythological Palestine
may be interpreted also as "colonial" in that they give a Hebrew shape to an
Arab space. When Mount Tabor is described as "beautiful in its fresh greenery
as if it were full of song, the song of everlasting life," or when the Sea of Galilee
and the Jordan River are made into lovers that are cursed by Allah, Smilansky
writes about geographic landmarks that are part of Jewish history.[49] At the same
time, he appropriates Arab folklore and combines it with the sights and sounds
of the untamed land to make a virtual image that fits his Romantic, European
imagination. These pictures had little, if anything, to do with the way Arabs saw
the same land, as they expressed a different level of consciousness that was not
part of the local culture at the time.

Moreover, Smilansky's appropriation of Arab folklore would seemingly fit into
what Boehmer describes as a typical colonial paradigm, in which colonizers
searched for non-European texts that would help them govern and legitimize
their control in the language of the natives. The very naming of a foreign land,
she writes, was an exercise of mastery. Yet, the case of Palestine was different,
of course, because in many instances Arab place names were derivations of
former "Jewish" biblical place names.[50]

Finally, it can be argued there was something ruthless in the way Smilansky
first stereotyped the native, then deprived him even of his imagined traits, and
finally replaced him with an alternative image of an invented native Jew, the
sabra. Such, for example, is Lazar, the Russian-Jewish giant in his story "Hawadja
nazar," who becomes a local superman by joining together his intimate knowledge of the local Arab culture, his physical strength, his skill as a laborer, and

48. Ibid., 305.
49. Smilansky, "Yillelat tsalhiya," 5:99; "Nikmat humadi," 5:129.
50. Boehmer, 19.

his dedication to the homeland. Ostensibly, the combination of racial superiority (Jewish ethnicity) and knowledge of the native culture (Arabic language and customs) makes Lazar an ideal colonial ruler, a white man who knows enough of the native culture to rule it effectively.[51] On the other hand, both Lazar and Avner admire the native Arabs and wish to mimic them. Avner even penetrates into the dark heart of the native territory when he goes into the mountain village of the Druze. But unlike Kurtz in Joseph Conrad's classic colonial novella *Heart of Darkness* (1902), Avner is not contaminated or corrupted by his contact with the natives.[52] On the contrary, through his cultural exchanges with them, he is baptized to become a new and better man, a Jewish-Druze or a New Hebrew.

Michael Gilsenan writes that at its height, in the beginning of the twentieth century, imperialism was characterized by a relentless and impossible search for an "elsewhere" that dissolved even the objective possibility of the exotic "except as fantasy, nostalgia, myth, self-deception, or the re-invention of tradition."[53] All these elements play an important role in Smilansky's work as well. But while the exotic attraction of the East in the West was escapist at best and destructive at worst, Smilansky and his Zionist contemporaries used Oriental exoticism as a real transformative power. The paradox of Jewish existence, which gave rise to Zionism in the first place, opened up Palestine for Jews as a real "elsewhere," where fantasy, nostalgia, and myth came together not for the purpose of domination and dispossession but in order to build a new Jewish identity and invent a new Jewish tradition in Eretz Israel.

51. Kipling often sets up this dynamic in his stories. See "Kim," for instance.

52. The most condemnable darkness of Kurtz's heart is obviously the corruption wrought by the greed of his Western employers, who are plundering Africa for ivory. But the proximity to the "savage" and "uncivilized" African natives removes all inhibitions he may have had before and unleashes these destructive forces in him.

53. Michael Gilsenan, *Imagined Cities of the East*, 5.

CHAPTER 4

A Jewish Noble Savage?

The Limits of Cultural Innovation

Frishman's one trip to Palestine at the end of his life epitomized his reluctance to see the East as much more than a symbol, potent and invigorating perhaps, but a symbol nevertheless. Although he was impressed with the developments he saw during his visit in 1911, Frishman did not believe that the Yishuv would amount to anything more than an inspiring example. The stylized biblical language and motifs he used in *Bamidbar* reflect these beliefs. Smilansky's immigration to Palestine as a teenager and his lifelong involvement in the development of the Yishuv left a different mark on his writing. The creation of the image of the All-Semitic Boy in *The Sons of Arabia* epitomizes his deep desire for Jewish integration into Arab Palestine; an integration that distinguished his own life. A third case, that reflects the limits to Smilansky's cultural innovation, can be found in the works of the writer L. A. Arielli (Orloff), whose skepticism of Zionism and suspicion of Orientalism as part of it stand at the center of this chapter.

Arielli was twenty-four when he arrived in Jaffa in 1908 and, like many young pioneers his age, first worked as a laborer (*po'el*), then as a watchman (*shomer*), until he finally became a teacher. His career as a writer was established fairly quickly in the small and intimate world of the young Yishuv. His painfully honest portrayals of pioneer life drew the attention of the literary establishment, and his works began to appear in almost every literary venue of the time. But despite his relative success as a writer, Arielli, like many of his peers, could barely support himself, and when family problems exacerbated the already harsh economic situation he decided to quit the country. In 1923, fourteen years after he came to Palestine, Arielli left his family and settled in the United

States, where he continued to write and teach until his death in 1943 at the age of fifty-seven.[1]

Emigration proved fatal to Arielli's literary career, and, notwithstanding his promising beginning, he remained a marginal writer in the United States, an artist who never regained the sophistication of the best works he produced in Palestine.[2] Angry and frustrated with the disappointing state of Hebrew culture in America, most of Arielli's American works are heavy-handed and acerbic critiques of Jewish life in North America.[3]

Unlike his unremarkable American work, however, the prose Arielli composed in Palestine was distinguished by an increasingly astute treatment of the Zionist pioneering experience. His first short stories were fashionably impressionistic, some even fantastic and surrealistic, but his subsequent Eretz-Israeli works dealt with the frustrating reality of early twentieth-century Jewish Palestine with uncommon maturity.[4] This was one of the reasons why Brenner, the supreme literary arbiter at the time and a staunch realist, encouraged Arielli, whom he considered as promising a writer as the young Agnon.[5]

Arielli's view of the Orient was never blurred by popular exoticism. A succinct example of his unflattering view of the Levant can be found in his 1916 short story, "Rainy Season" (*Biymot hagshamim*), about a family of Jewish shopkeepers who live in isolation among Arabs in Samaria and epitomize the

---

1. For a comprehensive account of Arielli's life and work, see Milton Arfa's preface to Arielli's collected works, *Kitve lamed alef arielli*, Milton Arfa, ed.

2. Shaked writes that, "we do not know what would have become of Arielli-Orloff had he not left Israel, at any rate, according to his own admission, he lost the immediate connection with readers in America. The transfer of the literary center to Palestine, and the fact that a viable center did not emerge in the 'golden Diaspora' [America], were very detrimental to this talented writer. Although Arielli left a desolate land and resettled in a great center of population, he in fact left a cultural haven for a desolate wilderness." Shaked, *Hasiporet ha'ivrit*, 2:119.

3. Arielli left Palestine primarily for personal reasons. From letters he wrote to friends and family, it seems that his wife, Bella, did not support his literary aspirations and he decided to leave her in Israel and move somewhere else. Three years before his death in 1943 he officially divorced Bella and married his longtime companion. His last few years of life with his new wife seem to have been happy. Shaked, 2:370, note 19. Shaked characterizes Arielli's American work as parochial and slight (127). Part of Arielli's bitterness stemmed from the fact that, unlike many of his contemporaries, he could not find a publisher who was willing to publish a collection of his writings. A partial anthology of his works was published posthumously in 1954. A complete edition of his works was first published in 1999 by Dvir.

4. Beginning in 1911, Arielli wrote almost one literary work for each of the years he lived in Palestine. For a complete list, see Gila Ramraz-Rauch, *Alef lamed arielli (orloff), hayav viyetsirato*, 224–27.

See also Gershon Shaked's article "Hate'om sheyarad" at the end of Arielli's anthology *Yeshimon*, 291.

5. S. Y. Agnon became Israel's most celebrated writer, winning the noble prize for literature in 1966. Agnon and Arielli were often paired at the beginning of their careers and their early stories were published simultaneously by Brenner in the periodical *Hapo'el Hatza'ir*. See Shaked in *Yeshimon*, 286, who acknowledges this in the title of his article. The twins referred to are Agnon and Arielli.

anomaly of Jewish life in the East. Menachem, the shopkeeper's neurotic son, cannot bear the dreariness of the stormy Palestinian winter and longs to be back in Russia. "*Nad amrachinim Petrogradam,*" he hums to himself in Russian a poem by Pushkin, "*dishal Noyabr assenim chladam*" (over the cloudy city of Peter / November blew a breath of autumn).[6]

> Ah, Menachem thinks, not even Petrograd is as miserable under the cold breath of November as this lonely and desolate Arab town, wrapped in a deadly pallor and forgotten by God and by people in the mountains, under the incessant rains of February. Ah, how stuffy is everything today! So depressing, depressing to tears, painfully depressing! Look at this land of eternal sun and summer! Menachem says, as if scolding himself. The East you read about in the poetry of northern bards is nothing but fraud, pure and simple. You'll read there about hot sand, palm trees that give shade to the customary camel, you will bask there in the sunlight to your heart's content, but nothing—you hear, nothing, not half a word, not even a hint will you find there about damned days such as these. . . . What should we, the denizens of the East, do then? Blur into the background? Evaporate? Or maybe emigrate to the southern hemisphere?[7]

The East in this scene is portrayed not as a promised land at all but as worse than exile. Arielli performs here a double inversion of the clichéd yearning for the East that was expressed in countless poems since the early Romantic period (not to mention the more traditional longing to the East within Jewish tradition that began with the Exile itself). He ridicules Gentile poets, whose ignorance may after all be excused, as well as Jewish poets who should ostensibly know better. From the lips of Menachem, Pushkin's words become a subtle parody of poets like Bialik, whose famous ode "To the Bird" opens with a heartfelt welcome to a bird that returns "from the warm lands to my window," that is, from the Land of Israel to his northern European shtetl.[8] But whereas the Land of Israel in Bialik's poem is a symbol, whose warm weather and eternal spring stand as a poetic contrast to the misery of Diaspora, Menachem's situation is a bit more complicated. Having settled in Palestine, Menachem now yearns for the harsh winters of Russia.

The irony in this passage extends to the pathetic attempts to romanticize the East through the sobering contrast with the miserable "eastern" winter day and to the parody of the longing itself. In an act of self-flagellation that accentuates his paradoxical existence, Menachem does not long for the cool, green summers of northern Europe but for its bitter, but "genuine" winters. The contrast he

---

6. From a poem called "The Brass Knight." See Arielli, *Yeshimon*, 93.
7. *Yeshimon*, 93.
8. See chapter 1 for a fuller discussion of this poem.

paints is not the more traditional complaint of the newly arrived immigrants to Palestine who, shocked by the scorching heat and the dusty yellowness, yearn for the cool and verdant summers of a temperate Europe. The alienation Menachem feels from his immediate, Eastern environment is reflected in the stormy weather and intensified by it. Like the cold and the rain, Menachem has no place in the East either.

Although pessimism about the success of the Yishuv characterized most of the realist writers of the Second and Third Aliya, Arielli went further than most in exploring this theme. In an earlier version of the previous story called "Troubles" (*Tsarot*, 1914), Arielli provides another unflattering view of the Levant, this time in summer:

> Like a symbol of the yearning, lazy East, the leaders of the town and its most respected citizens were crouching with half-shut eyes by the cactus hedges that lined both sides of the road, which was covered by a thick layer of hot dust, peels of fruit and miscellaneous other remnants of the country's crop. Around them hung countless, half naked young men and children. Some of them chewed on watermelon slices that they picked up from the dust and that extended all the way up to their ears, and some were shouting wildly in broken English the "Our Father in Heaven" prayer that they learned at the Mission. Some were beating each other vigorously with whatever they could lay their hands on, and still others—the ten year olds and older boys—bragged to each other with shouts and gesticulations . . . , about the money they had already collected in order to buy a bride. And over all of them, like hot and dulling summer bitterness, count-less swarms of flies buzzed around and around.[9]

The Arab village functions here as an epitome of parochialism, much as the Jewish shtetl often figured in contemporary Eastern European literature, and the detailed descriptions of the overall degeneracy conjure up a decidedly unro-mantic East.

Often, Arielli portrayed the failure of his Jewish protagonists to find a place for themselves in Palestine through their abortive relations with Arabs. This is true of the very first story Arielli published, "Heinrich the Pale" (*Heinrich hahiver*, 1909), in which the introverted protagonist, Itzhak Bloom, is visited by night-mares about Bedouins.[10] In another short story, "Young Bunia" (*Hana'ar bunya*, 1913), the sensitive adolescent hero is obsessed with the image of an Arab laborer, who died of yellow fever. Bunia's foolhardy and quasi-messianic attempt to resurrect the dead Arab, make light of the very Zionist project of revival.[11]

9. *Yeshimon*, 61.
10. See Shaked, in *Yeshimon*, 287.
11. Arielli, *Bentayim, kovets sifruti*, 50–77.

Arielli's most comprehensive critique of Zionism as an Orientalist project, however, can be found in one of his earlier works, his play *Allah Karim!* (Arabic for Allah the generous), which was serialized in the periodical *Hashiloah* during 1913. The play was Arielli's sixth published work, appearing after four short stories written in the neo-romantic style popular at the time and a novella titled *In Venus's Light* (*Le'or havenus*); an impressively complex work in which the writer's short experience in the czarist army is cast as a boldly modern version of a Joseph in Egypt story.[12] After *Allah Karim!*, Arielli published three more stories and another novella titled *Yeshimon* (*Wilderness*), all of which examine an increasingly complicated East, in which Jews are often damned and very seldom redeemed.[13]

One of the most remarkable aspects of Arielli's play, beyond the surprising genre itself, is its bold and almost revolutionary treatment of some of the most burning questions of the time, and by an immigrant who has barely spent three years in Palestine at that. For in *Allah Karim!*, the oppressive atmosphere of despair, self-criticism, doubt, and scorn surpasses even that of Brenner, who was famous for his harsh views on Yishuv life.[14] Chief among the vehicles of critique in the play is Arielli's devastating treatment of Oriental Romanticism, a fad that swept the Yishuv at the time and manifested itself in Arab dress, in the incorporation of Arabic words into Hebrew, and the imitation of Arab masculine bravado, as the works of Smilansky attest.

My analysis of the play, which comprises the rest of this chapter, will focus on three different aspects of Arielli's critique of Hebrew Orientalism. The first part of the analysis deals directly with the portrayal of the characters and their conduct as a general commentary on Zionism. The second part looks at Arielli's examination of the colonial nature of Zionism and the relations between East

---

12. Arfa writes that there were very few Hebrew works that presented Jewish protagonists who were so organically integrated into the Gentile society as Arielli's *Venus*, x.

13. The play first appeared in *Hashiloah* in 1913. It was published again as a booklet in New York in 1918, without knowledge or permission of the author. Apparently it was also performed in New York around that time, although I could not find a reference to it. It was performed again in Israel in 1982 as part of the Acre Theater Festival. See Arielli's collected writings, Arfa, 2:203–4.

There are three noteworthy analyses of the play, one by Abraham Epstein in *Sofrim 'ivriyim be'amerika*, 258–262, and an article by Ehud Ben-Ezer called, "Aravi ehad mokher tufinim," 20–21. The third analysis appears in Ramraz-Rauch's monograph. Gideon Ofrat discusses the play briefly as part of his survey of pioneering and land-worship myths in Hebrew plays of the settlement period in *Adama, adam, dam*, 41–52. Avner Holtzman also mentions the play in his article about self-consciousness in Second Aliya literature ("Al hatoda'a ha'atsmit besifrut ha'aliya hashniya") in a collection of research papers titled *Ha'aliya hashniya—mehkarim*, Israel Bartal ed. (Jerusalem: Yad Ben-Tzvi, 1997), 367–385. Because all of these discussions provide comprehensive insights into various internal, Jewish-political aspects of the play, my discussion will be limited for the most part to a study of what I consider its Orientalist themes.

14. Arfa, xxiii.

and West as they are reflected in the interaction between the Arab and Jewish characters. The third part is an analysis of gender relations in the play that includes a critique of both Zionism and Orientalism. At the end, all three parts are brought together to show some of the problems Arielli saw in Zionism as an Orientalist project.

The play takes place in Jaffa in 1905, four years before Arielli's actual arrival in Palestine. It has seven male characters, four Jews and three Arabs, and two Jewish women. The four Jewish men include Shmaryahu Fogel, a twenty-two-year-old watchman (*shomer*); Kalman Weinschenker, a fifty-six-year-old laborer (*po'el*); Noah Yunter, an effete twenty-four-year-old, who studies to become a teacher (*moreh*); and Shimshon Bronskul, a twenty-five-year-old dandy with literary pretensions (*sofer*). The four men share one big room in town, a sort of a commune, where most of the action takes place (two acts out of three). The two women include Naomi Schatz, a pretty eighteen-year-old girl, flirtatious, strong and imperious, and Tsipora Englebrandt, a tall, thin, soft-spoken and diffident secretary, aged twenty-two, who is in love with Fogel. The Arab characters include Ali, a young and dashing salesman of baked goods, and two other minor Arab characters, an old Muslim cleric called Abu-hawadi and his middle-aged assistant, Mustafa. The action of the play takes place on three different days that extend over a period of about a week.

As not many plays were written during the Tehiya, especially not in Palestine where there were no professional actors or theatrical venues at the time, the choice of genre begs attention from the start. The very artifice of a play as an art form, with its inherent confinement of space, time, and dramatic action, makes *Allah Karim!* an odd choice for its time and place. All the more so, when the matter of language is concerned. One of the most obvious advantages of theater over literature is the immediate access viewers gain to a play's characters, who speak to each other directly and in real-time. But in 1913, the year the play was published, conversational Hebrew was just beginning to form and many simple, everyday matters could not be negotiated easily and naturally in Hebrew.

The problem was not particular to Arielli. Hebrew writers since the Enlightenment struggled to find more natural modes of expression in Hebrew. But it is one thing to insert a few conversations in a fabricated vernacular as part of a story or novel, and quite another to write an entire work based on an invented, conversational idiom. Moreover, theater as one of the more refined expressions of bourgeois art seems somehow out of place in the fervently socialistic milieu of early 1910s Palestine, even as a vehicle of modernism. The profits that can be made from a play, and the very spectacle that is part and parcel of any theater production, seem unfitting somehow as part of the asceticism and the revolutionary idealism that characterized the society of Jewish pioneers in Palestine.

It may very well be that Arielli chose to write the play precisely because it was so alien to its time and to its place. The very nature of theater as a performative medium calls attention to some of the more problematic aspects of the Hebrew Revival, which the play presents in a highly ironic light as a grand theatrical act of self invention. The characters themselves are a case in point. The four Jewish men in the play make up a representative gallery of Yishuv society at the time, including a watchman, a laborer, a writer, and a teacher-to-be.[15]

The four men are at one and the same time poster images of the new Jewish culture in Eretz Israel and a parody of it. Fogel, for instance, whose name ironically means "bird" in Yiddish, is described in the stage instructions as a menacing Cossack, wearing high boots, a wide leather belt stuffed with bullets, and a soft, black hat whose wide brim hangs low from his head in "gracious disarray." Real-life watchmen were dressed in this fashion, and cut a dashing figure of a Jewish cowboy in the "Wild East" of Palestine. Yet Fogel's fancy hat, poised so deliberately on his head, throws his image out of balance and calls attention to the mannerist dress and the very theatricality of the *shomer* and his exaggerated signs of manhood (the boots, the bullets, the forceful gait). The incongruity of Fogel's exterior is reflected in his character as well. Once a social revolutionary, Fogel now laments that he has to stand guard over the private property of a wealthy orange-grove owner: "While in Russia everything is in a wonderful upheaval," he mutters to himself angrily, "I am asked to smack the cheeks of shepherds and farmers and confiscate their cattle to protect private property" (189). Fogel astutely observes how he has been co-opted to serve the Jewish bourgeoisie in the name of the Zionist revolution.

Kalman's image also suffers from inconsistencies. Although his enthusiasm to take part in the Zionist revolution and the zeal that made him leave his wife and daughters in Europe is made more impressive by his old age, it is also problematic. The harsh life of 1910s Palestine would have been much more difficult for a fifty-six-year-old man than for a person thirty years younger, as were most pioneers. At the same time, such an extraordinary commitment may be interpreted as an act of lunacy. Kalman is far more religious or traditional than any of the other Jewish characters, despite the fact that he has one of the most radically revolutionary occupations, that of a laborer. His conversation is peppered with rabbinical references, which he employs with wit to comment on a pioneers' life. The analogy that is created between the revolutionary Jewish society

---

15. Ramraz-Rauch designates the characters as archetypes without developing the idea further, 132.

in Palestine and the traditional Jewish society in the Diaspora is rife with ironies that Kalman embodies.

The image of young Noah Yunter is a parody of the fragile Jewish youth, whose chronic indecision, self-doubt, and insignificant existential concerns become farcical against the objective instabilities of the time, which are also reflected in his image. The fact that such a suicidal weakling (whose name is suspiciously reminiscent of the Yiddish derogative for a nagging, gossipy woman, a *Yente*), is part of the pioneering enterprise undermines the very concept of revival. Although Yunter's promise to kill himself is not taken seriously by anyone, his days in Palestine seem numbered.

The poet Shimshon Bronskul is equally absurd. His bourgeois fastidiousness and intellectual smugness are just as alien to the impoverished surroundings and to the idealism of the pioneers as Yunter's fashionable depression. Decked in a neatly ironed suit complete with a gold pocket watch, Bronskul is an unlikely member of the new Jewish frontier. He is a poseur from the pompadour he sports to the blue and white Star of David he displays prominently on his lapel. He is much more enamored with the appellation of a writer than with the craft itself, and when he finally sits down to write he composes clichés, for which Naomi rightly derides him.

To these fine Jewish speci*men*s, Arielli adds the Arab Ali, whose description reads as follows: "A twenty-year-old Arab peddler of baked goods. His face is oriental, handsome, and tanned. He is dressed entirely in purple (תכלת) and his shoes are red. On his hip he sports a short sword in a scabbard adorned with silver, and wrapped around his head is a blindingly white kerchief encircled by a black *Ajal* [fastening cloth ring] embroidered with silver. His entire being and conduct bespeak the pride of a handsome and strong savage of a distinguished family."[16]

Ali's campy attire is striking. The historical improbability of such fancy dress aside, which fits a sentimental operetta better than the streets of a desolate port city in Palestine, there is no reason why a street peddler would wear such clothes. They are too expensive for him and they are too impractical for his trade. The last part of his description is still more improbable because it assumes that Ali is well aware of the fact that he is both savage and noble. Arielli constructs here a highly ironic image, not just exotic, as most critics of the play contend: a savage who is aware of his savageness ceases to be savage.[17]

These inconsistencies probably occurred to Arielli, too. The point, of course, is that it is part of the parody of the Jewish pioneers and their attitude toward

16. *Yeshimon*, 182.
17. Most critics of the play seem to ignore this contradiction. See Ofrat, 45.

the East, as well as that of the Arabs themselves, who, like Ali, are willingly co-opted by Western culture. Both the Jewish and the Arab characters, then, are poster-like images. Their failure to negotiate their respective worlds underscores the theatricality, the performative quality of Orientalism and the pioneering project as part of it.

Arielli keenly uses the visual medium of the play as an art form to underscore this irony. When it opens, the viewers see the disorganized room of the four men. "The entire left wall of the room," read the stage instructions, "is three big windows, so wide and so low that through them, when the filthy curtains are drawn aside, a wide and spectacular panorama of an eastern city, with its mosques, minarets, flat-roof houses etc., appears before the viewer. Passersby in the street can be seen in their entirety" (181).

The sharp disparity between the disheveled room of the Jewish men and the beauty of the Eastern city in the distance is immediately apparent. Later on in the scene, the exotic exterior vista comes to life when a choir of dervishes marches across the window, followed by a distinguished-looking Muslim cleric, Abu Hawadi, and his assistant, Mustafa.[18] The two Arab natives sit to rest in the street, making up the last detail in this picture-perfect Orient.[19] During the first two acts, the Jewish characters gaze upon this framed Eastern exterior from inside the room, as do the readers or spectators, whose own gaze is filtered through that of the characters or actors.

When Naomi makes her entrance shortly thereafter, she bursts into this calm scene with great force. Having just landed ashore in Jaffa, she enters directly from the ship that brought her from Russia (i.e., the "West"). Sweeping majestically across the room, Naomi denigrates everything in it, including the brave Fogel, whom she finds asleep in his bed. "Is this mighty fighter with the bullets dead too?" she asks, and smacks him irreverently on the nose. "Oh, great fighter!" she calls out and turns to the others in the room, "What ideal did he give up his life for?" (197). Within the cultural context of the Second and Third Aliyah, Naomi's behavior is shocking, even scandalous. The *shomer* was one of the most revered symbols of the Zionist revolution, as illustrated by the stories

18. The Hebrew word Arielli uses is literally dervish (דרוויש).
19. For an example, see Jean-Leon Gerome (1824–1904), the French Orientalist painter, whose paintings from the Near East characterize the period. Benjamin, 3.
Ramraz-Rauch writes that "the eastern city, whose mosques, minarets and flat-roof houses can be seen through the curtains of the commune, invades the room very much like the invasion of Naomi, who comes from the sea [or west. The Hebrew word she uses is ים, "sea" Y.P.]. It seems, as if both East and West confound the heroes," 135. I disagree. I think the window is positioned so as to keep the interior Jewish space and the Eastern exterior separated and to emphasize the act of gazing. This relationship between exterior and interior is cleverly manipulated throughout the play, as I indicate in my analysis.

of Smilansky and others—a modern incarnation of a biblical hero come to life as an Eastern native. The fact that Fogel is shown lying in bed for all to see is already a breach of literary conventions that usually kept this hallowed symbol of early Zionism shrouded in mystery and seldom subjected him to the ignominy of everyday life, such as eating or sleeping. Naomi's irreverence toward him adds insult to injury.[20]

Naomi does not stop with Fogel; she treats everyone and everything around her with flippant ridicule. Her highest contempt, however, seems reserved for Ali and her mock flirtation with him becomes the most poignant parody of Orientalism in the play. Naomi's tongue-in-cheek coquetry is so amusing, and the ironies of her conduct so acute, that scene 8 of act 1 is worth quoting almost in full:

ALI: (*His voice sounds far off, filled with sweet sadness.*) Allah Ka-rim!

NAOMI: (*listening*) What is that?

ALI: (*closer*) Allah Ka-rim!

NAOMI: Who is calling?

YUNTER: It's an Arab . . . selling baked goods. . . .

NAOMI: A baked-goods salesman, you say? What a pleasant voice! (*runs to the window and looks out*)

ALI: (*very close*) Allah Ka-rim!

/ . . .

NAOMI: . . . (*sees Ali in the street; calls to him*) Hey, Allah Karim, come closer! Do you hear, Allah Karim? (*Ali comes to the window and puts his pastry basket down. Naomi turns to Yunter.*) Grandma! Come, be the go between us.

YUNTER: (*smiles shyly*) This Arab . . . is . . . a rarity . . . in some ways . . . hard to find. . . .

NAOMI: (*seriously*) How so?

YUNTER: He speaks Hebrew . . .

NAOMI: Indeed?—Do you, Allah Karim, speak Hebrew?

ALI: Yes, madam.

NAOMI: (*with eyes bright with wonder*) Tell me, then, what is the price of these "Allah Karims" (*selects a few pastries from the basket*).

ALI: Three pennies and a half. (*He pronounces the guttural letters with a heavy Arabic accent.*)

20. As part of his analysis of Hebrew drama in the first half of the twentieth century, Gideon Ofrat includes *Allah Karim!* in a group of works he calls Doubt Plays (מחזות הספק). At the heart of these plays are a group of pathetic characters, who represent the fulfillment of Zionist ideology. Into this group of existential "losers" bursts a passionate and dominant figure, who is supposed to bring redemption with it, and who usually represents personal fulfillment. This play provides an interesting variation on this theme. See Ofrat, 33–34.

NAOMI: (*coyly*) Ah, so expensive! You want to rob me of everything I have, Allah Karim, don't you? And when tomorrow you will pass by this house again, I shall follow you and your basket with my eyes, hungry and wretched, unable to buy even one little piece of "Allah Karim."

ALI: (*smiling cunningly*) There will be enough left for you. The Jews have enough *massari* [money, Arabic]. And tomorrow I will not come by here. . . . not any more. . . .

NAOMI: (*with interest*) Ah, and why not?

ALI: I won't go around with my basket anymore selling pastries. . . . never . . . (*shakes both hands in a typical Arab gesture*), *khallas* [enough] . . .

NAOMI: But why?

YUNTER: There's a rumor . . . his father . . . his father was killed. . . .

ALI: (*threatens him with his fist*) Keep quiet, *Abu-Dakan*, ["beardface," Yunter sports a goatee, Y.P.] don't speak of my father. . . . not . . . even *wakhad kalami* [one word] . . . what's my father to you? Do you think he's your rabbi?

KALMAN: Ha-ha-ha! "Abu-Dakan"! What a fine nick-name!

YUNTER: (*frightened and pale*) But I . . . I . . .

NAOMI: Why, why Allah Karim?

ALI: Why do you need to know, madam?

NAOMI: (*stubbornly*) I want to!

ALI: (*he likes her caprice, smiles*) *Ras bin-an*? [against my will?]

NAOMI: Yes. Banan, peaches, bananas, Mohammed, Karim . . . you must tell me why you are carrying your basket today for the last time?

ALI: Today, for the first time, I have enough money to buy a Martin rifle and a sword. . . . (*draws half a circle with his hand to indicate that the sword will be bent*) . . . plenty sharp. . . .

NAOMI: But you already have a sword.

ALI: (*dismissive*) *Mushanfi* . . . [bad one]

NAOMI: All right, then. But what do you want with a gun and a sword?

ALI: (*looks aside for a while and then begins to speak*) My mother was pretty, pretty *kathir shalbieh* [very pretty] . . . there are no *banaat* [girls, daughters] like her any more. . . . many sheiks and *effendis* [rich men] wanted to buy her. . . . they gave a lot of money and cattle. . . . but my father came from a high family, all of them *jidot* [brave] and rich men, and . . . she became his wife. But one Bedouin from Mt. Hebron, who wanted to buy my mother earlier, was . . . was . . . (*looking for words*) *kathir za'alan* [very angry] with my father for this. . . .

NAOMI: Zalan—that means, he meant to "kill and destroy"? [the words are Haman's, from the Book of Esther 3:13, Y.P.]

ALI: That's it. And once—two weeks before Ramadan, it was ten years later, my father rode to Hebron *mash'an* [because] . . . he wanted to exchange [mispronounces the Hebrew word, Y.P.] (*explains with his hands*) his horse for a younger one with a *sakheb* [friend]. . . . the Bedouins were already waiting for him. . . . (*suddenly his eyes flash with anger, he clenches his fists and thunders*) *Jehenom yahudhum!* [the hell with them] . . . they cut him *mathal* [as if] he was a piece of meat! *Mathal* they were butchers!

NAOMI: (*completely charmed with the story*) Well? . . .

ALI: Tomorrow I ride [mispronounces the word, Y.P.] to Mt. Hebron. . . . In the name of *Allah il Azim* [God all mighty] I ride! [mispronounces again, Y.P.] So that they shall know that Abdallah has a son! . . .

NAOMI: And you still hate your father's killers after all this time? Ten years you said, didn't you?

ALI: (*with pain*) Ten years . . . hatred . . . they too, for ten years . . . the *Khaj* [honorific] Abu-Khalil said, you need *mathal* they did . . . they—ten, I—ten . . . [His speech is confused and unclear in Hebrew, too, Y.P.]

NAOMI: (*Her eyes are bright with excitement.*) You're very brave, *Allah Karim!* Take me with you to the mountains! (. . .)

ALI: (*astounded, almost cannot believe his ears, whistles "no" with his tongue*) not possible . . .

NAOMI: But why not?

ALI: (*whistles as before*) It cannot be, madam. . . . Good-bye! (*mounts the basket on his head and leaves*)

NAOMI: Good-bye, *Allah Karim!* Don't forget to bring me the spinal bones of the Bedouin. I know how to make wonderful toys out of them.

/ . . . (204–207)

Naomi's initial delight with Ali's charming, far-off voice soon turns into a cutting parody of the young Arab, his image, and what it represents. Knowing full well that the salesman's name is not Allah Karim—one of Allah's honorifics—Naomi persistently calls him by it. She offensively calls even the little pastries he sells "Allah Karims." With her undiscriminating Western eye she is ostensibly unable to distinguish between these different cultural elements, reducing the Muslim god, the Arab man, and the Mediterranean pastry into commodities that are bought and sold on the open market. On the other hand, Naomi is not entirely to blame for her disrespect, as Ali's fancy getup deserves this kind of attention. With his purple clothes, red shoes, and miscellaneous Oriental paraphernalia, he too parades himself for sale as an exotic commodity. All the more so as the "savage nobility" his image still retains soon dissolves after he begins to flirt with Naomi with the expertise of a seasoned, drawing-room dandy.

Ali seems to like Naomi's petulance, and with a melodramatic flair he coyly returns her advances with the Arab expression *ras bin-an* [against my will]? His reply only complicates things, because Naomi, who does not understand Arabic, utters a cacophonous mixture of Arabic-sounding names in a frivolous parody of an Oriental bazaar. "Banan, peaches, bananas, Mohammed, Karim," she glibly retorts, dismissing Ali's culture, the culture of the Orient, by mixing fruit names with the Arabic names for God. She demands and expects the satisfaction of her petty curiosity according to the Western conventions of chivalrous courtship.

Ali's ready reply and his willingness to take part in the game Naomi plays further undermine his "native" qualities and underscore the fact that he is playing a role. Even the story of his intended blood revenge is a little overdone, calling attention to itself like a native performance for tourists. Ali specifies the brand name of the gun he is going to buy with juvenile bravado, and gestures the contours of a scimitar, a topos of the Muslim fighter and a symbol of its menace in the West. Then, when he recounts the history of the blood feud, he uses an inordinate number of Arabic words, which are designed to intensify the authenticity of his image and actions as a "native." As a result, his speech is just as contrived and exaggerated as his attire. The dramatic pauses, the choice Arabic words, the narrative predictability of the tale—his mother's inordinate beauty, her many suitors, his father's nobility, the inevitable jealousy of the spurned lover that ends in murder—all amount to a stylized formulation of Levantine savagery.

Naomi's voyeuristic delight is dismissive. After Ali completes his story, she congratulates his bravery a priori. Naomi's exclamation, "you are very brave, Ali," is patronizing, and, significantly, given as a reward for the simulated performance of the blood revenge, not for the act itself. Naomi's utter ignorance of the ways of the East and her disregard for it are revealed in her request of Ali to take her with him on his journey of revenge. The absurdity of the request must have occurred to her, too. Not only is this the personal business of Ali, which Eastern conventions mandate he must carry out on his own, but the inclusion of a woman in it is a humiliating affront. Nevertheless, Naomi cheerfully offers to accompany the young blood avenger, dismissing the venerated Eastern custom just as summarily as she smacked Fogel, the *shomer*, on his nose. Naomi's last words to Ali before he departs are the most devastating blow to his Eastern manhood yet. "Don't forget to bring me the spinal bones of the Bedouin [you kill]," she calls after him, "I know how to make wonderful toys out of them." This callous response to the bravado of the little pastry salesman shows his Eastern antics to be just as diverting and equally unreal as his clothes.

Naomi finalizes her "conquest" of the East when Ali returns to the window a few scenes later with an ashen face and confesses that he has been completely smitten by her, so much so, that he is now willing to take her with him to Mt. Hebron (!). Naomi, who after only three days in Palestine uses Arabic phrases freely, swears in the name of the prophet Mohammed and torments the vanquished salesman. "Did you see that?" she cries. "First he said 'it's impossible' . . . and now it is already possible. . . ." She then makes fun of Ali's affectation by joking about the grim journey he plans to take, making it sound like a fantastic tale from the Arabian Nights. "Shall you give me a horse and a sword?" she taunts him with studied excitement. "The harness, of course, shall be embroidered with gold, and the stirrups . . . shall naturally be of pure silver. . . . and the horses shall carry us . . . over the clouds . . . yes?" (223). Ali, who does not understand that Naomi is mocking him, answers her questions with complete earnestness by confessing that the journey is going to be far less glamorous than she imagines.

Finally, after she is done teasing him, Naomi changes her mind and demands that Ali prove his love for her by canceling his intended journey. Ali is naturally shocked by her contradictory request and protests: "I did not sleep for three nights. I did not eat for three days. . . . I thought only of you." Ali's agreement to take Naomi with him to avenge his father's death, his willingness to empty an ancient and venerable custom of its value, shows him for who he really is: not the fearless Eastern fighter he pretends to be but a simple, young salesman who is more interested in impressing a pretty women than abiding by his tradition. Moreover, his frustration does not seem to derive from the hitch in his plans for revenge as much as from the fact that he has been exposed as an empty talker. In reply, Naomi delivers one of her sharpest critiques yet, in which both East and West, Arab natives and Jewish pioneers, are indicted as a useless lot of idlers and pretenders. "You are wasting your time, *Allah Karim!*" she says. . . . "It is not enough to think . . . you see? It is not enough! . . . You will have no future until you learn to put the dead behind you," she exclaims in reference to Ali's former desire to kill in the name of his family's honor.

Naomi's words are not directed only at Ali's thirst for blood. They are also aimed at the four Jewish roommates. When she advises Ali that thinking is not enough, that action is needed instead, she is also referring to Bronskul, Fogel, and Yunter, whom she ridicules for their ineptitude as well. Naomi exposes the Jewish pioneers as a bunch of incompetents, who instead of practicing the high ideals of the revolution that brought them all the way to Palestine are preoccupied with selfish concerns and with the pettiness of everyday life.

Fogel is a miserable drunkard, a socialist revolutionary, who instead of defending the Jewish settlements from marauders, guards the property of a wealthy landowner and protects it from poachers. Bronskul is a dandy who is anxious about his own literary reputation. Kalman, the ascetic laborer, obsesses about buying new clothes for himself, and Yunter lives in the self-absorbed world of his own petty anxieties. Presumably, all four came to Palestine in the name of the many Jews who sanctified the land by their death throughout history. This has always been an important part of the Jewish claim to the Land of Israel. Naomi, however, thinks it a poor basis for a constructive enterprise. Ali's plan to kill one man in order to settle the death of another seems absurd to her, just as unreasonable as it would be for Jews to harm Arabs in the name of other dead Jews.

Naomi's suggestion of ending the morbid relationship between the land and the men who lay claim to it, both Arabs and Jews, unfolds in act 2 through a structural device. After the separation between East and West is strictly maintained throughout act 1, the two worlds collide when Mustafa and Abu Hawadi step out of the Eastern scenery into the pioneers' apartment. Up to that point, the Jews gazed upon the East from inside their room and even conducted their commerce with Ali through the window. The Arabs briefly set aside this divide in act 2 by physically entering the room.

Assuming they will be welcomed in their Jewish neighbors' house, as Eastern custom dictates, the dervishes innocently ask for some water. Unfortunately, however, the clerics arrive at a very inopportune moment. Just before they came in, Fogel had vented his anger about the damage that wandering Arab shepherds repeatedly cause the orchard under his watch. Frustrated at his inability to prevent it, Fogel jumps on the first Arabs he sees—the unsuspecting clerics. Although Mustafa and Abu Hawadi do not ask for much, Fogel retorts with a barrage of insults. "You Arabs are hypocrites and sycophants, all of you!" he yells at Mustafa. And when he sees him reaching for the bottle of water on the table he barks: "What, an earthenware jar is not good enough for the likes of you?" and sends the bewildered man to the kitchen to drink water from the jar. After this abysmal welcome, Fogel adds insult to injury by insisting on accompanying Mustafa to the kitchen because all Arabs, "from the sheik down to the poorest man, are thieves and robbers, pick-pockets and murderers" (235).

The disparity between Arabs and Jews in this scene cannot be greater. The Muslims are older, more respectable, and more moderate than the Jews, who are represented here by a young, drifting, and disillusioned revolutionary. This difference is almost insurmountable from the outset. But in addition to the generational gap that separates them, a vast cultural and political gulf stands between them; a distance that can be bridged only by understanding and good will, both of which Fogel sorely lacks. The Arabs seem willing to compromise. They empathize with Fogel and condemn the destruction of the orchard. But they fail to see the political connection that Fogel makes between the trespassing shepherds and themselves. For them, it is a common proprietary felony. Fogel, of course, sees it differently. As someone who has come to Palestine to reclaim it, all aspects of life there have a political meaning for him.

Most writers of the Tehiya ignored the Arabs of Palestine, idealized them, or wrote about them as obstacles to the Jewish settlement. However, Arielli's political engagement seems different. The miscommunication between the dervishes and Fogel is so profound, and the insults that Fogel hurls at the Arabs are so mean, that little hope remains for a peaceful future together, especially after Fogel's threat to kill one of the Arab shepherds materializes at the end of the play.

The physical dynamics between Arabs and Jews change once again in act 3, when both groups meet in a neutral place outside. The entire act takes place in a grassy patch near the orchard and opens with the news that Fogel shot and wounded an Arab shepherd the night before. This ominous information is then followed by the sound of digging and the voices of laborers who chant one of the most well-known ditties of the Second Aliya, signifying the heroic efforts of redemptive rebuilding: God shall build the Galilee / Blessed he who builds the Galilee / The mighty shall build the Galilee (גיבור יבנה הגליל / ברוך יבנה הגליל / אל יבנה הגליל). This jarring juxtaposition of destruction and construction, the wounding of the Arab and the cultivation of the orchard, is continued on a personal level when Naomi and Ali enter the meadow next.

Ali jumps out of the bushes with burning eyes and clenched fists and calls Naomi a devil-woman, blaming her for tempting him and ruining his life as a respectable Arab. Naomi is not impressed and calmly points a handgun at him to stop him from coming closer. The farcical fight between the domineering Jewess and the histrionic Arab underscores their incompatibility and illustrates Naomi's dismissal of Ali and the culture he represents. As long as Ali was a picturesque image viewed through a window, he fascinated Naomi and amused her. Once he stepped out of his designated place and became real, the connection between them becomes impossible.[21]

But Ali cannot be put back into the quaint East from which he came, of course. He insists on staying out in the real world and makes his presence painfully obvious by attacking Fogel. Naomi tries to stop him again, this time by firing her gun into the air. Unable to keep her cool detachment anymore, she expresses for the first time what she really thinks about the Orient of this young Arab nationalist; a man she had thus far suffered with amusement: "my face is not covered with a veil. . . . remember that, you wild beast of a man!. . . ." she

---

21. Ofrat calls this scene one of the most deceptive in the history of Eretz-Israeli drama. He writes that Arielli privileges here neither the pioneers nor the Arabs, and that "natural passion, simplicity and harmony are the answers" for the existential quest of the characters (45–46). I agree in principle, only I think Arielli arrives at that message primarily by presenting both the Jews and the Arabs as buffoons. The anti-romantic irony in the play is directed at both groups. This is also where the novelty of the play lies.

tells him (279). But Ali is just as resolute, and when he finally learns that the shepherd whom Fogel injured has died of his gun wound, he grabs a sword, stabs Fogel, and kills him in return.

The words of the dervish become relevant all too soon when Fogel, before he is killed by Ali, comes out of the orchard ecstatic that he finally managed to shoot one of the trespassing shepherds. "I feel so good," he says to Kalman, who replies with a grave air that there's nothing amusing about shooting someone. But Fogel insists that "happiness is called a knee, the knee of an Arab shepherd," and continues his gruesome speech by saying that, "tonight I shall try to shoot one of the shepherds, whether he is guilty or not [of trespassing], above his knee . . . or, what is better still, directly at his center. And the next night I shall be so much more experienced that I shall shoot the blue dot to the right of his nose. . . . experience is a pleasant thing. . . . as it is clearly written: Neudorf was created with experience, inspired by books and by dreams" (266–267).

Fogel is ironically referring here to Herzl's utopian novel *Altneuland*. Neudorf (literally: new village) is the name of a new and prosperous Jewish village in the futuristic Jewish state the book envisions. Arabs and Jews live harmoniously side by side in this village, which represents the benefits of cooperation between West and East. The experience to which Fogel is referring here is much different from the one Herzl had in mind, of course. Indeed, in his reply to him, Kalman sadly corrects him by saying that "this is not how Neudorf was created, and may it never be created so" (267).[22] But Fogel, in a delirious speech that mocks ideology in all its forms says:

> Still, we shouldn't give up even on Neudorf, since . . . There's no mightier than our God! I insist—there's no one like our God! And there are no limits to our possibilities! . . . Behold, the day shall come when Kropotkin[1] shall obtain a certificate of good behavior from Kaluga, the governor of the county, and build together with Godwin[2] a paper factory. But, being men of quick action, they shall not be squeamish about dealing in *ethrogim* [citrus fruit used ritually in the feast of Sukkot] for Sukkot and in fir trees for Christmas. . . . they will make me watchman and I shall use English gun-powder on any crook who will dare lay his hands on a piece of paper. . . . But Bronskul! I shall give him the best paper manufactured by the Kropotkin-Godwin factory, since he is destined to write a poem in white rhymes, titled "Neudorf," that shall excite the hearts of our young men and make our young women yawn, and dedicate it to me. And everything shall be fine! (267)

22. It is not clear if Kalman wishes such a village never to be created, or that he wishes that it will not be created in the manner indicated by Fogel. The Hebrew reads: ‏. . . . כך לא נברא ניידורף ואל ייברא לעולמי עד.-‏

1. The leader of the Russian anarchists at the time of the play.
2. William Godwin, English writer and philosopher, 1756–1836, considered the founder of Anarchism.

Fogel wraps together religion, capitalism, socialism, communism, and anarchism, and cheerfully dismisses Kalman's worries. Unlike Brenner's well-known motto, "Nevertheless" (ואף על פי כן), that epitomized the defiant spirit of the Hebrew Revival, Fogel's speech is far more morbid. Ideology itself is burnt on the stake of his sarcasm, in which traditional jingoistic expressions such as "there is no mightier than our God" (אין כאלוהינו), are mixed with bombastic Zionist slogans such as "there are no limits to our possibilities" (אין גבול לאפשרויותינו). Fogel's description of Bronskul as a national Hebrew poet in the service of capitalist industry is a vicious send-up of Zionist politics at the time. As far as Fogel is concerned, all of these slogans are meaningless, emptied by a harsh and bitter reality that no amount of ideology or self-deception can change. Fogel's own actions spell cruelty, destruction, anarchy, and abandon. As a participant in one of the most radical and potentially constructive attempts to change the course of Jewish history, Fogel, the watchman, is also one of the most destructive characters in the play. His death at the end is poetically justified as a punishment for murder. At the same time, as one of the most potent symbols of the new Yishuv, Fogel's death may also hint at the possible demise of the whole Zionist experiment.

Having killed each other, the Jews and the Arabs are even now, although none of them are satisfied. The ethnic-national hatred that gnaws at the bitter Fogel is gradually transferred to the Arabs as well. Sitting in the meadow, one of the dervishes comments on the development of the Yishuv by paraphrasing Pharaoh's admonition in Exodus 1 : 10, saying, "who knows what the future will bring if we do not deal wisely with them (אם לא נתחכמה להם)." With these words, the relations between Arabs and Jews are placed into a historical analogue that does not bode well for the future. Just as the Egyptian monarch sought to curtail the growth and prosperity of the sojourning Israelites, the Arabs wish to contain the Jewish development of Palestine. History, the play seems to suggest, repeats itself in inevitable and depressing cycles.

Indeed, the men who remain after Fogel's murder are not necessarily better than the dead watchman. None of them seems especially suited for the kind of sacrifice that a successful settlement enterprise would require. Bronskul remains a useless wordsmith, who arrives at the orchard swinging a shiny new walking stick. Kalman, the old laborer, loses his former composure and exhibits for the first time some of Fogel's animosity toward Arabs, if only as a reaction to his friend's death. Yunter finally delivers on his promise and tries unsuccessfully to hang himself by Naomi's silk necklace. His pathetic suicide attempt sends Naomi into a violent tirade directed at all men: "Go away! . . . Go away, all of you!" she screams with disgust at the top of her lungs.

> Don't let me see your face again! . . . I despise, despise all of you, you cultured worms! . . . From the savage Arab I learned something. He taught me two wonderful words: *"Allah Karim!"* . . . And you . . . and even Fogel . . . didn't teach me one positive thing, not even one good thing about life! . . . And as for death— this is not how heroes die. *(with new hope)* But the nightmare is over! . . . I am growing wings! . . . I feel it. . . . A land that nurtured strong and vigorous men like our ancient heroes, and even like this savage Arab, is worth living in—living and fighting. And I choose to live and fight! *"Allah Karim!"*—God is merciful! *(Exits resolutely toward the road in the distance. Yunter is paralyzed with shock).* Curtain. (283–284)

Naomi rejects Fogel, the recreated Jewish hero, as well as Ali, the Arab native who inspired his image. She wants nothing to do with either. At the same time, both images clearly inspire her. The lesson that she draws from the ignoble death of Fogel and the equally pathetic life of Ali is how *not* to lead her life. While it is not clear at the end what Naomi will do in the future, her denunciation of both the biblical and the native option, so characteristic of Hebrew Orientalism, brings this Romantic combination to a final rest.

Naomi's closing speech also highlights Arielli's radical redeployment of gender relations as part of his general critique. As the play clearly illustrates, Naomi cuts the most "masculine" figure of all the characters. All the men pale in comparison to her and are, in fact, subjugated by her. Naomi may even be considered mistress of a harem of men, with Bronskul, Yunter, and significantly Ali, as her "concubines."

The harem economy is suggested already in the play's opening scene, with its communal bedroom full of sleeping men, unmade beds, blankets, and pillows. The opening conversation between Bronskul and Yunter, who speak about their toiletries with an avidness that is typically associated with women, continues this theme on a textual level. As the curtain rises, Yunter is seen standing in the middle of the room looking into a mirror and lamenting his hair loss. Bronskul suggests he try a hair product that might help him. He proceeds to advise him on his dress, analyzing each and every article of clothing Yunter wears until he comes to the buttons on his cape. "This button," he says with delight, "was stolen by you from Kalman's underwear!" "Kalman! Kalman!" He laughs and runs over to the sleeping laborer, "Wake up . . . ! I found the man who stole your underwear button" (184). Not only do the two men discuss in detail points of fashion and toiletry; apparently they are also intimately familiar with each others' underwear. While there is no hint of explicit sexual connection between the men, the implication that Yunter may have handled Kalman's underwear and that Bronskul knows about it suggests an intimacy that is usually associated with women, not men, in Western culture.

Later on, when Bronskul and Yunter return from the dock with Naomi, the young woman majestically sweeps into the room followed by the two men. She runs around the room almost maniacally, criticizing the furnishings, belittling the occupants, laughing obsessively all the while. "Please, darling, stop that and calm down a little," Bronskul gently rebukes her. But Naomi pays no attention to him and continues as before, refusing resolutely to make love to Bronskul, who asks her at one point, "Did you really come here just for the sake of the Land of Israel?" Adding to the irony of the question about so-called Zionist motives, Naomi replies by saying that she simply wanted to see new places. "And nothing more?" Bronskul insists in a sad tone, continuing the jibe at Zionism by sacrificing his allegiance to it in favor of his ego.

Ostensibly, Naomi takes advantage of her privilege as a woman and manipulates the conventions of chivalry in order to control the men around her. She is amused to learn that Bronskul described her to his roommates as his fiancée, and acidly jokes about their impending marriage. Musing out loud in a mock-romantic tone, she describes an elaborate wedding ceremony in which she imagines Fogel as the rabbi, an iron clamp of a pickle barrel as the wedding ring, and the four friends as the poles of the wedding canopy. When Kalman points out that their company consists of four men in total, including the groom, which would leave out either one pole bearer or the groom, Naomi blithely replies: "Groom, pole—it's all the same" (201).

Naomi then taunts Yunter by giving him various women's names. "Grandma," she asks him, "would you like to stroll with me in the street holding hands, or do you have to stay home and help Bronskul . . . ?" (203). After the two go out together, Yunter soon returns alone, distraught by Naomi's treatment of him. "Ah, Shimshon," he complains to Bronskul, "you wouldn't guess what that girl of yours did to me! . . . she's not a woman but the devil. Just imagine, in front of all the shopkeepers she declared: '*Abu Dakan* for one penny and his hat for two'" (203). In a conscious subversion of Eastern custom, the Western Jewish maiden is not only selling her suitor as an object, she charges more for his hat than for the man himself. While the sale of women as sexual objects is used by Frishman in *Bamidbar* to describe the ancient biblical East, and while Smilansky uses it in *The Sons of Arabia* to describe the modern Levant, Arielli's inversion of it in *Allah Karim!* seems critical of the misogynistic custom and its literary use as titillating Orientalia.

This inversion reaches its climax in Naomi's romance with Ali, who is the last man to join her "harem." The initial attraction of the Western woman to the Eastern man is masculine in that Naomi notices Ali's "ornamental" qualities in the same way men usually look at pretty women, and her subsequent treatment of him is just as offensive.[23] When, earlier in the play, Ali tries to abduct the willful Naomi (act 2, scene 13) everyone is shocked and scandalized, except for the woman herself, who is thoroughly amused by it. Naomi never thinks it more than a show, a performance. As she is carried off by Ali, she readily participates in the charade by admiring the Arab's courage, as if she were a heroine in a melodrama (as he carries her off she calls him her "noble and fearless knight"). In the meantime, Bronskul is running helplessly about while Yunter looks on with paralyzed fear. Finally, Naomi puts an end to the farce by strangling Ali and physically forcing him to put her down. "Madam, oh madam," the vanquished savage pants, but Naomi laughs heartily and declares: "No one handles me with violence! I don't have a black veil over my face. . . . God forbid, I don't have a black veil yet! . . . On the other hand, I have here [points to her pocket] a loaded gun . . . yes, yes, [laughs] . . . And you didn't know, poor thing? . . . I forgive you. . . . [she laughs again]" (256).

The manipulation of the harem as a literary device finds an interesting expression in another of Arielli's works, the novella *Yeshimon*, his last and longest work, published in Palestine in 1922. The protagonist of the novella, David Ostrovsky, is a young flute player who joins a Turkish army orchestra somewhere in the arid south of Palestine toward the end of World War I.[24] David is a delicate and beautiful youth, who takes away the breath of the coarse Turkish soldiers, who lavish attention and privilege on him as if he were a pretty woman. The novella strikes a rather obvious homoerotic tone right from the start:

> All eyes were lifted from the cards and turned toward the entrance of the tent. . . . The canvass was raised and, bending his head in order to come in, the merry and drunken wide face of an officer appeared in the opening followed by a beautiful and delicate young man, about twenty-two years of age, dressed in a fancy, urbane suit. That outfit and that beauty dumbfounded the people in the tent. Only once before, when a kitten with a pink ribbon and a bell hanging from it showed up in these far away and desolate places among the tents, were the players so surprised. The card game was completely forgotten and everyone stared hungrily at the young guest. (107)

23. This is not to say that women do not look at men in the same way. Within the conventions of the time, however, certainly the literary conventions, Naomi's aggressive pursuit of Ali stands out.

24. The story is loosely based on the life of Arielli, who served as a musician in the Turkish army during part of World War I.

Later on, David and another flute player in the orchestra, Hamdi, become friends and carry on a sublimated but passionate affair.[25]

The tent in the opening scene may be read as a harem because of its typically Oriental setting, because of the sexual bonds that connect the group of men who are housed in it, and in the sense that it simultaneously confines and promotes sexual desire. The palpable sexual tension between the men is contained by the fact that it cannot be openly expressed. The attraction of the men to one another is an almost logical extension of the Western perception of the East as an orgiastic universe. At the same time, the homoerotic tension also subverts these conventions because it removes the hierarchical or power relations that are inherent in heterosexual relations, especially in the East. Perhaps this is the reason for David's happiness at the sight of his fellow soldiers dancing together passionately as the sun sets and a young moon shines softly in the darkening sky. "Ostrovsky very much liked this camp of young men, full of so much laughter and licentiousness (הוללות). His heart rejoiced with happiness and thanksgiving for the good fortune that brought him to there" (120).[26]

The harem analogy in *Allah Karim!* is valid only up to a point. In the last analysis, Naomi's subjugation of Ali, as well as her own manly ways, is not entirely complete. Ali maintains some of his native integrity when he avenges the death of the Arab shepherd killed by Fogel. Naomi herself senses that Ali is capable of doing so even before he kills Fogel. "Allah Karim is not an herbivorous animal," she tells Kalman, "and he will be right to kill me" (263). But although she cannot resist the temptation to tease him, she emphatically tells Kalman that neither Ali nor Bronskul understand that she is waiting for a truly dominant man; a man who will be able to command her and not the other way around, "Only then will I give up everything, everything" (263).

Compared with her usual rhetoric and actions Naomi sounds reactionary here. The death of Fogel seems to have touched her and made her serious for the first time. As she consoles Tsipora, she confesses that "I am as miserable as you, Tsipora. . . . I am not brave and strong anymore. . . . I am only an ordinary, wretched girl" (281). Whether she admits to having played a role before or she really is changed by the experience, Naomi speaks in a completely new voice. For the first time she also expresses the alienation that the other Jewish charac-

25. Adi Tsemach argues this point persuasively: "The sexuality in *Yeshimon*, not the one that is discussed in the work, but the sexual perception that underlines it, the writer's point of view, is homosexual. . . . *Yeshimon* impacts the reader not only by presenting a protagonist with homosexual tendencies. This would not be new. The innovation is that the author's stance privileges male-love and is deeply misogynic." "Min ve'ofi le'umi," 374.

26. For more on this theme in *Yeshimon*, see my book, *Derech Gever: siporet homoerotit basifrut ha'ivrit hahadasha, 1887–2000* (Shufra, 2003).

ters always felt toward Ali and the rest of the Arabs. "A wind came over from the desert," she says to Tsipora, referring to Ali's murder of Fogel, "and brought with it wild men from the desert (literally: desert savages, פראי-מדבר) who made us all unhappy" (281).

Naomi seems to side here with the Jewish pioneers, something she had never done before. Until now, she enjoyed her role as an enfant terrible, flirting with Ali with careless abandon, upsetting the boundaries between Arabs and Jews, and confusing the roles between men and women. The death of Fogel, however, forces her to take sides for the first time. As a Jewess, she can no longer continue her drawing-room affair with a man who killed one of her own people. But the pitiful sight of Yunter, whose effeminacy is underscored by his attraction to women's finery—Naomi's silk necklace, by which he tries to hang himself—shakes her out of her remorseful mood and makes her realize how sad and sorry the whole pioneering enterprise is. It is the pathetic picture of Yunter that prompts her to deliver her final, angry speech, in which she rejects both sides of the emerging Jewish-Palestinian conflict.[27]

Ultimately, Naomi's "masculinity" and the "femininity" of the male characters in the play become a critique of the Zionist attempt to change Jewish sexual stereotypes. Naomi is a strong woman of action, whereas the men in the play satirize the very diasporic ailments that Eretz-Israeli Jewish life was supposed to correct—physical inactivity, sensitivity, and economic dependence. The distinction Naomi makes between "real" men and the men of the Jewish commune paints not only Bronskul and Yunter but also Fogel, Kalman, and by extension all pioneers, in a negative light. After Naomi meets Ali, she adds the Arab to this category as well.

---

27. Naomi's final speech is quoted by all critics of the play, usually as an example of Arielli's contrived conclusion, whose positive note typified the literature of the period. Ehud Ben-Ezer sets the tone in his article when he concludes by writing: "In the last analysis, Orloff's work remains poised between two genres. On the one hand, it is romantic, naive, and not based on reality, which is also its major artistic flaw. On the other hand, . . . the work describes the tragic, and at times tragic–comic lives of fairly typical Second Aliya figures. . . . The play does not try to hide the gulf between Arabs and Jews in Eretz Israel. But by privileging the strange couple of Naomi and Ali, and by contorting the end so that the murderous Ali and not Fogel the watchman becomes the model hero, all of which is written from an allegedly positive, Zionist-nationalist point of view, the play gets mired in fairly false and at times ridiculous romanticism." Ben-Ezer, *Iton 77*, 21.

The only contrivance of Naomi's speech resides in the fact that it is far more conclusive than anything else she expressed up to that point. At the same time, it is dismissive of both Arabs and Jews. Calling Ali "an Arab murderer," as Ben-Ezer does, while modifying Fogel with the positive adjective "*shomer*" ignores Fogel's nationalistic hatred toward the Arabs that is part of his image throughout the play. Furthermore, Ali's killing of Fogel is motivated by a much more passionate and personal reason than Fogel's cold-blooded shooting of the Arab shepherd. This is precisely why Naomi rejects both Ali and Fogel at the end.

This is the point where Arielli's gender critique is joined to his overall appraisal of Zionism. Already in the beginning of act 1, Kalman delivers a monologue that exposes the pathos of the pioneering life. "This is a dog's life!" he mutters to himself as he gets up from bed, "you dig and work the land day after day, bending over your hoe, your hands chafe and get pricked by the thorns and thistles of the *vineyards and orchards of our redemptive revival . . .* so that finally you turn into a rag or an insect" (187).[28]

When Fogel enters the room, Kalman greets him with a hearty "greetings, watchman! How's the night?" (שלום שומר! מה מליל?), which is part of a well-known pioneering song that celebrates the valor of the New Jew as represented by the *shomer*. Fogel replies with the paraphrase: "greetings, laborer! How's the day?" The mock solemnity and politeness of the greeting and its paraphrase belittle both occupations, the watchman and the laborer, and their quasi-religious place in labor Zionism. Kalman goes even further to say that if conditions get any worse he will soon become a martyr, making light of the Zionist tendency to idolize and sanctify people like himself.

Only Bronskul and Yunter refrain from poking fun at Yishuv culture, perhaps because they never feel truly part of it. Both men are humorless, which may explain the smugness of the one and the existential discomfort of the other, and both relate to the Palestinian reality around them only after they are jolted by exterior circumstances. Bronskul's disappointment with Naomi suddenly makes him see the wretchedness of life around him, whereas Yunter's Zionism is awakened only after he escapes to Egypt in mid-play and meets a German botanist, who admires the Jewish colonization of Palestine. As Yunter tells Naomi after his return to Jaffa: "I felt guilty that at the very hour my people had awakened to a new life, . . . I was thinking of killing myself" (227). Here, too, perception plays a central role. Yunter cannot see the majesty of the enterprise he is part of until he removes himself abroad, because such an understanding is always easier from the vantage point of time or distance. Naomi, and to a lesser degree the Arab characters, play a similar role.

The Arabs in the play are not only given unprecedented speaking roles, their very message is remarkable in the context of the times. As he sits outside the orchard toward the end of the play (act 3, scene 9), Abu Hawadi rather surprisingly laments the development of the land around him and the disappearing wilderness. To speak against economic development and advocate wilderness preservation in 1910s Palestine, which was a desolate and undeveloped region even according to Ottoman standards, is very unusual not only for

---

28. The Hebrew reads "כרמינו ופרדסי תחייתנו," which is a parody of a typical Zionist locution. My emphasis.

an indigenous member of a traditional society but especially for a revivalist writer who put these words into his mouth. Read in 1913, the year the play was published, Abu Hawadi's sentiments can be understood as anticolonial. Read today, these sentiments become more postcolonial in nature. Quite apart from their self-perceived right to the Land of Israel in the name of their Eastern heritage, the Zionist pioneers also thought of themselves as harbingers of Western civilization. The Arabs of Palestine naturally felt displaced and alienated by the development of the Jewish Yishuv. Like American Indians, Africans, and other natives of the colonized world, they resisted the foreign emigration to their land with various acts of anticolonial terrorism (the damage to the orchard, the killing of Fogel). At the same time, these sentiments are also postcolonial, because their indictment of Zionism as an exploitative Western force comes from a Western pen. Instead of the usual glorification of the pioneers, this Jewish play, which significantly bears an Arabic title, acknowledges *and* criticizes some of the damage that Zionism caused the indigenous population of Palestine.

These complex issues are shrewdly expressed in the play through the physical relationship between the Arabs and the Jews. The three acts chart a gradual change in the physical dynamics between the two groups that follow the deconstruction of the concept of "East" in the play. Act 1 presents the Orient as an exotic Western construction, a distant and alluring vista that the European Jews gaze upon through a window. During this act, the contact between Arabs and Jews is minimal and predicated on preconceived notions of the East, exemplified by the operatic romance between Naomi and Ali. In act 2 the Arabs materialize as a real presence when they step out of the Eastern scenery and attempt to connect with the Jews. The East still remains an exotic background, and after the Jews (Fogel) reject them, the Arabs recede into it. In act 3, the privileged, Western perspective dissolves and both groups occupy the same space, albeit with disastrous consequences.

It is very hard today, when reading the literature of the revival, to lift the mythological veil that time has spun over it. This is especially true of works that were written in Palestine at the time and that deal with the actual lives of the pioneers who took part in the Sisyphean project of revival. The very adjective I chose to describe the period, "Sisyphean," illustrates the veneration that Israelis have for that era, even those who are critical of its achievements.[29] I mention this only because it relates directly to what I think is a general tendency

---

29. I am referring primarily to post-Zionist critics, who are mentioned throughout this study. Even Hanan Hever, a major post-Zionist literary critic, acknowledges the impressive literary output of the early Jewish pioneers. See his introduction to *Te'oria uvikoret* 20.

by many critics to invest some of their own admiration for the pioneers in the works of that period, including *Allah Karim!*[30]

These critical dynamics are made all the more interesting in the play because they involve the very issues of reality and perception. Many works that were written during the revival grappled squarely with the dire conditions of Yishuv life. *Allah Karim!* can be set apart not only because of its attempt to depict "truthfully" the lives of the pioneers. Other writers did that just as well, if not better. Few, however, wrote about the period with such a keen awareness of its imaginary or performative qualities. In *Allah Karim!* Arielli examines the Hebrew Revival as a grand act of self-invention based on the Jewish connection to the East, both the ancient and the modern. The play examines both possibilities but in the last analysis chooses neither the Hebrew Bible nor the Arab native as possible models for revival, leaving the matter open for various alternative possibilities.

---

30. In the most recent commentary on the play, Avner Holtzman writes that *Allah Karim!* should not be considered such a strictly anti-generic work, as Shaked suggests. Holtzman offers a more moderate reading that considers both the generic and anti-generic elements in the literature of the revival. Recapping previous readings of the play, Holtzman maintains that in *Allah Karim!* Arielli combines a "sober, 'low,' and cruel" look at the Hebrew Revival in Palestine with Romanticism and Vision (381). He goes on to write that in Naomi's final speech, "Arielli brings the desire to merge into the East and the wish to become like the Arabs, which is a common motif in Second Aliya literature, into an absurd extreme" (382). I agree with the first half of Holtzman's reading. As for the Romanticism and vision, those are very problematic in the play, as I discuss in my analysis.

Conclusion: The Legacy of Hebrew Orientalism

"In its limited and existential sense as a place of life and death, this place [Israel] is in the East. In the lofty and ideological sense of this place as an idea, it maintains a complex relationship to the East. Sometimes it is one with it, sometimes it only touches it, and at other times it aspires to be completely separated from it."[1] The allure that the East held for Jews since the end of the nineteenth century diminished progressively as the Jewish settlement in Palestine grew and the relations with Palestinian Arabs became competitive throughout the 1920s. Culturally, the strong ideological commitment of most Yishuv Jews to Zionism affected the nature of Hebrew literature as well, which, since 1930, reflected this commitment more and more. This change was not only political. It was due to the very success of the Hebrew Revival. The formation in the 1930s of an invented, native Hebrew culture in Palestine was unprecedented in modern history. As the Yishuv developed, Hebrew writers were no longer writing in a vacuum but for a growing number of readers. The reciprocal relationship between writers and readers—a natural part of any vibrant and living culture—finally began to shape the literature that was written in Eretz Israel. As a result, the general wish of most Jews during those years to establish an independent Jewish polity gradually drowned the voices that favored a cultural and political integration with the Arabs by encouraging the separatist tendencies that were always inherent in Zionism.

One of the most symbolic literary points of disengagement between Jews and Arabs can be found at the end of a short story by Ya'acov Steinberg, "The Haj from Heftsiba" (*Hahaj miheftsiba*, 1920). The story is an impressionistic account of a few days the writer spent with the founders of a new settlement near the town of Hadera in the Sharon Valley. The narrator is especially intrigued by

1. Yigal Zalmona, "Mizraha! Mizraha?" *Kadima: hamizrah be'omanut yisrael*, 91.

the Arab watchman, an old, religious Muslim (Haj) who remained behind after his tribe sold the land to the Jews and left the area. The solemn figure of the tall patriarch, who is engaged by the Jewish settlers as a night guard, fascinates the narrator. For several nights he gets up at midnight to watch the old man sitting motionlessly and looking blankly into the darkness. One night, the Arab watchman suddenly stirs with anger:

> Suddenly, his staff made a quarrelsome thump that startled me. I stopped and saw the old man rise quickly and angrily. With his coat disturbed, he moved a few steps toward me. He then stood, his staff began to pound the ground rapidly, and he hurled at me an incomprehensible growl. I knew he was cursing me, but I stood motionless. Suddenly, he wrapped his coat around himself and turned to walk toward the river bank. I looked after him, trembling with both wonderment and understanding. . . . I knew that he wanted to *recapture the motherland like I did.* Night after night I troubled him, filling the air with strange longings. Finally, he could not bear it anymore. Here he was, fleeing, his figure swayed, wrapped in vapors, he appeared hunched over, as if he descended into the netherworld. Only his dog barked a muffled bark at me.[2]

In a poignant meeting between the old native and the new Jewish immigrant, the Arab withdraws, making way for a new Jewish order. Yet the European narrator puts himself on par with the aboriginal Arab. He uses the word "homeland" (מולדת) to describe his and the Arabs' connection to the land, and talks about the urge or need of both to "recapture" it. The eventual retreat of the old Haj into the night signals his surrender and acknowledgment of the Jewish control of the land, at least in the mind of the Jewish-European writer.

Although Hebrew Orientalism as a literary phenomenon all but disappeared after the 1930s, some of the ideas that inspired the writers of the previous chapters later found expression in Israeli culture in more subtle and fragmentary ways. Several of the notions Frishman developed in *Bamidbar* about a Jewish renaissance in the East can be found in the works of S. Yizhar, one of the most influential literary representatives of the first generation of native Israelis. Smilansky's Orientalism found an equally romantic, though somewhat more sophisticated articulation in Canaanism, an innovative cultural movement that inspired the world of art and letters in Israel during the 1940s and beyond. And the awareness of the colonial nature of Zionism that resonates in Arielli's works eventually took two forms, the troubled engagement with the image of the Arab in Israeli literature and the development of a "non-Western" Mizrahi culture after the 1970s.

2. Ya'acov Steinberg, *Kol kitve ya'acov shteinberg* (Tel-Aviv: Dvir, 1957), 264. My emphasis.

Frishman's Oriental renaissance found an interesting expression in some of Yizhar's works, especially in his monumental opus, *The Days of Tsiklag* (*Yeme tsiklag*, 1958).[3] One of the defining works of the first generation of native Israelis, the 1948 Generation, *Tsiklag* chronicles a three-day battle over a hill in the Negev during the Israeli War of Independence in 1948. The very premise of the work, about a small group of resolute soldiers who attack an outpost in the middle of a hostile desert and then fight to hold on to it in the face of superior enemy forces is colonial. But while the desperate defense of the hill is justified by the foolhardy logic of a Zionist settlement mentality, the fact that not all soldiers abide by it undermines the imperialism of the aggressive action somewhat. This kind of ambivalence is typical of Yizhar, whose heroes are often tormented by the inconsistencies of their Zionist ideology.

At first, the soldiers feel alienated from the barren expanses around them. They compare unfavorably the brown, dusty hills to the greenery of their homes in northern Israel and note with aversion the wretched remains of the Arab village they capture. They comfort themselves with the civilizing prospect of bringing water to the desert and colonizing it, and they try to maintain their sanity by engaging in lively discussions about classical music, humming notes by Brahms, Bach, and Beethoven, which swirl surrealistically in the desert air: "hill 244 existed no longer, . . . and all the irregularities around them were suddenly straightened . . . there were no more dirty Arabs (ערבושים) fleeing or being injured—a spirit of good wholesomeness bound them together" (44–45). This striking picture of a Western outpost in the middle of an alien environment erases the local Arab culture as well as the biblical Jewish past, in the name of which the soldiers fight to capture the hill.

Yet the soldiers are never really presented as superior to their Eastern surrounding and their alienation is largely self-induced. The novel sets up a clear division between the beauty of the open countryside, graced by an ever-changing and fantastic spectacle of light, wind, and color, and the soldiers' wretched physical and emotional state. Against the peaceful domesticity of the Arab huts, still redolent of wood-burning bread-ovens; against the far-flung vista, with its ploughed fields and the golden remains of the last harvest; against skies that constantly display a magnificence of shapes and colors, the soldiers frantically burrow foxholes into the rocky hill pockmarking its surface in a metaphorical act of disregard for the natural beauty around them. These soldiers are often described as sweaty, smelly, unwashed men who ravish abominable pieces of pale, gelatinous canned meat with the greediness of ravenous animals. Confined to

---

3. S. Yizhar, *Yeme Tsiklag*. Parts of the book began to be published in various literary venues in 1956.

their foxholes, their world is literally limited. They are sunk to the ground, bogged down by a debilitating mixture of sloth, apathy, vulgarity, and fear.

But as the story progresses, the minute and lavish descriptions of the physical space, either by the soldiers or by the narrator, slowly change the contours of the strange landscape, soften it and familiarize it. As the men remain on the hill for hours on end, they come to know, appreciate, and finally belong to the country around them. They note the gradual change of light that alters the appearance of the land, and they marvel at the intricate filigree of canyons and the different kinds of wind and sky and clouds that surround them. This slow and almost imperceptible change that is created by the threads of words that are spun continuously over land and sky find a parallel in the very structure of the story. The battle over the hill is waged in three successive waves that are essentially identical. During the first attack the soldiers charge the hill in the morning and dig in. By night they retreat before an overwhelming enemy only to return the next morning, capture the hill again, and hold on to it.

The painstaking pace in which the thousand-page novel unfolds creates more of a spatial than a linear narrative, in the process of which the fighting men slowly mesh with the wilderness around them until they become one with it. Not surprisingly, many critics at the time faulted the novel precisely for that. The influential critic Baruch Kurzweill argued passionately against regarding the work as an epic and calling it a "novel" on the grounds that it did not have a developing linear narrative but a spatial one.[4] Kurzweill's assessment was shared by many critics, most of whom complained about the weakness of the architectural structure of Yizhar's work and his exaggerated descriptions of nature.[5] Some noted that these descriptions came at the expense of the human characters, who are mentioned only in passing.[6] Others, like Yosef Auerbach, protested that the natural descriptions take away from the main story and lamented that the young men in *Tsiklag* are egotistical and self-centered. They do not believe in national redemption (גאולת העם), and their blood is spilled for naught. Moreover, the disgruntled men are severed from their historical past and from any creative ideals, he writes, "even the countryside, *which is after all that of the patriarchs*, means nothing to these young men."[7]

All of these arguments are directly related to the point I am trying to make, which is Yizhar's attempt to transcend the biblical argument as a rationale for

---

4. "Trapped by the Present of his characters, who are inundated by time in their endless and uninhibited ravings," he wrote, "Yizhar effectively blocks the dimension of epic time." Baruch Kurzweill, "Great Disappointment" (*Achzava gedola*) in *Ben hazon leven ha'absurdi*, 376–403.

5. The comment is attributed to Yehuda Burla, no citation is given. See *S. Yizhar, Mivhar ma'amare bikoret al yetsirato*, Haim Nagid, ed. 15.

6. Shlomo Tsemach in Nagid, *S. Yizhar, Mivhar ma'amare bikoret al yetsirato*, 86.

7. Averbach in Nagid, *S. Yizhar, Mivhar ma'amare bikoret al yetsirato*, 134–137.

national redemption. While the biblical connotations of the space are retained in the reader's mind as an important backdrop—Tsiklag is mentioned in the Bible as part of King David's kingdom—the immediate and present connection that is forged between the men and the land gains precedence over it. The connection may have begun with the Bible, but it is now actualized through a physical and emotional contact with the land. Thus, a new meaning is grafted onto the eastern Israeli landscape, which derives its power from a very palpable present that flows through the consciousness of the young Jewish soldiers. It is in this sense that *Tsiklag* continues where *Bamidbar* left. If Frishman brought the ancient East into Europe and addressed the existential crisis of Diaspora Judaism with the help of the Bible, Yizhar may be said to have completed this move. Frishman strove to create an aesthetic and highly suggestive biblical universe in order to infuse Diaspora Judaism with some of what he perceived as the nation's ancient vigor. Yizhar actualized this aesthetic formulation by setting *Tsiklag* in a real, geographically identifiable desert, not an imaginary one. As a native Israeli, Yizhar took the New Hebrew and planted him into the landscapes of Palestine through a literary device that was equally effective. By inundating the Eretz-Israeli space in *Tsiklag* with a deluge of words, Yizhar breaks down the local landscape, strips it of its biblicism by deconstructing it, and then "colonizes" it by reorganizing it according to a new, native-Israeli sensibility.

In many ways, then, Yizhar can be seen as completing what Frishman set out to do by realizing the aesthetic formulation of the desert. Frishman, unlike Yizhar, was not interested in the political possibilities that the Eastern space held but used it as inspiration, a promise of another beginning with all its invigorating force. The rejuvenating power of the desert is inextricably connected in *Bamidbar* to its place in the history of the Jewish nation. Yizhar does not try to resurrect this essence in *Tsiklag* but translates the transformative power of the desert in ways Frishman probably never envisioned. Both writers are concerned with the moral and especially the personal meaning of "Eastern" space. But whereas Frishman released his characters into a symbolic space to imbue them with a new spirit, Yizhar placed his characters in a real and specific location. The rich descriptions of the wilderness in *Bamidbar* are reflected in the incredibly intricate depictions of the land in *Tsiklag*. In both works the desert is dramatized by different devices that call attention to the very act of literary production. Frishman uses a highly contrived but extremely evocative biblical register and nomenclature to conjure up a passionate national past. Yizhar ostensibly discards that past but at the same time weaves it into the rich descriptions of every shade and contour of the vast, open land, until it vividly materializes before the reader.

There is no doubt that Yizhar's attempts to construct a native identity in *Tsiklag* are far more violent than the attempts his uncle, Moshe Smilansky, made in his work. Indeed, the novel is premised on the very act of a forceful establishment of sovereignty and national identity. In this respect, *Tsiklag* and Yizhar's work in general, stand in direct opposition to much of the post-Zionist criticism of Hanan Hever, for instance, who contends that the encounter with the Palestinian space and the violent attempt to merge with it in Hebrew literature is repeatedly elided and blurred in order to mitigate it. "The national story is almost always an identity story in which the space is represented after the violent event," writes Hever, "a colonial space that is represented from a postcolonial perspective," in order to cover up the aggressive act leading to the occupation.[8] But the national identity Yizhar constructs in *Tsiklag* is inextricably connected not only to the "foreign" countryside but also to its former Arab inhabitants, even though they are physically absent from the story.

Hever is most exacting in reading Yizhar's best-known work, the short story "Hirbet Hiz'a," about the moral qualms of a soldier-narrator who witnesses his unit's expulsion of Arabs from their village in 1948. The narrator's view of the expelled Arabs as "wandering Jews," his ability to understand their trauma by filtering it through the Jewish experience of exile, is not considered empathetic by Hever but ethnocentric. "The identity of the Other is understood in this story according to Jewish identifying characteristics," he writes, "characteristics that neutralize the histories of the Palestinian space in order to prepare it for its Israeli permeation."[9] Moreover, because the eradication of the Arab in Israeli literature is almost never complete, his presence as a perpetual Other is used for the establishment of a Jewish, Israeli identity and ensures his control. Frequently, such moral identifications, contends Hever, enable Israeli writers to distance themselves and even eschew their responsibility for the suffering of others through maudlin expressions of helplessness.

Again, the argument with Hever would be about meaning not content. Within the context of the Arab-Israeli conflict, "Hirbet Hiz'a" is perhaps one of the most existentially ethical texts in modern Hebrew literature. Writers are usually regarded as the moral conscience of their communities, not as politicians who are expected to suggest platforms for political action. Hever's charge therefore, that the story's hand-wringing empowers readers to avoid their responsibility for the violent actions they or their country perform, seems misplaced. Another way of understanding Yizhar can be found in Brenner's words about the relations

---

8. Hever, "Mesifrut Ivrit lesifrut Yisre'elit," 168. Hever does single out Yizhar as an anomaly in that his stories usually try to grapple with this rupture, although usually to assuage the Jewish conscience; Ibid., 174.

9. Hever, 174.

between Jews and Arabs, quoted in chapter 1 about a soulful connection that has no aim or purpose, except for Jews and Arabs to be brothers and friends.[10] The incomplete processes of eradication that, according to Hever, Arabs are often subjected to in Hebrew texts, can also be seen from a different perspective. As veiled or silenced as the Arab presence may be in Zionist narratives, the very fact that it is there may be the means as well as the promise of a future return. It is a commonplace that the act of creation always involves a process of selection during which some parts of a culture are included and others are left out. While post-Zionist critics choose to focus on what Zionism left out when it sought to create a new Jewish identity in the Land of Israel, this book looks at some of the elements from the local Arab culture that have been incorporated into it.

Although some of Frishman's Oriental sensibilities imbue the work of Yizhar and others of his generation (Hazaz, Shamir), Smilansky's romance of the Orient found a highly original but equally romantic expression in the innovative ideas of the Young Hebrews: a small group of writers, artists, and intellectuals who made a significant imprint on the Israeli world of art and letters during the 1940s. In many ways, the Young Hebrews, known popularly as Canaanites, brought the anti-religious sentiment that was always inherent in Zionism to its culmination in their call for the creation of a pan-Semitic polity in the Middle East, comprising the various non-Islamic ethnic groups in the region. While the Canaanites' political vision—severing the ties between Israeli Jews and Jews in the Diaspora, disavowing exilic Jewish history, and creating a separate Hebrew nation in Palestine—never caught on, their aesthetic innovations did. The Canaanites called for the creation of a native, Hebrew art rooted in the local landscape and devoid of any foreign, especially diasporic, Jewish elements. The movement's founder and chief ideologue, the poet Yonatan Ratosh, believed that such art can be achieved by adopting a strict secular ethos, by using only a "pure" Hebrew vernacular (biblical or contemporary but not rabbinic), and by focusing mainly on current, native-Israeli issues or themes.[11]

As a staunch secularist, Ratosh rebelled against the spirituality of Judaism, its adherence to "history and memory" over "nature and matter."[12] His development of what he termed as Canaanite Aesthetics was aimed at breaking the old religious mold of Judaism and at grounding Hebrew culture in a specific space,

10. Chapter 1, note 57.
11. For two comprehensive studies of Canaanism, see James S. Diamond, *Homeland or Holy Land?* and Ya'acov Shavit, *Me'ivri ad kna'ani* (Domino, 1984). See also Anita Shapira, who comments on both these studies from a more contemporary perspective that includes postcolonial considerations as well in *Alpaim*, 25, 2003, 9–54. Shapira claims that Canaanism had a fairly wide appeal for the 1948 Generation, especially among the young men who fought in the War of Independence.
12. Diamond, 122.

that of the old–new Near East. This impetus was characteristic of Zionism as well, but Ratosh wished to sever the ties between Israel and the Jewish world abroad and erase postexilic Jewish history, something mainstream Zionism was never willing to do.

The most obvious Oriental element of Ratosh's poetry was its distinct linguistic features, characterized by a strict adherence to what he regarded as "Semitic purism." This was expressed not only in his use of biblical language and syntax, and in the incorporation of ancient Near Eastern elements, such as Ugaritic epics, but also in his use of neologisms. The creation and use of new words and phrases in Hebrew was a common literary practice since the revival. For Ratosh, however, it was not only a lexicographical necessity borne out of the need to modernize an ancient tongue. It was also a way to secularize the language, release it from its religious past, and cleanse it from what he considered foreign linguistic influences.[13]

Ancient Middle Eastern cultural influences also found expression in the visual arts in Israel, although the Canaanite identification of the painters and sculptors who used them is not always clear. The works of sculptors Avraham Malnikov and Yitzhak Danziger, for instance, are generally considered to be inspired by ancient Assyrian and Egyptian aesthetics. Malnikov's famous stone statue of the roaring lion, commemorating the martyrs of Tel-Hai, has been compared to lions that appear in Assyrian palace stone carvings.[14] Danziger's equally well-known sculpture of the ancient Hebrew hunter Nimrod (Gen. 10: 9) has become one of the most identifiable visual symbols of Canaanism. Although Danziger's political affiliation with Canaanism has been limited, a picture of his Nimrod statue adorned the first issue of the Canaanite journal *Aleph* that came out in 1948, symbolizing Canaanite ideology in its modern rendition of ancient Egyptian and Assyrian elements.[15]

---

13. "Language and literature thus became for Ratosh and his followers important loci of the *Kulturkampf* they wished to precipitate. This is why, for example, Ratosh proposed at one point abandoning the conventional 'Assyrian' style of Hebrew script in favor of recasting it in Latin characters. This conversion would formally express the transformation of Hebrew from a sacral Jewish tongue into a secular Western one. It would also serve in a practical way to drive a wedge between the younger generations, who would grow up using the new script, and the sacred texts of biblical, rabbinic, and medieval Judaism. It is on this basis, too, that we must understand the energy Ratosh invested in developing Hebrew neologisms. . . . While this cultural agenda was directed at promoting the secularization of Hebrew as a language, it also, at the same time, was intended to preserve its linguistic independence and autonomy. For Ratosh, this meant being zealous about purifying the language and purging it of foreign influences in vocabulary and spelling. This pursuit was really a working out in cultural terms of what Canaanism called for in its broader vision." Diamond, 109.

14. The direct inspiration has never been conclusively established, although it is generally assumed. See Tamar Manor-Friedman, "Yamenu kakedem," in Tzalmonas *Kadima: hamizrah be'omanut yisrael* (Jerusalem: Israel Museum, 1998), 100.

15. Ibid., 104–105.

Aside from the inspiring aesthetic vision it offered, one of the chief political values of Canaanism was that it channeled the founders' revolutionary zeal toward a new ideological venue. Rather than deal with the less glamorous aspects of state building after the bloody but glorious fight for independence—the Israeli War of Independence lasted a whole year—Canaanism offered an opportunity to continue the Zionist revolution.[16] The ideology also offered a convenient Jewish connection to the East without the complications of contemporary politics. By conjuring up the pre-monotheistic, mythic past of the Hebrews, the Canaanites offered a viable bond with the region that conveniently ignored contemporary Muslim culture. At the same time, the Canaanite ethos also enabled the ruling European, Ashkenazi classes and the new non-European, Sephardi, or Mizrahi immigrants to forge an alliance as "Hebrews" without addressing their increasingly problematic cultural differences.[17] But despite these attractions, Canaanism remained politically marginal, perhaps because inde-

16. Diamond is quoting Boaz Evron, a convert to Canaanism, who reflected in a 1984 interview that "the fact [is] that this sense of a Hebrew homeland sought out an ideology for itself. Zionism is an ideology of an ethnic group that lacked a territory and sought one in order to solve its problems. But from the moment a territorial structure was created . . . , from that moment on they were in need of an ideology that would express this movement. . . . and this is the explanation for the joy and the relief that we felt when we first encountered [the Canaanite] ideas. . . . This ideology was important [evidence] of a tremendous intellectual hunger of which we were not even conscious. It defined for us why we rejected Zionism, why we felt that we, children and products of this land, were intrinsically different from Jews in the Diaspora, whose thought processes and sensibility seemed qualitatively foreign." Diamond, 80.

See also Tzalmona, who writes: "Different artistic, cultural, psychological and political needs were channeled into the so-called Canaanite myth, which became a meeting point of various spiritual purposes. It was the means for a purifying return to the Dionysian essence of Judaism; it was the fundamental history of Israeli being; it was the key to a collective self-discovery of a political being in search of its identity; it amounted to a moral ideal that dictated a spiritual, cultural, personal and public conduct. At one point, it also provided the answer to the question 'who is an Israeli?' and thus alleviated anxieties relating to problems of authenticity. The unifying communion with it became the spiritual and personal solution for those who were deprived of a normal past and a normal present. The alchemist laboratory that was supposed to create a distinctly Israeli artistic style ex nihilo was established under the wide wings of this phoenix." Tzalmona, "Mizraha!" *Kadima: hamizrah be'omanut yisrael* (Jerusalem: Israel Museum, 1998), 68–69.

17. The designation "Sephardi" to denote non-Ashkenazi Jews became prevalent after the expulsion of Jews from Spain (Sepharad in Hebrew) in the fifteenth century. The term became increasingly inaccurate as an identification of origin as time went by. After the mass immigration of Jews from the Muslim countries of North Africa and the Middle East to Israel it became meaningless because many of these Jewish communities had no connection to Spanish Jewry whatsoever. While the term "Mizrahi" (meaning Eastern) that replaced it was initially an artificial designation that lumped all non-Ashkenazi immigrants into one group, it eventually became a more meaningful political and cultural marker. After a while, the marginalized groups of Moroccan, Iraqi, and other Jews from non-European countries forged a common, non-Ashkenazi local Israeli culture that was defined primarily by their anti-establishment status. For more on this, see *Mizrahim beyisrael*, Hanan Hever, Yehuda Shenhav, Pnina Mutzafi-Heller eds. (Hakibutz Hame'uhad, 2002).

pendence proved to be exceedingly demanding after all and the opportunities it offered too tempting to forgo.

Although the fervently partisan society of the Yishuv and the new State insured Ratosh's continued marginality as a poet, the influence of Canaanism on Israeli arts, letters, and politics was significant, much more than the cultural and political establishment of the country cared to admit.[18] And while there may not have been a direct connection between Ratosh's ideas and those of Smilansky, their consideration of spatial and linguistic elements seems strikingly similar, a testament to some of the issues that stood at the center of the new Jewish society in Eretz Israel and its relation to the East.

As the conflict with the Arabs escalated during the 1950s and 1960s, the promise of the Canaanites' fantastic political vision evaporated almost completely and their cultural ideas did not fare any better. A decade after the establishment of the State, the connections of Israelis to the East, to the geographic location of their state, were chiefly military and demographic and very rarely cultural. On the international front, the alignment with France, Germany, and finally with the United States placed Israel firmly in the West; a political position that was eagerly adopted by the European-born leadership of the country. On the domestic front, the cultural and political ties with the West were reflected in the marginalization of Jewish immigrants from Muslim countries by the Ashkenazi cultural and political elite.

As a result, references to the contemporary East in Israeli literature and culture took on two different shapes after the establishment of the State; shapes which in many ways continued the [post]colonial concerns that Arielli raised in some of his works thirty years earlier. The first and more political expression of these concerns was the preoccupation with Arab characters and themes in Hebrew literature and their presentation as either grotesque creatures or as victims of Zionist aggression.[19] The second phenomenon was the creation of a genuine Mizrahi culture in Israel, which was forged locally on the margins of the hegemonic Ashkenazi culture—Mizrahi music and later poetry and

18. Ratosh's ill repute was even used against Yizhar, who, as one critic accused him, presented the new, Hebrew generation in *Tsiklag* as rootless, petty, and *Canaanite through and through*, a generation that does not believe in the Zionist cause it gives its life for. See Auerbach in Nagid, 134. Although *Tsiklag* may indeed have some Canaanite elements, these are not necessarily part of the characters' worldview. The Canaanite sensibility of the work resides in what Miron calls a simplistic belief in the anticultural ideal of freedom that permeated the work, and in the strong desire to become one with the open spaces. See Miron in Nagid, 35 and Mordechai Fechter in Nagid, 177.

19. The creation of grotesque Arab characters was especially pronounced in children's literature, like Yigal Mosinsohn's popular detective series, *HASAMBA* (חסמב"ה), about a group of Israeli teenagers who help defend the country by thwarting various Arab villains who plot against it.

literature began to surface in the 1970s as part of the Mizrahi cultural and political revolution that marked Israel's growing pluralism. Both of these trends were reactions to the legacy of Zionism as a dominant Western movement. While the particular references to Arabs in Israeli literature can be seen in some respect as an expression of guilt that characterize other colonial literatures, the creation of a unique Mizrahi culture can be seen as a reaction against what has been problematically termed at times as the cultural colonialism of the Ashkenazi hegemony.[20]

The presentation of Arabs as victims of Israeli aggression is especially pronounced in the literature of the State Generation, the generation of writers who came into prominence after the establishment of Israel. In works such as A. B. Yehoshua's *Facing the Forests* (*Mul haye'arot*, 1963) and *The Lover* (*Hame'ahev*, 1972), David Grossman's *Yellow Wind* (*Hazman hatsahov*, 1985), and Yehoshua Kenaz's *The Way to the Cats* (*Baderekh el hahatulim*, 1991), the Arab characters often figure as a protest against the tragedy of the Palestinians and their continued misery as a result of the Arab-Israeli conflict. In other works, like in some early short stories by Amos Oz, the moral dilemmas of Jewish nationalism (dilemmas raised by Yizhar a decade earlier), are developed into a strident criticism of Zionism. Oz's short stories from the 1960s reveal a turbulent struggle between East and West, embodied in the tension between the kibbutz as an isolated community of Western immigrants and the consuming Eastern wilderness around it; a struggle that usually unfolds through a metaphoric fight between mighty natural elements that symbolize the two sides.

Oz's first short story, "Where the Jackals Howl" (*Artsot hatan*, 1963), about incest and sexual assault on a kibbutz, opens with a poetic attempt of the Western wind to drive a heat wave eastward:

> In the early evening the westerly wind grew stronger. The heat wave was pushed to the east, from the plain to the Judean mountains, and from the Judean mountains to the valley of Jericho, and from there to the scorpion deserts east of the Jordan.[21]

The climatic change is cast in the mold of a vengeful fight between West and East; between Western forces of progress and those of the local Eastern wilds that predated them. And although at the beginning of the story the heat is pun-

---

20. I say "problematic" because the colonial paradigm has been applied by post-Zionists not only to the treatment of Arabs in Israel but also to that of Mizrahi Jews. But as I showed in chapters 3 and 4, this analogy does not always obtain and it often does a disservice to Zionists, Arabs, and Mizrahis alike.

21. Az, *Artsot hatan*, 9. My translation.

ished and driven away to a remote and deadly penal colony, it soon comes back in a different guise. As night falls, the darkness takes up the initial fight of the easterly wind and closes in on the isolated island of civilization, menacing it with wild jackals and the specters of an untamed world:

> Our land betrays us every night anew. It is not familiar and yielding now, criss-crossed by water pipes and dirt roads. Our fields defect to the enemy now, releasing waves of strange and alien smells at us. Before our eyes our land bristles at night with a menacing hiss and takes on again the shape it had before we came to this place.
>
> An internal circle, a circle of lights, protects us from the gathering plot against us. But this is a weak wall that cannot stop the smells and sounds of the enemy at night.[22]

Ironically, the Eastern space that tries to shake off and expel its Zionist colonizers in Oz's stories, is the same East that Frishman enlisted to inspire and invigorate his generation; the East that Yizhar painstakingly made familiar and that Ratosh sought to permeate.

In other stories by Oz, this tension is strengthened and complicated by adding Arab natives to the onslaught of the natural forces that threaten to undo fifty years of Zionist cultivation. In the story "Nomads and Viper" (*Navadim vatsefa*, 1963), for instance, an especially dry winter drives clans of Bedouins from the south toward the cultivated northern regions. Like the seven lean cows of Pharaoh's dream, the dark, hungry, and relentless Bedouins come out of the desert to consume the fat of the land. Their black goats pockmark the kibbutz fields like a terrible disease, threatening to destroy them and return the land to its former desolation. Their slow invasion is completed one night during a chance meeting between a Bedouin shepherd and a young woman from the kibbutz. Unable to consummate her powerful attraction to the young nomad, the woman returns home where she is bitten by a viper. Penetrated in a symbolic act of vengeance by a messenger from the very earth the kibbutznik and her community sought to husband, and not by the attractive young native she desires, the woman slowly dies.

"Nomads and Viper" deals not only with the alienation of the Zionist settlers from the Eastern space they occupy but also seems to justify it. The very meeting between the Bedouin shepherd and the kibbutznik takes place in a lush orchard, to which the snake lends an unmistakable meaning. Potentially, their meeting also could have been that of an Arab Adam and a Jewish Eve. The girl's own fantasies about the shepherd hint at such a possibility ("Maybe she should go to him, find him among the wadis, forgive him and never return," 42). But the

22. Ibid., 15–16.

chances for it are either missed or they were never real to begin with. This, too, is what Oz seems to be saying about Zionism and the East.

One of the most interesting postcolonial commentaries on Zionism by another member of the State Generation can be found in Yehoshua's 1990 novel, *Mr. Mani (Mar Mani)*, which looks at Zionism as an Ashkenazi phenomenon.[23] Unlike most works that deal with the immigration of European Jews to Palestine, *Mr. Mani* examines it from the privileged perspective of a Sephardi native of the East. The result is a new understanding of time and space, in which Zionism loses its place as one of the pinnacles of Jewish history and becomes a passing episode in the eternal life cycle of a harmonious East.

Mr. Mani is a pseudo-historical novel about five generations of a Sephardi family that begins in present-day Jerusalem and goes back in time to 1848. Shaked writes that Yehoshua examines in this novel the Sephardi element in pre-Zionist Palestine from an Ashkenazi point of view, which looks at the Palestinian Sephardis with a mixture of admiration, bewilderment, and anxiety.[24] The Ashkenazis sense the almost mythic ability of the Sephardis to survive in an ever-changing world, an ability that is sustained by their native attachment to the land and their natural relations with the Arabs. The novel pays homage to the deep affinity of the Sephardis to Eretz Israel, irrespective of politics. The characters in *Mr. Mani* are a natural part of the Mediterranean world. They know it intimately and move through it freely. For them, Zionism is just another regional political phase that does not determine their relation to the Land of Israel. The Ashkenazi point of view, through which events are narrated in the novel, calls attention to the nature of Zionism as an artificial, and perhaps even a harmful development in Jewish history. The natural attachment of the Sephardis to the Mediterranean, Muslim world questions not only the validity of Zionism but its overall benefit to Jews. The novel seems to say that, unlike their Ashkenazi brethren, the Sephardis never really had a Jewish problem.[25]

23. Beginning with his 1977 novel *Hame'ahev*, Yehoshua increasingly developed Sephardi themes in his works. See his novels *Molkho*, 1987, *Mar Mani*, 1990, *Journey to the End of the Millennium*, 1997. Shaked writes that in his short stories and in Yehoshua's first novellas there is no mention of his ethnic background or of the world of his father, who wrote about the Sephardi community of the old Yishuv. Shaked notes that in the preface to his father's memoir, Yehoshua confesses his conscious decision to stay away from his ethnic background so that he can become purely an "Israeli" writer. It seems to me that Yehoshua's conscious decision alone qualifies his inclusion in a discussion about Orientalism. See *Sifrut kan, az ve'akhshav* (Zmora Bitan, 1993), 153–154.

24. Shaked, *Sifrut kan, az véakhshav*, 163. The novel has been read in other ways as well. See for instance Bernard Horn, *Facing the Fires*.

25. This may also be where Yehoshua and the post-Zionist critique converge. Judging from his literary corpus and from many essays and interviews he published throughout his life, Yehoshua probably did not write the novel with that critique in mind. Yet the novel should also be read within the cultural context of its time, and as such, post-Zionism should be considered as an influence, even if indirect. See for example Yehoshua's collection of essays and interviews, *Hakir ve'hahar*, and the more recent one by Horn.

The other phenomenon mentioned above, the emergence of a distinct Mizrahi culture, can be traced to the early works of writers like Sami Michael and Eli Amir, Iraqi-born Jews who began writing about their experience as non-European, Western immigrants in an Ashkenazi-dominated Israel in the 1970s. Both writers dealt with the absorption pangs of their community in an Israel that was largely dismissive of their non-Western cultural sensibilities, which were deemed Arab-like and therefore primitive and inferior. Some of their earlier works are didactic biographies about the hardships of these immigrants to fit into a culture that was fundamentally alien to theirs. These works, like Michael's 1974 *Equal and More Equal (Shavim veshavim yoter)*, and Amir's 1983 *Scapegoat (Tarne-gol kaparot)*, combine a litany of the Ashkenazi establishment's well-meaning but clumsy efforts at absorption with an apologia about the merits of Eastern or Arab culture.

Michael and Amir were among the first to bring the existence and concerns of a Mizrahi community to the attention of mainstream Israeli culture. Their attempts to deal with the tension between their own Eastern culture and the European culture of the Israeli State through the biographical genre were later picked up by second- and third-generation Mizrahi writers—Ronit Matalon, Koby Oz, Dorit Rabinyan—who dealt with this theme in more diverse ways. Two novels by Dorit Rabinyan, an Israeli of Persian descent, are illustrative examples of such treatments. Rabinyan's first novel, her 1995 *Persian Brides (Simtat hashkediyot be'omrijan)*, is the story of a Persian Jewish community in northern Iran at the dawn of Zionism in the beginning of the twentieth century. Her second novel, *Strand of a Thousand Pearls (Hatunot shelanu,* 1999), takes place in Israel and follows the lives and loves of a Persian-Jewish family after their immigration to Israel. Although both works are fictional, Rabinyan readily admits they are based on her family's background and history. "I've written about my mother, my grandmother, my aunts—actually all the female options I could come up with [because I did not] have the courage of peering straight inside of me."[26]

That many Mizrahi writers, the older as well as the younger generation, use biography as a substantial literary device in many of their works to date seems at least in part to be a compensation for the long silence of non-European Jewish immigrants in Israel. As such, this may be viewed as another indication of the ongoing legacy of Zionism as a Western phenomenon, with which Arielli dealt in the 1910s.[27]

26. From an internet interview with Dorit Rabinyan conducted for Random House Publishing by Jenny Lee at http://www.randomhouse.com/boldtype/0702/rabinyan/interview.html.
27. To some extent, the literary category "Mizrahi" is reductive and perhaps even tautological, as a work is usually considered "Mizrahi" only if it includes a preponderance of biographical infor-mation that identifies it as such and if the drama in it is based directly on it. Otherwise, I don't know of identifiable literary devices that may be termed "Mizrahi" in and of themselves.

In the last two decades of the twentieth century, the emergence of a substantial Mizrahi literature, and even Israeli-Palestinian literature and poetry in Hebrew—by Anton Shamas, Emil Habibi, Kashu'a Sayed—makes it increasingly difficult to define Israel's place with respect to the East.[28] This is why Hebrew Orientalism as a literary phenomenon was so short-lived. One hundred years after the emergence of Zionism, and fifty years after the establishment of the State of Israel, the tensions, connections, influences, and counterinfluences between East and West in Israeli culture are becoming ever more complex and harder to discern.

Consider, for example, two recent novels, one by Meir Shalev, an "Ashkenazi" writer, and another by Ronit Matalon, a "Mizrahi" writer.[29] Shalev's 1988 *The Blue Mountain* (*Roman rusi*) deals with one of Zionism's central foundational myths—the settlement of the Jezrael Valley during the Second Aliya in the 1920s. Matalon's 1995 novel, *The One Facing Us* (*Ze 'im hapanim elenu*) deals with a different foundational myth in the history of Israel, that of the Mizrahi immigration to Israel after 1948. Shalev's magic-realist novel is an ode to the extraordinary sacrifice of the pioneering men and women who dried swamps, tilled the land, and literally built the country from the ground up with their own hands at a great personal cost. But the half-imagined novel is also a send-up of the sheer lunacy and folly of some of these pioneers, whose grandchildren fulfill their legacy in highly ironical ways: they profit from their inherited farmland not by continuing to cultivate it but by selling it at exorbitant prices as burial ground for those seeking eternal rest in the shadow of the myth.

Matalon's novel tells the story of a different group of immigrants, who were just as vital for the creation of Israel. Like Shalev, she too bases her narrative on half-imagined truths to tell the story of her Egyptian family before and after World War II. The novel makes clear that in a postcolonial world easy divisions between East and West no longer obtain. This becomes obvious as the writer's extended Jewish-Egyptian family disperses all over the globe after the war. While the Israeli branch of the family is considered Eastern or Mizrahi in Israel, those family members who went to Africa become representatives of the former Western, colonial powers, and those who left for France and North America become sophisticated cosmopolitans, harking back to the very place that the Jewish family occupied in colonial Alexandria before the war. By placing old family photographs at the head of each chapter and telling the stories behind

28. For a comprehensive and detailed summary of these trends, see the articles by Ariel Hirschfeld, Garsiella Trachtenberg, Yigal Tzalmona, and Tamar Manor-Friedman in *Kadima*.

29. In all of her interviews, Matalon strongly disagrees with such facile divisions. Her disagreement supports my contention, that such divisions are indeed increasingly meaningless. For a representative interview, see Rolly Rosen, "Soferet. Nekuda," *Kol Ha'ir*, March 20, 1992.

those pictures, Matalon conjures up the rich life of the immigrants' vanished world. At the same time, some of the admittedly imagined details she invents about the pictures question the validity of the harmonious lives Mizrahi Jews allegedly led among Muslims before their so-called ruinous immigration to Israel.

Both novels rely on ethnic references and folklore to tell two different stories about two different communities. Yet despite the distinct cultures—Eastern European pioneers and Egyptian Jews—the ethnic references highlight the similarities, not just the differences, between the stories as reconstructed mythologies of Jewish communal life. Shalev and Matalon are native Israelis who feel far enough removed from their ethnic communities to go beyond the narrow East–West or Ashkenazi–Mizrahi divide. Mixing reverence and irony these writers elevate and at the same time debunk the grand foundational myths they write about.

Writing in 1913, Yosef Haim Brenner hypothesized that "in fifty, a hundred, or even two hundred years from now, if the Land of Israel will be populated with hundreds of thousands of Jews, and life will flourish and be stable, with well-defined traditions, character, and shape—both old and new—then there surely will be a natural, Eretz-Israeli and Jewish" literature.[30] Both Shalev and Matalon seem to exemplify Brenner's prediction, especially because of the historical dimensions of their narratives. Unlike revivalist writers such as Frishman and Smilansyk, who tried to create a mythological Jewish *future*, Shalev and Matalon no longer have to resort to such literary contortions. As two writers who are rooted in a flourishing and stable culture, with well-defined literary traditions, character, and shape, they can finally mythologize the Jewish-Israeli *past*, which may yet be the last triumph of the Hebrew cultural revival.

30. Yosef Haim Brenner, "Mitokh pinkasi," *Ktavim* (Hakibutz Hame'uhad, 1985), 4:1024.

Selected Bibliography

Alboim-Dror, Rachel. *Hamahar shel ha'etmol: mivhar ha'utopia hatsiyonit*. Yad Yitzhak Ben-Zvi, 1993.

Almog, Shmuel. *Tsiyonut vehistoria*. Hebrew University, Jerusalem: Magnes, 1982.

Alter, Robert. *The Art of Biblical Narrative*. New York: Basic Books, 1981.

Ansimov, Zecharia. "Yehudei heharim." *Hashiloah* 18 (1908), 467.

Arac, Jonathan, and Harriet Ritvo, eds. *Micropolitics of Nineteenth Century Literature. Nationalism, Exoticism, Imperialism*. Philadelphia: University of Pennsylvania Press, 1991.

Arielli, A. L. *Kitve lamed alef arielli*. Ed. Milton Arfa. New York and Tel-Aviv: Keren Israel Matz Ltd. and Dvir, 1999.

———. *Bentayim, kovets sifruti*. Ed. Yehoshua Feldman. Jaffa, 1913.

———. *Yeshimon*. Ed. Dan Miron. Tel-Aviv: Dvir Publishing, 1990.

Ashton, Thomas. *Byron's Hebrew Melodies*. University of Texas Press, 1972.

Auerbach, Yosef. In *S. Yizhar, mivhar ma'amarim 'al yetsirato*. Ed. Haim Nagid. Am Oved, 1972, 134–137.

Avineri, Shlomo. *Hara'ayon hatsiyoni ligvanan*. Tel-Aviv: Am Oved, 1991.

Avni, Abraham. *The Bible and Romanticism*. The Hague, Paris: Mouton, 1969.

Azoulay, Ariella, and Adi Ophir. "100 Years of Zionism, 50 Years of a Jewish State." *Tikkun* 13, no. 2 (March/April 1998).

Barash, Asher. "Arvi'im." In *Kitve asher barash*. Tel-Aviv: Massada, 1952.

Bartal, Yisrael. "Kozaq ubedvi: olam hadimuyim hale'umi hahadash." In *Ha'aliya hashnia*. Ed. Yisrael Bartal. Jerusalem: Yad Ben-Tzvi, 1997.

Bar-Yosef, Hamutal. *Maga'im shel dekadens: biyalik, berdichevsky, brenner*. Ben-Gurion University, 1997.

———. "Afterword" in *Professor Leonardo*. Yaakov Hurgin, Jerusalem: Keter, 1990.

Barzel, Hillel. *Shirat hibat tsiyon*. Tel-Aviv: Sifriyat Po'alim, 1987.

Barzilai, Yehoshua. "La'atidot hamizrah." *Hashiloah* 29 (1913–1914), 340.

———. "Me'erets yisra'el." *Hashiloah* 31 (1914–1915), 171.

Bassok, Ido. "Psikho'analiza beheksher tarbuti ufoliti, 'iyun vehadgama besipure bne 'arav shel smilansky." *Bikoret ufarshanut* 29 (Sivan 1993).

———. *Betsel pardesim 'al adama metsora'at: 'al yetsiratam hasifrutit vehapublitsistit shel moshe smilansky ve'uri tsvi greenberg*. Hakibutz Hame'uhad, 1996.

Belkind, Yisrael. *Eretz yisrael*. Hame'ir Publishing, 1919.

———. *Ha'aravim asher ba'aretz*. Hermon Publishing, 1969.

———. *Bintiv habilyuim: zikhronot.* Misrad Habitachon, 1983.

Ben-Arye, Yehoshua. "Perceptions and Images of the Holy Land." In *The Land that Became Israel: Studies in Historical Geography.* Ed. Ruth Kark. Magnes Press, Yale University Press, 1989.

Ben-Ezer, Ehud. "Kol ha'ema shebadavar." *Davar,* November 5, 1979.

———. "Aravi ehad mokher tufinim." *Iton 77* 18 (Nov.–Dec. 1973), 20–21.

———. "'Al kanfe hehalom, mimar'ot ha'aretz." *'Al hamishmar,* September 24, 1976.

———. "Mavo." In *Bemoledet haga'agu'im hamenugadim.* Zmora-Bitan Publishing, 1992.

Ben-Gurion, David. "Leberur motsa hafalahim." In *Ha'aravim asher ba'arets.* Ed. Uzi Ornan. Hermon Publishing, 1969.

Benjamin, Roger, ed. *Orientalism, Delacroix to Klee.* Art Gallery of New South Wales, 1998.

Bentwich, Norman, and John Shaftesley. "Forerunners of Zionism in the Victorian Era." In *Remember the Days; Essays on Anglo-Jewish History Presented to Cecil Roth by Members of the Council of the Jewish Historical Society.* Eds. Norman Bentwich and John Shaftesley. 207–239. Jewish Historical Society of England, 1966.

Ben Yehuda, Eliezer. "Hahalom veshivro." In *Kol kitve eli'ezer ben-yehuda.* Jerusalem, 1943.

Ben-Yisrael, Hedva. "Te'oryot 'al hale'umiyut umidat hahalatan 'al hatsiyonut." In *Tsiyonut: pulmus ben zmanenu.* Eds. Pinchas Genosar and Avi Bar-eli. Ben-Gurion University, 1996.

Ben-Zvi, Rachel Yana'it. *Anu Olim.* Am Oved, 1959.

Berdichevsky, Micha Yosef. *Kol kitve mem yod berdichevsky.* Tel-Aviv: Dvir Publishing, 1964.

Bergman, Shmuel Hugo. *Toldot hafilosofia hahadasha.* Jerusalem: Mossad Bialik, 1973.

Berkowitz, Y. D. *Kitve yod dalet berkovitch.* Tel-Aviv: Dvir Publishing, 1959.

Berlowitz, Yaffa. *Lehamtsi erets, lehamtsi 'am.* Hakibutz Hame'uhad, 1996.

———. "Ha'otopia hatsiyonit: hathalat hame'a—sof hame'a." In *Iyunim bitkumat yisrael, me'asef liv'ayot hatsiyonut ve'eretz yisrael,* Ben-Gurion University, 1997, 7:601–618.

———. "Haseder hashlishi—tor yisrael be'artso. Yetsirato hasifrutit shel Ze'ev Yavets bir'i hashkafato hahistorit." *Katedra* 20 (1991), 165–182.

———. "Dmut hatemani ba'aliyot harishonot." *Pe'amim* 10 (1982), 99.

———. "Reshita shel hasifrut be'retz yisra'el vezikote'ha leshirat sefarad, hatsa'a lemodel tarbut yehudi-'arvi." *Bikoret ufarshanut* 32 (Winter 1998).

———. "Sifrut utehiya le'umit, bne 'arav lemoshe smilansky—hasipur hapatroni." In *Iyunim bitkumat yisra'el.* Ben-Gurion University, 1994, 4:409.

Bialik, Haim Nachman. "Lekhinusa she ha'agada ha'ivrit." *Hashiloah* 18 (1908), 19.

Birenbaum, Natan. "Milhemet hakoltura be'retz yisra'el biyme kedem." *Hashiloah* 1 (1896–1897), 293.

Blubstein, Rachel. "Megilat kedem: reshimat bikoret." *Hashiloah* 37 (1920), 595.

Boehmer, Elleke. *Colonial and Postcolonial Literature.* Oxford University Press, 1995.

Boyarin, Daniel. *Unheroic Conduct, the Rise of Heterosexuality and the Making of the Jewish Man.* Berkeley: University of California Press, 1997.

Bram, Dijkstra. *Idols of Perversity, Fantasies of Feminine Evil in Fin-de-Siecle Culture.* Oxford University Press, 1986.

Brantlinger, Patrick. *Rule of Darkness. British Literature and Imperialism, 1830–1914.* Ithaca, N.Y.: Cornell University Press, 1988.

Brenner, Yosef Haim. *Kol kitve yod het brener.* Tel-Aviv: Hakibutz Hame'uhad, 1985.

Brinker, Menachem. *'Ad hasimta hatveryanit: ma'amar 'al sipur umahshava biyetsirat brener.* Am Oved, 1990.

Buber, Martin. "Hithadshut haye 'am." *Te'uda viyi'ud* 2 (1959–1961):175–191.

Burla, Yehuda. *Ishto hasnu'a.* Davar-Massada, 1951.

Cantor, Paul A. *Creature and Creator: Myth-Making and English Romanticism.* Cambridge, New York: Cambridge University Press, 1984.

Diamond, James S. *Homeland or Holy Land? The "Canaanite" Critique of Israel.* Bloomington: Indiana University Press, 1986.

Dinur, Ben-Zion. "Be'ayat halukatan shel toldot yisra'l litkufot bahistoryografia hayhudit." *Dorot ureshumot* (1978), 30–48.

Domb, Risa. *The Arab in Hebrew Prose, 1911–1948.* Vallentine, Mitchell, 1982.

Dor, M. "Mizraha! Mizraha!" *Ma'ariv*, November 11, 1974.

Dudley, Edward, and M. Novak, eds. *The Wild Man Within: An Image in Western Thought from the Renaissance to Romanticism.* University of Pittsburgh Press, 1973.

Ehrenprize, M. "Le'an?" *Hashiloah* 1, no. 6 (1897), 490.

Eliot, George. *Daniel Deronda.* Clarendon Press, Oxford University Press, 1984.

Epstein, Abraham. *Sofrim 'iwriyim be'amerika.* Tel-Aviv: Dvir Publishing, 1953.

Epstein, Y. "She'ela na'alama." *Hashiloah* 17 (1906–1907), 193.

Ergang, Robert. *Herder and German Nationalism.* Columbia University Press, 1931.

Ernst, S., ed. *Sefer yavetz.* Tel-Aviv: Achi'ever Publishing, 1934.

Even-Zohar, Itamar. "Tsemihata shel tarbut 'ivrit be'eretz yisra'el 1882–1984." *Studies in Zionism* 4 (1981).

Fairchild, Neale Hoxie. *The Noble Savage.* New York: Russell & Russell, 1961.

Fechter, Mordechai. In *S. yizhar, mivkhar ma'amare bikoret 'al yetsirato.* Ed. Haim Nagid. Am Oved, 1972, 177.

Fichman, Ya'acov. "Sefer hamar'ot." *Hashiloah* 46 (1926), 68.

Finkelkraut, Alain. *The Imaginary Jew.* Trans. Kevin O'neal and David Suchoff. Lincoln: University of Nebraska Press, 1994.

Francis, David G. *Arabian Nights.* New York: David G. Francis Pub., 1869.

Frishman, David. "Hayadata et ha'arets? Reshimot masa be'eretz yisrael." *Hatzfira*, May 22, 1911.

———. *Bamidbar.* Tel-Aviv: Dvir Publishing, 1990.

———. *Mikhtavim 'al hasifrut.* Jerusalem, Tel-Aviv: M. Newman Publishing, 1968.

———. *Kol kitve david frishman.* Warsaw-New York: Lilly Frishman Publishers, 1938.

Furst, Lillian. *Romanticism.* Methuen, 1976.

Gerhardt, Mia Irene. *The Art of Story-telling; A Literary Study of the* Thousand and One Nights. Leiden: E. J. Brill, 1963.

Gertz, Nurit. *Hirbet hiz'a vehaboker shelemoharat.* Tel-Aviv: Hakibutz Hame'uhad, 1984.

Gesenius, Wilhelm. *Hebrew Grammar.* Oxford: Oxford University Press, 1966.

Giddings, Robert, ed. *Literature and Imperialism.* London: Macmillan, 1991.

Gilboa, Menucha. *David frishman, mivkhar ma'amare bikoret 'al yetsirato.* Tel-Aviv: Hakibutz Hame'uhad, 1988.

Gilsenan, Michael. *Imagined Cities of the East: An Inaugural Lecture Delivered before the University of Oxford on 27 May 1985.* Oxford University Press, 1986.

Gorni, Y. "Hayesod haromanti ba'idi'ologia shel ha'aliya hashniya." *Asufot* 10 (1966), 55–74.

Govrin, Nurit. *Dvash misela.* Tel-Aviv: Misrad ha-Bitahon Publishing, 1989.

———. *Maftehot.* Tel-Aviv University: Hakibutz Hame'uhad, 1978.

Gramsci, Antonio. *Selections from the Prison Notebooks of Antonio Gramsci.* International Publishers, 1972.

Gur-Ze'ev, Ilan. *Likrat hinuch legalutiyut rav tarbutiyut ve hinuch she keneged ba idan ha post moderni.* Resling Publishing, 2004.

Hacohen, M. B. H. "Yisrae'l ve'artso behazon hasipurim." *Hashiloah* 11 (1903–1904), 117–124, 334–339, 521–528.

Hanani, Yisrael. "Reshit hasipur ha'eretz yisra'eli." *Molad* 19, no. 161–162 (December 1961), 645.

Harshav, Benjamin. *Nekudot tatspit, tarbut vehevra be'rets yisra'el.* Ed. Nurit Gertz. Tel-Aviv: University Press, 1988.

Heine, Heinrich. *The Romantic School.* New York: H. Holt & Co., 1882.

Helman, Yom-Tov. "'Avar vehove." *Hashiloah* 37 (1920), 1.

Herder, Johann Gottfried. *The Spirit of Hebrew Poetry.* Transl. James Marsh. Burlington, Vt.: Edward Smith, 1833.

Hermoni, A. "Tsiyonut mukdemet." *Hashiloah* 21 (1919–1920), 52.

Hershberg, A. SH. "'Al hasfaradim be'rets yisra'el." *Hashiloah* 18 (1908), 170.

Herzl, Theodore. *'Inyan hayhudim, sifre yoman 1898–1902.* Jerusalem: Mossad Bialik, 1999.

Hess, Moshe. *Roma viyerushalayim.* Warsaw: Tushiya, 1899.

Hever, Hanan. *Sifrut shenikhtevet mikan, kitsur hasifrut hayisre'elit.* Yedi'ot Aharonot—Sifre Hemed, 1999.

———. "Mesifrut Ivrit lesifrut Yisre'elit." *Te'oria uvikoret* 20 (Spring 2002).

———. "Tnu lanu badranim veyanuhu beshalom—sifrut yisraelit bizman shel kibbush." *Alpaim* 25 (2003).

Hirschfeld, Ariel. *Kadima: hamizrah be'omanut yisrael.* Jerusalem: Israel Museum, 1998.

Hissin, Haim. *Masa ba'aretz hamuvtahat.* Ed. and transl. Haim Ben-Amram. Tel-Aviv University, 1982.

Holtzman, Avner. "Hasifrut, hametsi'ut umish'alot halev." *Katedra* 87 (Nissan 1998), 175–183.

———. "'Al hatoda'a ha'atsmit besifrut ha'aliya hashniya." In *Ha'aliya hashniya—mehkarim.* Ed. Israel Bartal. 367–385. Jerusalem: Yad Ben-Tzvi, 1997.

Horn, Bernard, ed. *Facing the Fires: Conversations with A. B. Yehoshua.* Syracuse, N.Y.: Syracuse University Press, 1997.

Hout, Syrine Chafic. *Viewing Europe from the Outside: Cultural Encounters and Critiques in the Eighteenth-Century Pseudo-Oriental Travelogue and the Nineteenth-Century 'Voyage en Orient.'* New York: P. Lang, 1997.

Idelsohn, Avraham Zvi. "Negina shemit." *Hashiloah* 37 (1920), 492.

Jordan, Mark. *The Invention of Sodomy in Christian Theology.* Chicago: University of Chicago Press, 1997.

Kagan, Tsipora. Afterword to David Frishman's, *Bamidbar.* Tel-Aviv: Dvir Publishing, 1990.

Kahn, Ludwig. *Social Ideals in German Literature, 1770–1830.* New York: Columbia University Press, 1938.

Kaniel, Yehoshua. "Anshe ha'aliya hashniya uvne ha'eda hasfaradit." In *Ha'aliya hashniya—mehkarim.* Ed. Yisrael Bartal. Yad Ben-Tzvi, 1997.

Karni, Yehuda. "Ha'omanim bamoledet." *Hedim* 1, no. 1 (1922), 36–38.

Kedar, Aharon. "Letoldoteha shel brit shalom bashanim 1925–1928." In *Pirke mehkar betoldot hatsiyonut mugashim leyisra'el goldstein.* Ed. Yehuda Bauer, Moshe Davis, and Yisrael Kolat. Jerusalem: The Zionist Library, 1976.

Kipling, Rudyard. *The One-Volume Kipling, Authorized.* New York: Doubleday, 1930.

Klausner, Yosef. "Yehudim hadashim." *Hashiloah* 14 (1905), 95.

———. "Hashash." *Hashiloah* 17 (1917), 574.

———. "'Olam mithave." *Hashiloah* 28 (1913).

———. *Historia shel hasifrut ha'ivrit hahadasha.* Jerusalem: Ahi'asaf, 1949.

Kleinman, Moshe. "Hashpa'at avraham mapu." *Hashiloah* 20 (1919), 49.

Kornberg, Jacques. *Theodore Herzl: From Assimilation to Zionism.* Bloomington: Indiana University Press, 1993.

Kornblatt, Judith. *The Cossack Hero in Russian Literature.* Madison: University of Wisconsin Press, 1992.

Kramer, Shalom. *Frishman hamvaker.* Jerusalem: Mossad Bialik, 1984.

Kreus, Shmuel. "Bet kuziva." *Hashiloah* 10 (1903), 35.

Kurzweil, Baruch. *Ben hazon leven ha'absurdi.* New York: Schocken Publishing, 1966.

Lachower, Fishel. *Toldot hasifrut ha'ivrit hahadasha.* Tel-Aviv: Dvir Publishing, 1946.

Laesk, Nigel. *British Romantic writers and the East: Anxieties of Empire*. Cambridge University Press, 1992.

Layton, Susan. *Russian Literature and Empire*. Cambridge N.Y.: Cambridge University Press, 1994.

Lazar, Menachem. "'Aseret hashvatim." *Hashiloah* 9 (1902), 46.

Leighton, Lauren. *Russian Romanticism: Two Essays*. The Hague: Mouton, 1975.

Lipshitz, Eliezer-Meir. "Lish'elot halashon, 'Aravit ve'ivrit." *Hashiloah* 32 (1916).

Lowa, Lisa. *Critical Terrains: French and British Orientalists*. Ithaca, N.Y.: Cornell University Press, 1991.

Lubetzky, Y. A. "Roman tsiyoni." *Hashiloah* 18 (1907–1908), 176.

Luidor, Yosef. *Sipurim*. Massada Publishing, 1976.

Lunz, Avraham Moshe. "Masa be'eretz pleshet." In *Sal 'anavim, sipurim Eretz yisre'eliyim bitkufat ha'aliya harishona*. Ed. Galya Yardeni. Jerusalem: Mossad Bialik, 1967.

Majeed, Javed. *Ungoverned Imaginings: James Mill's The History of British India and Orientalism*. Oxford: Clarendon Press, New York: Oxford University Press, 1992.

Malter, Zvi. "Hafilosofia ha'aravit vehashpa'ata 'al hayahadut." *Hashiloah* 6 (1899–1900), 38, 16, 99.

Melman, Billie. *Women's Orients, English Women and the Middle East 1718–1918: Sexuality, Religion, and Work*. Ann Arbor: University of Michigan Press, 1992.

Mendes-Flohr, Paul. *Divided Passions: Jewish Intellectuals and the Experience of Modernity*. Detroit: Wayne State University Press, 1991.

Miron, Dan. "He'arot lishne sipurim." In *S. Yizhar, mivhar ma'amarim 'al yetsirato*. Ed. Haim Nagid. Am Oved, 1972.

——. *'Arba panim basifrut ha'ivrit bat zmanenu*. New York: Schocken Publishing, 1975.

——. *Bo'a layla*. Tel-Aviv: Dvir Publishing, 1987.

——. *Bodedim bemo'adam*. Am Oved, 1987.

——. *Yonatan ratosh—shirim*. Ed. Aharon Amir. Zmora-Bitan Publishing, 1991.

——. *Kivun orot: tahanot basiporet ha'ivrit hamodernit*. New York: Schocken Publishing, 1979.

Morris, Benny. *The Birth of the Palestinian Refugee Problem, 1947–1949*. Cambridge: Cambridge University Press, 1987.

Mosse, George. *The Image of Man: The Creation of Modern Masculinity*. New York: Oxford University Press, 1996.

Montefiore, Judith. *A Private Journal of a Visit to Egypt and Palestine*. Yad Ben-Zvi, 1975.

Myers, David. *Re-Inventing the Jewish Past: European Jewish Intellectuals and the Zionist Return to History*. Oxford University Press, 1995.

Nagid, Haim, ed. *S. Yizhar, mivhar ma'amare bikoret al yetsirato*. Tel-Aviv: Am Oved, 1972.

Ofrat, Gideon. *Adama, adam, dam*. Gomeh Publishing, 1980.

Oueijan, Naji. *The Progress of an Image: The East in English Literature*. New York: P. Lang, 1996.

Oz, Amos. *Artsot hatan*. Am Oved, 1980.

Oz, Koby. *Moshe hawata veha'orev*. Keshet, 1996.

Parush, Iris. *Kanon sifruti ve'idi'ologia le'umit*. Jerusalem: Mossad Bialik, 1992.

Polack, A. B. "Motsa'am shel arviye ha'aretz." *Molad* 3, no. 213 (November 1967), 297–299.

Pratt, Mary Louise. *Imperial Eyes, Travel Writing and Transculturation*. London: Routledge, 1992.

Rabbi Binyamin. *'Al hagvulin*. Vienna: Appel Bros. Publishers, 1923.

Rabinowitz, Ya'akov. *Nedude 'amasai hashomer*. Jerusalem: Mitzpe Publishing, 1929.

Rabinowitz, Yisrael. "Be'retz yisra'el." *Hashiloah* 16 (1907), 40.

Rabinyan, Dorit. *Simtat hashkediyot be'omrijan*. Am Oved, 1995.

Ramraz-Rauch, Gila. *Alef lamed arielli (orloff), hayav viyetsirato*. Tel-Aviv University: Papirus Publishing, 1992.

——. *The Arab in Israeli Literature*. Bloomington: Indiana University Press, 1989.

Reiss, Hans Siegbert. *The Political Thought of the German Romantics, 1793–1815.* Blackwell, 1955.

Reuveni, A. *Kol sipure alef re'weni.* Jerusalem: Reuveń Mass Pub.

Rozen, Haim. *Contemporary Hebrew.* The Hague: Mouton, 1977.

Rubinstein, Eliezer. *Ha'ivrit hakduma veha'ivrit shelanu.* Ed. Yoel Reppel. Sifriyat Universita Meshuderet, 1980.

Ruskin, Jonah. *The Mythology of Imperialism.* New York: Random House, 1971.

Sadan-Loebenstein, Nilie. *Siporet shenot ha'esrim be'eretz yisra'el.* Jerusalem: Sifriyat Poalim, 1991.

Said, Edward. *Culture and Imperialism.* New York: Knopf, 1993.

——. *Orientalism.* New York: Vintage Books, 1979.

Sapir, A. "Harhavat sfatenu veha'arvit." *Hashiloah* 4 (1898–1899), 328.

Schneidau, Herbert. *Sacred Discontent.* Baton Rouge: Louisiana State University, 1976.

Schorsch, Ismar. "Ideology and History." In *The Structure of Jewish History.* Heinrich Graetz, Jewish Theological Seminary of America, Ktav Publishing, 1975.

——. "The Emergence of Historical Consciousness in Modern Judaism." *Leo Beck Institute Year Book* 28 (1983), 413–437.

Schulman, Kalman, ed. *Sefer halihot kedem.* Y. R. Rom Publishers, 1858.

Schwab, Raymond. *The Oriental Renaissance: Europe's Rediscovery of India and the East, 1680–1880.* New York: Columbia University Press, 1984.

Schweid, Eliezer. "Hashiva el hahistoria bahagut hayhudit shel hame'a ha'esrim." In *Hevra vehistoria.* Ed. Yehezkel Cohen. Jerusalem: Misrad Hahinuch, 1979–1980.

Schweid, Elly. In *S. Yizhar, mivhar ma'amarim 'al yetsirato.* Ed. Haim Nagid. Am Oved, 1972.

Shafer, Boyd. *Nationalism: Myth and Reality.* New York: Harcourt, Brace, 1955.

Shaffer, Elinor. *"Kubla Khan" and the Fall of Jerusalem: The Mythological School in Biblical Criticism and Secular Literature, 1770–1880.* Cambridge, New York: Cambridge University Press, 1975.

Shaked, Gershon. *Gal hadash basifrut ha'ivrit.* Jerusalem: Sifriyat Poalim, Hakibutz Hame'uhad, 1971.

——. *Hasiporet ha'ivrit, 1880–1980.* Hakibutz Hame'uhad, 1977.

——. *Safrut kan, az ve'akhshav.* Zmora-Bitan, 1993.

——. *Yetsirot venim'anehen, 'arba'a prakim betorat hahitkablut.* Tel-Aviv University, 1987.

Shalev, Meir. *Roman Rusi.* Am Oved, 1988.

Shami, Yitzhak. *Nikmat ha'avot.* Tel-Aviv: Yachdav Publishing, 1975.

Sharafuddin, Mohammed. *Islam and Romantic Orientalism: Literary Encounters with the Orient.* Tauris, 1994.

Shavit, Ya'acov. "Ben tarbut le'umit letarbut yelidit." *Masa,* June 5, 1992.

——. "Hatsiyonut ben shki'at hama'arav utehiyat hamizrah." *Moznayim* 36 (1973), 139–141.

——. *Me'ivri ad kna'ani.* Tel-Aviv University: Domino, 1984.

——. "Tarbut umatsav kulturi." In *Ha'aliya hashniya—mehkarim.* Ed. Yisrael Bartal. Yad Ben-Tzvi, 1997.

Shepherd, Naomi. *The Zealous Intruders: The Western Rediscovery of Palestine.* New York: Harper & Row, 1987.

Shimoni, Gideon. *The Zionist Ideology.* Hanover: University Press of New England, 1995.

Silman, K. L. "Sha'ot." *Revivim* 3–4 (1913), 125.

Sloshetz, Nachum. "Ever ukna'an." *Hashiloah* 37 (1920), 237.

Smilansky, Moshe. *Kitve moshe smilansky.* Tel-Aviv: Hitahdut Ha'ikarim Be'eretz Yisrael, 1935.

Soloweitchik, M. "Hamidbar betoldotav vehashkafat 'olamo shel 'am yisra'el." In *Dvir, me'asef lehokhmat yisra'el* (Dvir), 2nd book. Tamuz-Elul, 1923.

Sontag, Debora. "In Israel, Free To Be Personal, Not Political." *New York Times,* October 24, 1999, Sunday edition, Arts & Leisure section, 33.

Steinberg, Ya'acov. *Kol kitve ya'acov shteinberg.* Tel-Aviv: Dvir Publishing, 1957.

Steinman, A. "Birshuti." *Ktuvim,* July 30, 1926, A–B.

Tabayov, Y. CH. "Sfat 'ever hahadasha." *Hashiloah* 10 (1903).

Thompson, James. *The East Imagined, Experienced, Remembered, Orientalist 19th Century Paintings.* National Gallery of Ireland, 1988.

Trevor-Roper, Hugh. *Jewish and Other Nationalism.* Widenfeld and Nicolson, 1962.

Tchernichovsky, Shaul. *Kol kitve sha'ul tchernichovsky, shirim uvaladot.* Am Oved, 1990.

Tsemach, Adi. "Min ve'ofi le'umi." In *Moznayim* 6-5, Tishre-Hesvan, 1982.

Tzalmona, Yigal. "Mizraha! Mizraha!' 'al hamizrah ba'omanut hayisre'elit." In *Kadima: hamizrah be'omanut yisrael.* Ed. Ariel Hirschfeld. Jerusalem: Israel Museum, 1998.

Werses, Shmuel. "Ha'agadot 'al 'aseret hashvatim vehasambatyon vedarke klitatan besifrutenu hahadasha." In *Mimendale 'ad hazaz.* Jerusalem: Hebrew University Press, 1987.

——. "Ne'umo ha'aharon shel nahman be *le'an?*" In *Mimendale 'ad hazaz.* Hebrew University Press, 1987.

White, Hayden. "The Historical Imagination in 19th Century Europe." In *The Uses of History; Essays in Intellectual and social History Presented to William J. Bossenbrook.* Detroit: Wayne State University Press, 1968.

Whitleman, Keith. *The Invention of Ancient Israel: The Silencing of Palestinian History.* London and New York: Routledge, 1996.

Willson, A. Leslie. *A Mythical Image: The Ideal of India in German Romanticism.* Durham, N.C.: Duke University Press, 1964.

Winks, R., and J. Rush, eds. *Asia in Western Fiction.* Honolulu: University of Hawaii Press, 1990.

Wislivsky, Zvi. "'Al miftan hamitos." *Gilyonot* 8, no. 3 (1938).

Yanaìt (Ben-Zvi), Rachel. *Anu olim.* Am Oved, 1959.

Yardeni, Galia. *Ha'itonon ha'ivrit be'eretz yisrael.* Tel-Aviv University, 1969.

Yavetz, Zeev. "Haravot le'itim." In *Sal 'anavim, sipurim eretz yisra'eliyim bitkufat ha'aliya harishona.* Jerusalem: Mossad Bialik, 1967.

——. *Leket ktavim.* Jerusalem: Salomon Publishing, 1943.

——. *Pri ha'aretz.* Warsaw: Schuldberg Bros. Press, 1892.

Yehoshua, A. B. *Kol hasipurim.* Tel-Aviv: Hakibutz Hame'uhad, 1993.

——. *Hakir ve'hahar.* Tel-Aviv: Zmora-Bitan, 1989.

Yelin, David. "Melitsat yishma'el besifrut yisra'el." *Hashiloah* 5 (1898).

——. "Ginze teman." *Hashiloah* 2 (1897).

Yevin, Shmuel. "Hakor'an." *Hashiloah* 42 (1924), 354.

Yizhar, S. "Hashavuy." In *Sipur Hirbat hizah, Hashavuy.* Merhavia: Sifriyat Po'alim, 1949.

——. *Yeme tsiklag.* Tel-Aviv: Am Oved, 1958.

Yovel, Yirmiyahoo. *Hida afela, hegel, nitshe vehayehudim.* New York: Schocken Publishing, 1996.

Zioni, A. "Hate'ologia hale'umit." *Revivim* 3-4, 1913.

Zmiri, M. "Lemekoriyuta shel yetsiratenu." *Gazit,* 2:A (second year, second ed.), 1934.

Index